All

Robert Marshall is a writer and producer of more than a 100 titles for TV and cinema, and the author of 4 books. He spent 20 years at the BBC, ran independent production companies, pioneered live screening of the performing arts and was an Executive Producer for Shakespeare's Globe. He returned to his native Australia and now lectures at Curtin University, and is still writing.

Also by Robert Marshall

Light in the Dark
All the King's Men

ROBERT MARSHALL

ALL THE KING'S MEN

■ CANELOHISTORY

First published in the United Kingdom in 1988 by William Collins Sons & Co. Ltd

This edition published in the United Kingdom in 2022 by

Canelo
Unit 9, 5th Floor
Cargo Works, 1-2 Hatfields
London, SE1 9PG
United Kingdom

A CIP catalogue record for this book is available from the British Library.

Print ISBN 978 1 80032 644 6
Ebook ISBN 978 1 80032 643 9

Look for more great books at www.canelo.co

Printed and bound in Great Britain by Clays Ltd, Elcograf S.p.A.

1

To the memory of my mother

and the love of my wife

Preface

During the summer of 1943, Britain's wartime secret service, the Special Operations Executive – SOE – suffered a major collapse of its networks in northern France. It was a disaster of monumental proportions, a disaster from which the SOE never properly recovered. The story of that collapse lies at the very heart of the history of Britain's secret war alongside the French Resistance. It is a story that is engraved upon the memories of those who were there and survived. For apart from the terrible loss of life and *materiel*, the collapse precipitated a serious crisis of confidence. After the war, stories proliferated – on both sides of the Channel – of betrayal, deception and English perfidy. An official history went to considerable length to silence these rumours, and for a while it succeeded. But the passing years nurtured old suspicions. If one picks up a well-read copy of *The SOE in France*, it will invariably fall open at the events surrounding the collapse of the northern networks and the role played by an individual by the name of Henri Déricourt. What makes these few pages so fascinating is that they raise more questions than they answer.

In fact all accounts of the events in France during 1943 are less than satisfying simply because authors have been hampered by the singular inaccessibility of the relevant material. All SOE's records are held in perpetual custody by the Secret Intelligence Service (MI6). Time, a little good fortune and a great deal of effort have shaken some of this material free. This development, coupled with the recollections of veterans and survivors and of many others not previously connected with the story, now makes it possible to produce a realistic, though hardly agreeable, explanation for SOE's very worst disaster.

The research for this book began when Roy Davies, editor of the BBC's history series TIMEWATCH, suggested I look into the subject as a possible item for that programme. In the course of its making an enormous amount of new material was uncovered – too much to be squeezed into one hour of television. This volume is, therefore, a golden opportunity to present that material in as much detail as the narrative will allow. I am indebted to a great many people who contributed much to the research and who deserve proper recognition. Daniella Dangoor, who combed the French archives exhaustively; Dr Stephen Badsey, military historian, who volunteered his time and knowledge in areas that were remote from my experience; Dr Katherine Herbig at the US Naval College in Monterey, California, an expert in strategic deception, who allowed me access to many papers unavailable in Britain; and finally – but most importantly – Larry Collins, author of *Fall from Grace*, who allowed me to read the typescripts of a great many invaluable interviews that were recorded with people now long dead.

The most valuable archival material that was uncovered was found in the private papers of Henri Déricourt. These contain his pilot's log books and licences, birth and marriage certificates, letters, financial records, military records, forged documents, a manuscript for a novel together with a vast quantity of miscellaneous trivia – even a receipt for his coffin. The name Déricourt is perhaps not so well known as Burgess or Maclean, but nevertheless he deserves to be recognized as one of the most accomplished intelligence agents of all time.

The bulk of the detail contained in this book is drawn from interviews with over fifty veterans and survivors of the secret war. These included some half dozen SS and SD officers in Germany; a number of pilots and crew who flew with Déricourt over the years; SOE officers; and countless members of the French Resistance. A surprising number of retired MI6 officers have also spoken to me freely about their work, and about Claude Dansey in particular. In fact it was the character of Dansey that proved the most difficult to unravel. A great deal of unhelpful hagiography has been written about this man, a complex individual who remained an enigma even to those who worked closest with him. Trying to weave one's way between those who thought him a god and others who believed he was the Devil incarnate proved a difficult task. Whether he was a madman or a genius is one of those MI6 mysteries that remain at best only half answered.

Robert Marshall
Perth, Australia, March 1987

I

'The French Kid Glove...'

During the winter of 1946, locked away in Fresnes Prison in the southern suburbs of Paris was a bleak and friendless community of souls. They had been thrown together by the final scenes of an exhausting war. Down the long central gallery, dimly lit by pools of grey sunlight, hundreds of wretched Frenchmen took their regular stroll from the cells to the little cubicles where they could meet their lawyers. A disparate group of frightened and bitter men, united by a single crime – collaboration. Paradoxically, just three years before, Fresnes Prison had echoed to the sound of jackboots and the inmates who padded along the gallery then also shared a common charge. They called it Patriotism. The world had been turned upside down. Of course, not all the inmates the Germans imprisoned there in 1943 were true patriots and nor indeed were all those imprisoned in 1946 guilty of treason.

The prisoners in Fresnes were part of a larger society that was gradually steeling itself for a painful period of self-examination. France was emerging from one of the darker chapters in her long history. She had not been united by war, but shattered into a hundred fragments. The presence of the Nazi occupiers had encouraged some Frenchmen of a fascist persuasion to embrace the invader – in the name of France. Although the vast majority, faced with the reality of defeat, had quietly accepted collaboration as the prescribed antidote to national humiliation, a few, a very few, presumed to resist the invader and live as underground terrorists.

As the tide of war had turned, the ranks of the resisters swelled, the collaborators became more unwilling and the Fascists were isolated. French society was wrenched first one way and then the other.

Isolated from the great social upheavals, there inevitably flourished a few who cared nothing for the politics of the thing, but who saw the whole great conflict as nothing more than a fabulous game, to be played either for profit or glory – or just for the thrill of it. And if they found themselves on the wrong side of the wall at Fresnes, it was often no reflection on how well they had played the game.

Prisoner Déricourt – number 13.181 – spent hours at his tidy little desk in cell 1/459, agonizing over the words to address to his uncomprehending wife. The monthly letter had become something of a struggle between what he would have liked to have said and what she needed to hear.

> My beautiful chicken…
> I've just received your letter of Wednesday. My poor chicken's nerves are having a hard time. And as you say, when will it end? For myself I don't know, for it's not me who decides. But they will have to release me for I have done nothing wrong.[1]

On 22 November 1946, he and his wife had been sitting down to their dinner when three officers of the

DST (Département de la Surveillance du Territoire), the French equivalent of Britain's MI5 (the Security Service), arrived to arrest Henri Eugène Alfred Déricourt on a charge of treason. They apologized for having called at such an inhospitable hour, then splayed themselves across the armchairs and waited for the couple to finish their meal. Occasionally they made an attempt at conversation but Déricourt was utterly taciturn and gave the impression of a man absorbed in his meal. His wife, Jeannot, or his 'little chicken', as he called her when trying to comfort, was temperamentally a different person. Petite and somewhat nervous, she had tried but failed to disguise her terror and so Henri had leant across the table, taken her hand in his and held it there.

When he had finished, Déricourt packed a small bag with toothbrush, soap and towel. Then he was driven to Fresnes.[2] On 29 November he was taken to DST headquarters and before the Commissaire de Police, René Gouillaud, he was charged with having had 'intelligence with the enemy', for which the punishment was death. Twelve months later, he was still awaiting trial.

> My affair will have to come to an end and
> I will have to be released. I have many great
> projects to do and many good things in store.
> Perhaps we could just pack our bags and go
> to that little corner and breed ducks. I send
> you kisses and caresses.[3]

France was still divided, suspicious, resentful and in the mood for revenge. Behind their flinty walls, the prisoners of Fresnes knew very little about the political currents that were flowing around them. This man in particular, isolated in his little cell, was drifting unaware towards the centre of a storm that threatened relations between Britain and France. The *entente cordiale* was being chilled to the bone. But Déricourt knew nothing of that, he was no more in control of his 'affair' than he was in control of Jeannot's nerves. His fate was being shaped by stealth, by the silently grinding wheels of an organization far beyond the reach of the DST. Behind his presence in Fresnes lay an extraordinary history of intrigue and deception within the British secret services.

Who was Déricourt and how had he come to be at the centre of that storm? The man whom an officer in the DST once described as the 'French kid glove over the hand of Albion'[4] was the subject of a vivid array of stories.

> ...the son of a respected French family related to nobility. At the Lycée he excelled in mathematics and science and set his heart on becoming an aviator. He was trained as a civil airline pilot and in 1933, at the age of 24, held the post of captain-pilot with Air France.[5]

> ...he had worked during the 1930s as a trapeze artiste in Germany, there he made contact with a number of useful people...[6]

> ...he had been to America on secret business, having escaped from France by crossing the Pyrenees...[7]

There was only one consistent theme in Déricourt's own account of his background: he never told anyone the truth about it. Once he had escaped his roots, he proceeded to bury them thoroughly. He cultivated a vaguely romantic air about his home and family and when pressed about his origins he would feign a pained silence, glance away and whisper 'Château Thierry'. It was terribly effective.

Henri Eugène Alfred Déricourt was born at twelve-thirty in the morning of 2 September 1909, in the little hamlet of Coulognes-en-Tardenois, near Reims in the département of Aisne, some 100 kilometres north-east of Paris. South of the fields of Picardy the country rolls gently between the rivers Aisne and Vesle before running into the industrial outskirts of Reims. It is country that has periodically seen the arrival and departure of foreign invaders since the time of Julius Caesar, and they would come twice more during Henri's lifetime.

The tiny community into which Déricourt was born worked under the feudal patronage of the local aristocracy. His father, Alfred, had been a peasant labourer until a stroke forced him off the land and into the Post Office. His mother, Georgette, was a domestic servant most of her life and worked as a concierge on the Thierry estates. Henri was the youngest of three boys. The eldest, Felix, was an ebonist – a craftsman skilled in working thin ebony veneers into cabinets or tables. Marcel, the second son, became a decorator.

Henri never had the slightest intention of labouring for his living. He showed some academic promise in his early years, which led his mother to cherish a dream that her favourite son would eventually become a teacher. But Henri had nothing so bourgeois in mind. Either by accident or design, Henri spent a lot of time in his mother's company at the Thierry estates, and from behind her apron, so to speak, he glimpsed the world of the local aristocracy. It was a world he liked very much. At 'Thierry' he found a sort of second family who seem to

5

have adopted him as a kind of mascot. At any rate he began to absorb something of the culture of that society and to develop a view of himself as someone separate from the 'little people' of the world. By 'little people' he meant anyone whose life was ruled by others, like his family and their neighbours. This view of himself as an individual divorced from his origins was perhaps the most important early development in what was to become a complicated character. Eventually he would distinguish between two kinds of 'little people': those who were vulnerable, who relied on him and somehow deserved his affection – like his mother; and those who had failed to improve themselves, deserved to be where they were and consequently barely figured in his view of the world – like his father.[8]

Every evening Henri and his mother would return to their very humble house and to a man who was, at least in Henri's eyes, the very worst type of time-server – a postman, a minor functionary of the state, a failure. Déricourt despised him. For some unknown medical reason, his father developed a bizarre and unfortunate complication after his stroke – he became appallingly obese. Henri, who always took a great pride in his own appearance, found his father's physical disintegration repulsive.

At the age of 16 he sat his baccalaureat, but his mother's hopes were dashed. Too indisciplined to cope with the necessary study, he failed his first exams, threw the rest in and left home for Paris. The only influence his father managed to exert on his youngest son was to ensure him employment by getting him a position with the PTT (Postes Télégraph et Téléphone). Henri started at the very bottom – 'supernumerare', literally a supernumerary. From this he progressed to the dizzying heights of 'clerk'.[9]

On 26 May 1927, in the company of nearly a hundred thousand of his countrymen, Déricourt went to Le Bourget airfield to cheer the young American, Charles A. Lindbergh, who had just flown non-stop across the Atlantic. It's difficult today to imagine the kind of prestige that was enjoyed by the pilots of the 1920s. In fact they were not pilots, they were aviators – flyers. They commanded the respect of presidents and kings – and the adulation of millions. The following day, outside the Hotel de Ville, Déricourt again watched as the President of France shook hands with Mr Lindbergh, and the postal clerk hit upon his first avenue of escape.

Déricourt liked to say he'd won a scholarship to a pilots' school, but in fact it was his mother's employer who had engineered his admission. Henri was privately sponsored to the Farman Air School at Toussus le Noble near Paris, the training school for the Military air service. On 10 May 1930 Déricourt had his *Baptême de l'Air*.[10] He flew for six minutes. By the end of the month he had clocked up over four hours' flying time and had already shown himself an uncommonly good pilot. By 1931 he had progressed to the rank of Corporal second class, then to Chief Corporal.

In 1932 he left the military to take up the life of an aerial showman. With a group of like-minded flying-fools he established the *Aéro Club de Paris*. From their base at Toussus le Noble, they moved about the countryside in a peripatetic fashion, producing impromptu 'Fêtes Aeriennes'.

In each new town they would land in a nearby field, distribute a few posters, then for six francs entertain the local country folk to a display of wing-walking, parachuting, dare-devil dives and, of course, the opportunity for a *Baptême de l'Air*. The glamorous twenty-three-year-old flyer developed a reputation as a witty, self-confident and extremely persuasive charmer, particularly with the ladies. It was really his talent on the ground that kept the Aero Club in the air, long after flying circuses had become passé.[11]

By 1935 the Depression put an end to their barn-storming. After trying to make a living as a salesman for a company that sold scientific instruments, Déricourt finally settled down to what he would have called a steady job. A new airline was created specifically to transport mail over the vast distances of France, a task previously dealt with by Air France. A fleet of silver-grey Caudron Simouns, the new fast monoplane, and some six or eight pilots and radio operators were gathered at Le Bourget to form Air Bleu. Déricourt was not a person who fitted easily into an organization. He had virtually no respect for authority and little patience with procedure. Air Bleu employees were required to wear a uniform of navy blue trousers, a white shirt and a navy blue tie. Déricourt turned up for inspection on the first day wearing white trousers, a navy blue shirt and a white tie.[12]

Unfortunately, within just a few months of getting financially off the ground, the airline almost crashed. In May 1936 the Renault family prematurely removed their investment and the pilots and crew were forced to stand down and await possible government help. It was during this hiatus in the airline's history that Déricourt first demonstrated an art for which he later became quite famous, the art of disappearing. Air Bleu had come to value him as one of their best pilots and were keen to keep in touch, should the company suddenly become solvent again. Throughout August and September, there

8

was a steady stream of Air Bleu correspondence to all of Déricourt's known addresses, each letter a little more anxious than the last as the company grew more alarmed by his absence. Air Bleu never received any explanations.[13] On this particular occasion, he was secretly down at Chambéry, near the Italian border, doing a bit of aerial photography.

In the spring of 1936 Déricourt had made the acquaintance of André Borrie, an officer in the Deuxième Bureau – the French intelligence service. At that meeting Borrie had approached him with an offer of some easy cash in return for taking some documents to a contact at Déricourt's destination. The contact would give him a similar sum on receipt. It was the start of an unofficial relationship with the Deuxième Bureau that eventually extended to flying Borrie over sensitive military sites in neighbouring countries. For instance, during his absence from Air Bleu they did some aerial photography over Italian naval docks and were held up by bad weather. On other occasions they flew over German territory to photograph stretches of the famous Siegfried Line.[14]

During the 1930s it was very common for pilots (by then no longer aviators) to perform the occasional clandestine operation. It was virtually considered a perk of the job. The Spanish Civil War in particular was a great opportunity to earn a little bit of extra cash. During the summer of 1936, soon after hostilities had begun, the buccaneering figure of Wing Commander Arthur Lord Granar arrived at Le Bourget airfield with an American Lockheed aircraft. He made a semi-official approach to Air France pilots asking them if they would be prepared to fly this and other aircraft across to the Republicans in Barcelona. It was all highly unofficial and just a tiny bit illegal, but he had no problems getting enough volunteers. Two of those were Léon Doulet and a contemporary of his called Rémy Clément.

They would arrive at Le Bourget before dawn to collect their contraband aircraft, which had enough fuel to get them to Toulouse. They carried no radio operator or engineers. At Toulouse they refuelled for the stretch across the Pyrenees and down to Barcelona. Having handed over their Lockheeds, they were then flown back across the border to Toulouse, from where they took the sleeper-train back to Paris. At an apartment in Boulevard Pasteur, a colonel in the Spanish Republican Army would hand over an envelope containing some 5000 francs.

Déricourt often told this story as though it was his own. But he was not one of those hard-working Air France pilots.[15]

By 1937 Air Bleu was off the ground again and Déricourt settled down to the routine of flying the mail from Paris to Toulouse, Marseilles and so on. His radio operator, Robert Marotin, recalled what it was like to fly with him.

> Once, en route from Rouen to Le Havre, we flew into a cloud. The wings and windshield iced over and Déricourt could only see out of a tiny clear spot in the glass. We dropped down below the cloud and found ourselves flying just above the waves and beneath the tall cliffs just out of Le Havre. Déricourt couldn't climb back up again because of the weight of the ice and so we followed the line of the cliffs round until we found the gap that led to the runway and got down safely. We

> dashed into the mess, had two quick brandies
> and then ran out again to chip the ice off the
> wings, and were off again within the hour.[16]

Déricourt had developed a taste for danger. He seemed to flourish during moments of stress and Marotin often felt he pushed the system to its limits, just to see when everything would fall apart. There was extra pay for night flying and in those early aircraft there were no sophisticated navigational aids. They used to steer themselves by following the roads and rivers by moonlight.

On one occasion, while on a long overnight flight to Perpignan, Déricourt's engine suddenly cut out and the aircraft began to go into a stall. Instead of bailing out Déricourt decided to glide the aircraft in to Perpignan. Somehow he was able to control their descent towards the aerodrome. As the landing lights appeared before them, he ordered Marotin into the back of the aircraft with the mail-sacks – 'There's no point in the two of us getting killed.' He made a perfect touch-down.

Henri began to believe there was actually something special about himself, that he had some gift for surviving where others would have perished.[17] He didn't feel protected, it wasn't a case of divine intervention, but he was sure it was something more substantial than mere luck.

Sometime during 1937 Déricourt met a young British journalist who had spent a little time in Barcelona during the war and was full of tales of intrigue and derring-do. Nicholas Bodington was an extremely bright, extremely entertaining bon viveur with a taste like Déricourt's for the fast lane. He was born in Paris, was completely fluent in French and was the very embodiment of the

Continental Englishman. His father, Oliver Bodington, was an eminent international lawyer based at the British Embassy in Paris. Nicholas, the youngest of three boys, was educated at Cheltenham and Lincoln College, after which he returned to Paris in 1929 to take up the position of chief correspondent with the *Daily Express*. He resigned from the *Express* in 1933 after they threatened to transfer him to London, a city he disliked. He managed to get a similar post with the *Daily Sketch*, but left in 1935 to join Reuters.

In 1936 the Chief Editor of Reuters cabled his Paris office requesting that Bodington be sent to cover the war in Spain. The Paris Bureau Chief advised against it, as Bodington was recovering from an illness and, besides, he was more valuable in Paris.[18]

Nevertheless Bodington, who spoke Spanish nearly as well as he spoke French, went to Barcelona and while there he got a taste for the world of espionage. Someone had put him in touch with one Otto Punter, a Swiss journalist who operated a network of intelligence agents from Switzerland and who in 1936 became the Republican Government's link with the international press. Bodington enjoyed the society of spies and would boast of being on terms with many of the 'clandestine figures' of the day. He also liked to give people the impression that he too was engaged in espionage, not an uncommon hobby for Reuters agents in the Thirties.[19]

Déricourt and Bodington became good friends. Henri found Nicholas's urbane and well-informed company a pleasant change from the flyers' club at Le Bourget. And Bodington was so well informed. He was always full of gossip from the Embassy, intrigue in the diplomatic world, whispers about secret signals, the comings and goings of the law makers and their messengers. In fact Bodington was a secret agent *manqué* and the little he knew about the diplomatic world was what he caught in the form of crumbs at his father's table.

There was enough political gossip and intrigue in Paris during the late Thirties to satisfy all the secret agents *manqués*. The dramatic political changes that had occurred on three of her borders had rocked the fragile socialist coalition which had governed France for more than fifteen years. Right-wing or fascist groups had begun to flourish and political debate had degenerated into violent demonstrations, mass rallies and at times open gang warfare. The increasingly repugnant Nazi regime in Germany had let loose a wave of refugees from the east, while the Civil War in Spain sent even more refugees from the south. Large concentration camps were constructed to cope with these human tides and a mood of xenophobia crept through French society. Déricourt's radio operator, Marotin, was a member of the right-wing Action Français and tried on a number of occasions to get Henri to enlist. But Déricourt was utterly unmoved by political arguments. At best he was remotely aware of the threat of some major conflict, but only very remotely.

During the spring of 1938, Paris prepared itself for a royal visit from the British monarch. King George VI was responding to an invitation the President of France had extended to him back in 1936, to visit the wargraves and generally do whatever Heads of State do to cement good relations. As the date for the visit approached there was a new outbreak of street violence, especially among the communist and fascist groups, that threatened to disrupt the royal occasion. The French authorities were convinced that much of this unrest had been imported by political refugees from Germany. During that spring a senior German police officer arrived in Paris as a guest of the French authorities. Krimminalrat Karl Boemelburg was a founder member of Interpol.

The German Embassy had offered the services of one of their most highly regarded criminal investigators, someone who had an excellent record for flushing out radicals and political dissidents. Krimminalrat Boemelburg was allowed carte blanche in his search for any disaffected German refugees who might wish to vent some ancient grudge against the British monarch.

He exercised his relative freedom with prudence. Though he enjoyed semi-diplomatic status, he kept himself at a distance from the German embassy staff. He preferred to take a room at a hotel in the Paris suburb of Neuilly where he could entertain his contacts with perfect discretion. He was not just an ordinary policeman.

Born in Elberfeld in 1885, Boemelburg had worked in Paris from 1906 to 1911, during which time he became fluent in French and developed a deep attachment for the city. He served in the 'Kaiser's Army' throughout the Great War, was wounded once and awarded the Iron Cross, second class. During the 1920s he settled in Berlin and went into business for himself. But the young entrepreneur became increasingly alarmed by the political currents of the day, in particular the activities of the Communists and the threat of a much-heralded revolution. On 1 December 1931 he joined the National Socialists. (Party No. 892239.)

His first political activities were with the *Sturmabteilung*, or SA – literally Storm Detachment. These were the familiar brown-shirted thugs who attended most Nazi political meetings. However, Boemelburg had the presence of mind to quickly sense which way the wind was blowing, and left the ill-fated SA after just six weeks to join the SS (SS No. 47269). He was assigned to the security section, the *Sicherheitsdienst* – or SD, where he was quickly recognized as 'a highly disciplined Teutonic Knight with a passionate loathing for Communism'. He rose quickly through the ranks, graduating from the SS Leadership School in Charlottenburg in 1938 as SS-Obersturmfuhrer, just before being sent to Paris.[20]

Though Boemelburg was ostensibly on the lookout for German dissidents, he was in fact engaged in intelligence work. His real purpose was to seek out and make contact with those elements of French society who might be sympathetic to the Nazis, or who might just wish to earn some cash. Sometime during that summer of 1938, Déricourt and Herr Boemelburg were introduced. There is a story that Boemelburg's son, who was a student in Paris at the time, met Déricourt at an aerobatic display and later introduced him to his father. But that story is apocryphal[21] – it was Bodington who made the introduction, 'How would you like to meet a real German spy?'[22]

This was the start of a very important relationship and what an odd trio they were. A 28-year-old French pilot who dabbled in a bit of clandestine aerial photography and courier work, a 30-year-old English would-be spy, and the 53-year-old Nazi intelligence agent, dining together away from the gaze of Parisian society out at the hotel in Neuilly. These two individuals – Nicholas Bodington and Karl Boemelburg – were the most fortunate acquaintances Déricourt ever made. How Bodington knew who Boemelburg was is anybody's guess, but it wasn't long before the secret was shared by others and the little summer idyll was brought to an end.

About the time of the Munich crisis, in September 1938, the French authorities finally tumbled to Boemelburg's real purpose and he was summoned to the office of the Director-General of the Ministry of the Interior in the Rue Saussais, where he was informed in the classic language of the diplomatic world that his activities conflicted with his official status and that he was henceforth *persona non grata*. He left Paris that night.

Two years later, in June 1940, the newly promoted Sturmbannfuhrer Boemelburg returned to Paris. He drove down the Rue Saussais, entered the Ministry building and marched into the same office where in 1938 he had been humiliated. He confronted the same unfortunate individual and ordered him out from behind his desk with the words, 'That is my desk from now on!'[23]

II

'...The Hand of Albion'

At the beginning of 1939, Whitehall government departments received a number of alarming reports from MI6 which claimed that the long-held view that Hitler planned to invade Russia and capture the Ukraine was out of date. The German Chancellor, claimed MI6, had recently switched his plans to a surprise attack on the West. During the remaining nine months of peace the reports that followed varied wildly and helped to confuse government planners about any real threat of war.[1] MI6, today the Secret Intelligence Service (SIS), was the secret service charged with the responsibility of providing the British government with intelligence from abroad. It gathered this material through an extensive network of agents scattered about the globe who operated as secret receptacles for the kind of information foreign governments prefer to keep to themselves. At the beginning of 1939, MI6 operated two separate networks of agents. The first was, by secret service standards, conventional while the second was very unconventional, very extensive and very, very secret.

This 'other' network was controlled by an extremely powerful man within MI6, Claude Dansey, whose career with the service reached back almost to its roots. He had a reputation within the service as a man of great charm and wit who was utterly devious, extremely dangerous and occasionally downright terrifying. His pedigree, like that of the service, was a bit ropey.

The Secret Service Bureau was created in 1909 by a government alarmed by a series of reports (completely false) that there were extensive networks of German spies at work in Britain. The first head of the secret service was a retired naval commander named Mansfield Cumming who had a distinctly swashbuckling view of the business of intelligence gathering. He told one of his recruits, the author Compton Mackenzie, 'Spying is capital sport!'[2] Cumming travelled around Europe, usually in a disguise he had purchased from Bermans and Nathans, armed with nothing more lethal than a swordstick. He quickly earned a reputation as a tough advocate for his new profession, though at first the Bureau owed more to the traditions of the Boy Scout movement than to anything we would recognize today as espionage. The First World War changed everyone's attitude towards secret intelligence, though at some cost.

The single most important 'intelligence' lesson that emerged from the trenches – a lesson that virtually became an operational article of faith – was that there should be one and only one organization responsible for operating networks of secret agents abroad and that organization must have a complete monopoly over the evaluation and distribution of secret intelligence. In the chaos of Flanders, three, and sometimes four, separate British networks operated side by side, not counting the networks operated by the Belgians, the French and eventually the Americans.[3]

In July 1917, Claude Dansey, a forty-year-old veteran of the late colonial wars, transferred from MI5, the War Office department responsible for security at home, to Cumming's secret service to try to sort out the confusion that reigned within the networks in Holland.

> Low-class agents [sell] the same information and [draw] pay from more than one service. The professionals in Holland have now brought their competition to such a pitch, that nearly every third man is a Secret Service agent working for one of the belligerents, if not for both. If they [agents] find an allied service is getting better information than they do, some of them are not above giving information to the Germans about their successful competitors.[4]

Secret agent disloyalty aside, there was a far greater risk of disaster from information that was corrupted before it ever reached the chiefs of staff, simply because it came from too many disparate and unco-ordinated sources. Any piece of news that came from two or more separate sources was automatically considered to have been corroborated and was therefore given a higher degree of credence. Because agents sometimes sold the same piece of information to as many purchasers as were available, it was often the case that a very insignificant piece of intelligence was given an extremely high rating. Consequently it wasn't long before the military lost confidence in *any* intelligence that was delivered to them. Cumming, a classic megalomaniac, sought to change all that. By the end of the war, largely due to Dansey's efforts in Holland and an equally brilliant controller in Belgium, Captain Henry Landau, Cumming's ambitions were realized and the quality of intelligence improved beyond measure.[5]

Paradoxically, the advent of peace actually threatened the very existence of the secret service. With the 'German monster' crushed, the government could see no obvious threat from abroad that warranted the retention of an organization which it felt was an embarrassment. The very idea of an official British organization secretly engaged in opening foreign government mail had never sat well with English sensibilities. In the event, however, the secret service was rescued by the Russian revolution.

Cumming successfully convinced the government that the Bolshevik dictatorship in Russia was engaged in a vast scheme to infiltrate and subvert British trade unions and so export the revolution. The government had been handed a *new* threat from abroad and the future of the secret service was assured.

By 1921, when Cummings moved his headquarters to 1 Melbury Road, in London's Holland Park, he had created a professional organization built around a framework that has survived until today. In June 1923, when he died on his favourite office couch, Cumming bequeathed to his colleagues an expanding empire that would eventually become one of the most powerful and influential organs of government. He also bequeathed his own title. He was known throughout the service as 'C', and since then every director of MI6 has borne the same initial. More importantly he had secured for MI6 an absolute monopoly over all secret foreign intelligence gathering *and* the means to do it. MI6 had been placed, for administrative purposes, under the control of the Foreign Office. Through that august institution

MI6 agents were provided with diplomatic cover and were attached to British Embassies as Passport Control Officers. Their ostensible role was to issue passports and visas, whereas their real function was espionage.

By the 1930s, however, that arrangement had begun to fail. The hideous spectre of international Communism, so skilfully conjured and then exploited by Cumming ten years before, had effectively obscured the government's perception of developments in Germany. Very few British politicians were greatly disturbed by the political turmoil in that country, though one man who was, Winston Churchill, relentlessly badgered MI6 for a clearer picture of events in the old enemy's camp. Unfortunately, the current 'C', Admiral Hugh 'Quex' Sinclair, found it difficult to oblige. Successive governments had pared MI6's budget to the bone. The Passport Control network had been allowed to run down and was virtually an open secret within the diplomatic world, while Churchill's demands for better intelligence only served to highlight MI6's complete lack of penetration in Germany. MI6 was virtually bankrupt and many of its staff were being paid out of Sinclair's own pocket. In 1936 he sought a solution with the man who was at that time the PCO at the embassy in Rome, Claude Dansey.

Claude Edward Marjoribanks Dansey was born on 21 October 1876 in London's South Kensington to Captain Edward Dansey, an officer in the Life Guards, and the Honourable Eleanore Dansey, a daughter of the second Lord Gifford. The young Dansey's childhood was spent at innumerable addresses, in both Britain and France, as the family fortunes tended to fluctuate with his father's success on the Turf. With the promise of a career in his father's regiment, young Claude was enrolled at Wellington

College, an institution that provided an 'education of a military tenor'. Unfortunately, this period of relative stability was interrupted by an outbreak of diphtheria in 1891 which killed two boys and closed the school. Dansey was removed to Belgium, where he was entrusted to the care of the English College at Bruges.

But it would seem the young Claude was not destined to complete a normal education, for in 1893 Dansey was discovered to be involved in a homosexual ménage that rocked the college to its foundations. Claude admitted to having been seduced one holiday weekend at Windsor by Mr Robert Ross, one of Oscar Wilde's more notorious lovers. His father, infuriated by the risk of scandal, removed his son from boarding school education and from any hope of the Life Guards too. The entire affair was swept under the carpet and Claude was sent abroad.

He enlisted in the British South African Police, saw action in Rhodesia against the Matabele and Mashona in 1896 and further action in Sarawak with the British North Borneo Company Police in 1899. He returned to Africa, was involved in the relief of Mafeking in 1900 and soon after joined the Intelligence Department of the British Army's General Staff. Then from 1904 to 1909, in what was one of the last of Britain's colonial wars, the young Captain Dansey served as an Intelligence Officer with the British Somaliland Protectorate in operations against the so-called 'Mad Mullah', Muhammad 'Abdille Hassan.

Sometime around 1911, Dansey seems to have slipped unobtrusively into the newly formed secret service and under the robust influence of Mansfield Cumming. At the end of the Great War, Dansey left intelligence work, preferring to make a career in the business world, and during the 1920s made a great many important contacts in America and Europe. But fortune failed to smile and following the Wall Street Crash in 1929 he returned to Britain and to what was by then MI6.[6]

As the Passport Control Officer in Rome, Dansey quickly appreciated that the resources available to him were completely inadequate to fund any sort of professional intelligence operation, so he established an unofficial network of informers from his contacts in the business world.[7] These businessmen, most of whom had dealings in Germany, supplied him with information on Germany's re-armament programmes and, more significantly, on the clandestine flow of currency loans to Germany through the Swiss banking system.

During 1936, MI6 discovered that its continental networks had been penetrated by German intelligence. 'Quex' Sinclair decided to tackle his problems of failing resources and German penetration by exploiting Dansey's unofficial links with the business world. During the autumn the PCO Rome was summoned to London on the pretext that some financial irregularities had been discovered in the Rome accounts. (This was in fact quite true.) Nothing was said officially, but it was tacitly understood that Dansey had been caught with his hands in the till and had been cashiered. It was generally thought that ultimately he had gone abroad, which in a sense was also true.[8]

In fact it was a typical piece of deception, the kind of thing Dansey made a speciality. Rather than scrap the PCO network, which would have signalled to German intelligence that MI6 knew it was compromised, it was decided to leave everything as it was – and create a completely new network from scratch. The Z Organization was constructed by Dansey around his well-established business contacts and through these gradually spread across Europe with its operational headquarters in Switzerland and Holland. The cashiered Dansey became 'Z-1', the controller of the network, and apart from Sinclair virtually no one else at MI6 knew of its existence.[9] From his headquarters in a suite of offices on the eighth floor of Bush House, Dansey's network had the added advantage of being virtually self-financing, thanks to the benevolence of patriotic businessmen.

This network of 'Z men' extended right across the commercial spectrum: Rex Pearson from Unilever, Basil Fenwick from Royal Dutch Shell, William Stevenson of the Pressed Steel Company, even the film producer Alexander Korda who established London Film Productions. Being in sole charge, Dansey ran the network as his own personal fiefdom, far from the gaze of his colleagues. He took advantage of the Z Organization's anonymity to employ a number of irregular operatives. Petty criminals, forgers, brothel keepers and embezzlers all took Dansey's shilling. He acknowledged that criminals, perhaps more than any other social type, were naturally suited to employment in an undercover operation. Dansey had created in a very short space of time an extremely sophisticated and flexible organization that spanned the breadth of Europe. Impressive though this was, the quality of the intelligence it gathered was, for some reason, very inconsistent.[10]

On 1 September 1939, Hitler's troops crossed the Polish frontier. Inside the British intelligence community, events moved almost as swiftly as the German Panzer divisions across the Polish countryside. The sudden reappearance of Claude Dansey at MI6 headquarters in London was a stunning shock to those who had presumed him to be in disgrace 'living abroad'. They were equally surprised by the revelation that he was the head of an extensive network of agents. There was no time for explanations.

As the Prime Minister, Neville Chamberlain, was preparing to announce to the nation that 'Britain is at war with Germany', Dansey and his assistant Kenneth Cohen (Z-2) were hurriedly preparing for a lightning dash across the Continent to their advance action stations. With code-books and other material, Cohen travelled to Paris, where he set up shop alongside the PCO man there, Commander Wilfred (Biffy) Dunderdale. Meanwhile Dansey made for Zurich in Switzerland. Just before his departure, he signalled to his Z man in Holland to drop previous security precautions and proceed to liaise with the PCO man in The Hague. It was a critical error.

When back in 1936 MI6 first received evidence that its PCO networks had been penetrated by German intelligence, that evidence had come from Holland. Up to September 1939 the Z man in Holland, Sigismund Payne Best, had operated with complete anonymity beside the PCO man, Major Richard Stevens. MI6 had no reliable evidence that the PCO network was any more secure in 1939 than it had been in 1936, so the decision to open the curtains was an odd one. Dansey's orders were for Stevens to supply Best with finance and communications facilities with London. This link inevitably compromised all MI6's operations in Europe.

The German military intelligence organization, the *Abwehr*, had identified a succession of MI6 station chiefs in Holland. Ever since Stevens's arrival in 1937, his headquarters, his movements and those of his operatives had been carefully monitored and catalogued. In a move that was to be repeated throughout the war, the Nazi

Party's own security service, the Sicherheitsdienst, or SD, assumed control of German counter-espionage operations in Holland, with devastating results.

In 1938 a Dr Franz Fischer, an SD informer who was keeping an eye on German refugees in Holland, succeeded in winning the confidence of one of Claude Dansey's operatives. Dr Fischer was engaged in much the same kind of work as Karl Boemelburg, though Fischer had so far evaded detection. Dansey subsequently recommended Dr Fischer to his Z man, Best, insisting that he would lead them to some valuable contacts in the German air force. Best was suspicious of this Dr Fischer, but was encouraged by 'C's' deputy Stewart Menzies to maintain contact. Dr Fischer claimed to be in contact with a dissident Luftwaffe officer who was involved in a military plot against Hitler. If there was such a plot, then it may prove an avenue towards peace. By October, Best had met this officer, a Major Solms, at a small hotel in the Dutch border town of Venlo. Solms was in fact a German counter-intelligence officer by the name of Johannes Traviglio. With Best and Stevens working together as a team and the two of them being led further up the path by their German contacts, everything now depended on how Whitehall interpreted the signals from Venlo. By 19 October a meeting had been held between Best and Stevens and two other 'dissident officers' where they discussed the sort of terms under which Britain would consider peace.

But in the meantime, back in London, a battle for succession caused a certain amount of distraction at a point when no one in MI6 could afford to take their eye off the ball. Admiral Hugh Sinclair, 'C', died on 4 November. Claude Dansey dropped everything and returned to London to declare his candidacy for the new head of MI6. His main rivals were Stewart Menzies and Rear Admiral Godfrey, the Director of Naval Intelligence. But on this occasion both the Navy and Dansey were out-manoeuvred when Menzies produced a sealed envelope containing a letter from Sinclair which recommended his deputy for the post. Dansey quickly appreciated that his own cause was lost and threw his support behind Menzies. As they waited for the Cabinet to make up its mind, attention switched back to the town of Venlo.

Best and Stevens had arranged to meet the key figures in the anti-Hitler conspiracy on 7 November. Further meetings were arranged for the 8th and again for the 9th at a small café situated between the frontier gates, though still officially on Dutch soil. On the 9th, Best and Stevens went to the café and watched as a black Mercedes proceeded from the German gates. Before they realized what was happening, the doors of the Mercedes swung open and an SD snatch squad leapt out and bundled Best and Stevens into the back of the car.[11]

At first, reports from Holland led Dansey to presume that Best and Stevens were dead. Long before the 9th, MI6 had established radio contact with the 'conspirators', and as these contacts continued and seemed to give no mention of any arrests, they concluded that the dissident officers were still safe and were proceeding with their plot against Hitler. But then on 22 November, MI6 received another message informing them that they had been duped from the beginning. What became known as the Venlo incident had been a brilliant piece of counter-espionage work that had a major psychological effect on both sides.

The effect on MI6 and on Claude Dansey in particular was to highlight the gradual emergence of the SD as a serious intelligence adversary when up till then they had been seen as little more than a particularly obnoxious secret police force.

From the outside, the Sicherheitsdienst and the Gestapo appeared identical. In fact the SD was far more ruthless and effective. It had begun life as the security section of Himmler's SS, with the responsibility for ensuring that no political influence, other than National Socialism, established a presence in the new Reich. During the early Thirties it was concerned with the business of monitoring the mood and thoughts of the population, which it did by controlling an army of informers from the countryside to the universities, and processing a vast archive of secret information on millions of German citizens. By 1936–7, under the influence of its head of counter-intelligence, Walter Schellenberg (the architect of the Venlo incident), the SD adopted a new role as guardian of the nation's moral wellbeing and conducted a number of investigations into corruption within the Party. In this new guise the SD began to attract a large number of young intellectuals, doctors, philosophers and lawyers who saw it as an opportunity to correct unnatural faults in German society. In truth they were attracted by a more fundamental instinct – power. Nevertheless, as a result of this influx of intelligentsia, the SD became almost overnight a creature with two personalities.[12] It was at once the secret tool of the Party and at the same time an intelligence organization. It was described by Schellenberg as 'The versatile instrument for use against all opposition circles and in all spheres of life, the people's sense of touch and feel.' In the grand scheme of things, 'the SD was destined to become the Intelligence Service of the Great German Reich'.[13]

Oberfuhrer Reinhard Heydrich, the head of the SD, even began to identify himself on his correspondence as 'C'.[14]

In August 1938, five months after Hitler's troops had occupied Austria, the SD tracked down and arrested the head of the MI6 station in Vienna, Captain Thomas Kendrick. In spring 1939 the Czech network collapsed. Then there was Venlo, which subsequently compromised all the Continental networks. Schellenberg's ambitions were fast coming to fruition and the new secret service was proving to be a most deadly adversary. To Dansey, the full import of these developments was only just beginning to sink in.

Despite the Venlo débâcle, Menzies was confirmed as the new head of MI6 and, surprisingly, Claude Dansey was made assistant chief. They moved into offices on the fourth floor of MI6 headquarters at Broadway Buildings, 54 Broadway, just opposite St James's Park tube station. The sign at the entrance announced 'The Minimaz Fire Extinguisher Company'. Menzies inherited all the trappings of his post: a beautifully appointed house at 21 St Anne's Gate which was connected by a secret corridor to the rear of Broadway Buildings and then by private staircase to his elegantly furnished office. Inside was a vast antique desk that Mansfield Cumming had brought with him from the Admiralty, a full-length portrait of the original 'C', and copious quantities of a green ink with which he signed all his documents. (The portrait still hangs in the present-day 'C's' office and he still employs the green ink.)

Dansey's office was next door to 'C's', but he rarely occupied it. He preferred to operate away from Broadway, either from his own flat at 3 Albemarle Street or at one of

MI6's addresses such as the flat at 5 St James's Street. The first priority was to amalgamate the Z Organization and the PCO networks and then get down to examining the damage. However, as the phoney war slowly ticked away, the SD's interrogation of Best and Stevens was gradually opening up the inner workings of MI6.

By the end of 1939, Dansey still stood at the head of an extensive organization, though its effectiveness was diminishing each day. He had been given responsibility for all network operations, while Menzies had overall control of the service and specific responsibility for the relatively new field of signals intelligence. The relationship between the two men was close but not friendly. Menzies had links with the landed gentry and divided his private life between riding to hounds, the Turf and White's. Dansey on the other hand was something of a loner. Though blessed with great quantities of charm he could not disguise a cold hard centre which discouraged admiration or sentiment. He seemed to harbour a brooding resentment for something – though precisely what, no one knew – which he often vented through the most vitriolic and withering criticisms of his colleagues. He preferred the society of Boodle's and the Savoy, where he would hold court before terrified young recruits.[15] For the first few years Menzies was somewhat in awe of Dansey, who at 63 was four years older than his chief. It became impossible for anyone to see Menzies without Dansey's intimidating presence, causing visiting intelligence officers from Poland and France to comment on how 'C' seemed to defer to his deputy.[16]

But the MI6 to which Dansey had returned was not the same outfit he had known five years before, the domain of ex-Indian policemen and naval types. There had been a vast influx of new recruits, mostly graduates and intellectuals, a breed he particularly disliked. He once wrote: 'I have less fear of Bolshies and Fascists than I have of some pedantic but vocal university professor.'[17] He was a man who had a passionate dislike of many things. He distrusted women agents and was convinced they were a liability rather than an asset; he disliked counter-intelligence officers, positively hated the French and utterly despised Americans.[18] He held a very cynical, though some would say pragmatic, view of humanity, claiming, 'Every man has his price and every woman is seducible.'

The creation of the Z Organization was by any standard a remarkable feat, though apart from having provided a springboard for Dansey's own ambitions it achieved very little else – except in one particular respect. It was an exceptionally well-kept secret. Its inner workings mirrored 'Z-1' himself, utterly mysterious and impenetrable. Nevertheless, by the end of 1939 he was arguably the most powerful individual in the British intelligence community. It remained to be seen how he would wield that power.

III

The Fall

During August 1939, as the last few weeks of peace slipped away, there was in France an unsettling mood of ambiguity. Had there been an obvious threat to the nation, her citizens would have risen up as one. Instead she was taking up arms because of her commitments to other countries. There seemed nothing clear about any of the issues, and to the average Frenchman it made no sense at all. 'Was not the plight of Poland no different than Czechoslovakia – and what had we done for Czechoslovakia?'[1]

Throughout France scenes of farewell were played out in homes, at hotels and at railway stations. Twenty-five years before, open displays of emotion had been considered unmanly or a disgrace to the family, but in August 1939 men and women embraced and wept openly at the prospect of separation. The only comfort was that at least it would be for only a few months. Twenty-five years earlier, when the French soldier last marched through the streets to war, his brass buttons glinted in the sunlight, there was a red slash down his trousers from his belt to his puttees and the sight of that sea of uniform blue invariably evoked a great cheer from pavements choked with waving tricolours. Now the army was a sea of muddy khaki, the colour that blended so well with the harvest. The buttons were green; the scarlet slash, such an excellent target for the enemy, was gone; and the pavements were now empty but for the odd group of veterans who had stirred themselves for the occasion.

Many civilians questioned the usefulness and even the legality of the mobilization, while many commanders complained of a lack of patriotic ardour amongst the junior officers. In fact, throughout the military hierarchy there were doubts about morale.

On the day that Germany invaded Poland, Nicholas Bodington watched a parade of the uncommitted and complaining new army, from his window at the Hotel Philadelphia. His only preoccupation, and that of most journalists, was what exacdy was France going to *do* about Poland? The French established a 'general formation of strength' around the Alsace-Lorraine border, and Bodington received permission to travel up to where they appeared to be making their first move.[2] On 9 September he reported the movement of a number of French Army groups into the Saar district of Germany, effectively straightening a number of sinuous kinks in the frontier and taking some thirty-six German villages in the process. The Germans retaliated by firing a few exploratory artillery rounds and then retreating to pre-determined positions, behind concrete defences. The whole performance was conducted exactly as French military planners had hypothesized months before and was intended as simply a warning manoeuvre. As this charade was taking place, in Poland thirty-five Polish divisions were being chased across the open countryside by an apparently omnipotent military juggernaut.

Despite the news from Poland, the French seemed pleased with the disciplined, though limited, manoeuvre in the Saar. Press reports were full of how the French Air Force had dealt with twelve Messerschmitts in one day. But the public were indifferent. The average peasant, now barracked and clothed in khaki, was thinking of his fields and who would deal with the ploughing and the planting. What would become of his family if the work was neglected?

When Bodington returned to Paris he learnt that Déricourt too had been swept away in the preparations for war. They were not to see each other again for another three years. Paris now seemed populated with an ever-expanding Press Corps straining to get news from the east. But the atmosphere of war, or the promise of war, made him feel out of place just reporting it. He felt a particular sense of wasted potential, especially after a humiliating incident that had occurred in April. Using his father's contacts at the British Embassy, Bodington had managed to get an interview with one of the officers at the MI6 station and made a formal application to join the secret service. The secret agent *manqué* wanted to make an honest man of himself. Bodington's application was sent to London, but to his utter amazement London was not interested.[3] His big mistake was in having told Déricourt about his intentions so that after his rejection he had to laugh the whole thing off: 'Who knows what London wants these days.'

Soon after his return to Paris, he had been informed by his editors that he could either stay in Paris as long as he wished or be transferred to the UK. London at least offered the opportunity of some kind of involvement in the war, whereas Paris promised intrigue. He was in two minds about what to do.

As the last few embers of resistance were being stamped out in Poland, Karl Boemelburg received a message at his office in Prague. The message, from SS Sturmbannfuhrer Horst Kopkow at Reich Central Security in Berlin, invited Boemelburg to consider a position in Warsaw within the next few months. Boemelburg had been in Czechoslovakia since the end of 1938, where he was Head of the Political Department and had been operating a campaign against communist partisans and foreign intelligence networks, most notably MI6's. He was of an age and reputation, if not rank, where he could almost decide his own posting. He declined Kopkow's offer, having decided to stay in Prague until something a little more conducive came along.[4]

–

Meanwhile, in France, the British Expeditionary Force was renewing old acquaintances. For months they marched back and forth, presented each other with medals and kissed each other fraternally on the cheek. Déricourt's role during what the French came to call the 'Drole de Guerre' was equally uninspiring. He had been dismissed from the Air Corps reserve in January 1937 for another of his unaccountable absences, and so on 3 September he was disappointed, but hardly surprised, to be ordered to report to the Séction Aérienne de Transport (SAT) at the military airfield at Étampes. There would be no combat flying for him.[5]

But before his war officially started, he too received a signal. On the following day, his birthday, he was about to get into his little car and drive out to the airfield, when the vehicle was destroyed by a heavy truck that collided with it. He was not hurt. That evening, while he was in a restaurant, a fight broke out between some people at the next table, one of whom pulled out a gun and fired a shot. The bullet passed clean through Déricourt's hair, and again he was not harmed. He noted these events in a diary, perhaps some time afterwards, describing them as a premonition that the war would spare him.[6]

Promoted to the rank of sergeant, Déricourt was thrown into a squadron with the Air France pilot Rémy Clément – now a captain, and given the task of flying any of a dozen different craft that had been commandeered to transport men and equipment up to the line. They were a support unit for a fighter group, accompanying it to the border each day where they would take up battle stations, and then flying back again at dusk to Etampes.[7] Déricourt tired of this job very quickly and managed to get transferred to a position as a test pilot with the Lloret Olivier company in Marseilles. The French aircraft industry had been nationalized in the 1930s and then broken up into geographical divisions. In Marseilles, Déricourt was employed by the *Société Nationale de Construction Aeronautiques de Sud Est* – or SNCASE, of which the old Lloret Olivier company was now an anonymous member. They were about to commence a long series of trials of their new Leo 451, a high-performance bomber, and a strange new craft called an Autogyro.

In April 1940 Déricourt began familiarization sessions on the new Leo, at about the same time as reports were being received in Paris that the Germans were planning an attack across the river Meuse, sometime between 8 and 10 May. A column of armour, sixty miles long, was snaking its way towards the Meuse, but despite all the visual proof, the French High Command refused to believe the Germans would attack at that spot.

In London, MI6 had more than sufficient intelligence of what was to come, some of it passed on through secret links with the Vatican. The Deuxième Bureau was equally well informed, but despite peppering the French High Command with reports during the first week of May, tens of thousands of men were either sent on leave or were already absent.

On 10 May, Déricourt took the gleaming new Leo up for the first time. The testing schedule was a modest one: climb to 10,000 feet, which he did in less than ten seconds, and then cruise out over the Mediterranean at a blistering 300 miles an hour.[8] The Leo 451 was one of the stars of the French aircraft industry. It had a range of over 1600 miles and could carry up to 2400 lb of bombs. The flight lasted eighty minutes and was a great success for both aircraft and pilot. Back in the wardroom, watching the sunset glistening on the wings of the Leo in the distance, Déricourt listened to the radio from Paris announce that massive German armoured divisions had attacked Holland and Belgium that morning. It seemed to Henri as though the war was on the other side of the world.

Every day for the rest of that week, Déricourt took the Leo up to put her through her paces, and every day the German forces punched their way deeper into the south and west. On 11 May the Germans crossed the Albert Canal, overwhelming the Belgians. On the 13th Rotterdam surrendered and on the following day, when Holland capitulated, the Germans crossed the Meuse. Déricourt took the Leo up for two separate tests that day and by the time he brought her down for the second time[9] the Germans had forced a breach in the French line fifty miles wide and were pouring Panzer divisions across the country. On the 15th Déricourt took the aircraft up for an unprecedented two and a half hours,[10] during which time the French Prime Minister telephoned the new British Prime Minister, Winston Churchill, 'We are beaten. We have lost the battle.'

–

Cruising well above 12,000 feet in the late spring sunshine, in the specially sound-proofed cockpit, Déricourt was insulated from the carnage below. Life continued as though he were travelling on a different stream. On the 19th, the day he took the Leo up three times to solve a transmission problem, he met an attractive married woman in the foyer of his hotel.[11] Mme Jeanne Gamerre was in fact the telephonist at the Hotel Noailles and was just leaving for the day as Déricourt was coming in. Henri's reputation had gone before him and at first Mme Gamerre was not interested. 'Most men would take a guitar and serenade a woman from beneath her window,' Rémy Clément once said; 'Henri used to take the guitar up into her bedroom.'[12] But within three weeks she had moved into Henri's room.

As May became June, nothing seemed to stem the rush of the catastrophe in the north. The remnants of the British Expeditionary Force plus a few thousand French were evacuated from the beaches at Dunkirk and France felt the first pangs of abandonment. Mute and stunned, citizens stood in the streets and watched the columns of Germans march deeper into their country. On the day the enemy paraded down the Champs-Élysées, many of the staff at SNCASE got drunk and cursed their soldiers, their commanders and their government. The latter was at that time scattered in various châteaux in the Tours area and trying to regroup at Bordeaux. Having done so, they swiftly brought the first part of France's war to an end.

On 22 June Déricourt climbed into a brand new Leo 451, just off the production line.[13] Its bright silver fuselage trembled as he started each of the Hispano-Suiza engines and slowly began the process of running them in. Gradually building up compression, keeping an eye on the oil pressure and temperature, he opened the throttle. He could feel the strain on the aircraft frame increase and double checked that the brake pressure was high enough – he didn't want the aircraft rolling down the runway. A bit more throttle and then he let it idle until he received the signal from the ground crew that they were satisfied with the sound of the engines. Once he got the thumbs-up, he switched off the engines and waited for all the noise and trembling to stop.

That evening they learnt that an armistice had been signed with the Germans, in the same railway carriage at Compiègne that had been the scene of Germany's humiliation at the end of the last war. Compiègne was not far from Déricourt's home, but it would be months before he knew his parents were safe.

All activity at SNCASE came to a temporary halt. The staff were stood down, but not dismissed. That evening Henri waited for Mme Gamerre to come off duty and they walked down oddly silent streets to their favourite restaurant. It was closed in mourning, so they went back to their room. Jeanne Gamerre was separated from her husband, who was one of the humiliated ranks of khaki choking the roads of France. She had not seen him in over a year, and as far as she was concerned he was lost. Now there was Henri, a few years younger than herself and very glamorous with it.

Jeanne's small frame and childlike features contained an infectious spirit that could at once be overwhelmed with joy or the darkest despression. She was a simple individual who knew nothing about why the war had been fought and understood even less about why her country had been thrown into this situation. All that really mattered at that moment was that Henri was a pilot, incredibly brave and knowing by her standards, who preferred to call her Jeannot and who seemed to care for her. In the coming months, when there would be little news of any comfort, they were insulated. Even when the management of the hotel, scandalized by their flagrant cohabitation, asked them both to leave, it was of no consequence at all.[14]

During July and August, as France began to collect herself round the comforting figure of Maréchal Pétain, the Germans built up a massive invasion force for an operation they called Sea Lion. Thousands of landing craft, tanks and men were gathered at the port of Calais; their objective was the island of Britain and they were scheduled to embark no later than the first week of September.

As France looked on, fed on a growing diet of Nazi propaganda, she waited for the news that Britain had capitulated, and that the Pax Germanica had been extended to the Irish Sea. As every Briton knows, what was expected abroad was never delivered. The RAF's finest hour, specifically the last two weeks of August and the first week of September 1940, effectively extinguished Hitler's ambitions in the west. By the end of September, intelligence could report that the massive invasion force was being dismantled. The psychological effect that was left in its train had far greater significance for both sides than anyone could have imagined at the time. The month of September and the port of Calais became lodged together in the collective sub-conscious.

Occasionally, while Déricourt was aloft in the bomber, he was caught up short by the sight of roads choked with human misery, of the refugees heading south. Everyone, it seemed, was going south. These, he told others afterwards, were 'the little people'. Landing at the Marseilles airfield at Marignon had become far more difficult, littered as it was with hundreds of aircraft that had been part of the exodus.

At the end of September Déricourt took up a proto-type Autogyro called the C301. The Autogyro was a strange craft which the local manufacturers had seen as their great white hope. It had a fuselage like an aircraft, but had no wings. Instead there was a set of rotor blades, like a helicopter's, mounted just behind the cockpit. In front was a straightforward engine and propeller, which dragged the craft forward, and this movement in turn forced the overhead blades to rotate; the faster forward the machine moved, the faster the rotation of the blades, until the craft lifted almost vertically into the air. The concept was not original, but the French manufacturers had made a number of important design advances which made the craft particularly fast.

In October, Déricourt demonstrated the C301 to a number of representatives of the German Armaments Commission. The demonstration took place on precisely the same day as Maréchal Pétain shook hands with Adolph Hitler at Montoire and later announced to the French public that he would take France down the road of collab-oration. At the end of that day, 24 October, Déricourt brought his flight log up to date at 3518 hours and 38 minutes and did not fly for SNCASE again.[15] He was paid up to the end of November and then joined a massive army of unemployed Frenchmen and -women, whose industries had been closed down or were being re-harnessed to the German war effort.

The winter of 1940–1 was one of the hardest in living memory. German demands for food and fuel created chronic shortages and great hardship. Petrol became a currency in itself. Soup kitchens appeared in the streets of all the major towns and cities, homes were rarely heated, queues formed at *boulangeries* for rationed bread while the conquerors turned Paris into a 'German Babylon'. Henri and Jeannot survived on what she earned as a telephonist, but even this dried up in November. They discovered Jeannot had been pregnant for three months, but the embryo was extra-uterine and had to be aborted. There were complications and Jeannot was ill for some time. Déricourt needed to earn some money.

Many enterprising individuals took advantage of the situation to make a living from the black market. The Germans, while not actually encouraging it, did little to prevent it from flourishing. For the black market was food and drink to the established criminal organizations and these were important allies of the Gestapo and the SD. Déricourt occasionally earned some money in the employ of the notorious Corsican gangsters Paul Carbone and François Spirito,[16] whose fortune had been made in narcotics traffic with America. But there was more money to be made where the Germans were in greater numbers, and so, very soon after Jeannot's abortion, Déricourt got permission to travel into the occupied zone.

Déricourt was devoted to Jeannot, but never faithful. During this and other trips to Paris, he invariably stayed with a woman who was separated from her husband, Mme

Julienne Aisner. They had known each other for a good many years and for some of that time had been lovers, but by 1940 they were what Henri described as 'comfortable friends'. Julienne, or 'JuJu' as Henri called her, was at that time beginning to see someone else, a young lawyer by the name of Charles Besnard. But JuJu and Henri had known each other so long that Besnard was no obstacle to their friendship.[17]

Déricourt's business was with one of the great Paris black-marketeers, Bladier. This enterprising gentleman was making his fortune by supplying the occupying forces, and anyone else who could afford it, with whatever they needed. Abandoned or confiscated apartments, vehicles scattered all across the city and petrol were the mainstays of his trade. Bladier not only did well out of the wealthy Parisians, but also out of his special relationship with the local office of the SD.[18]

The Sicherheitsdienst were establishing themselves with great efficiency at an extremely luxurious set of apartments between numbers 78 and 84 Avenue Foch, near the Port Maillot Metro station. (By the end of the year, the Avenue Foch had become known as Avenue Boch.) Among the very first to arrive was of course Sturmbannfuhrer Karl Boemelburg, who was for some time the highest-ranking SD man in France. He was formally head of Desk IV a2, Counter-Sabotage, and was senior to Heinrich Reiser, Desk IVa, Counter-Espionage.[19] Following Boemelburg's self-gratifying confrontation with the Director General of the Ministry of the Interior, his men laid hands on the most comprehensive secret police records outside Nazi Germany. Every criminal, every terrorist, every foreign intelligence operative whom the French had kept under surveillance was listed here – it was a treasure-house of French low life. Once Berlin heard of the discovery, *all* the files were sent to Heidrich's headquarters at the Reichssicherheitshauptamt – RSHA (Reich Central Security Office) – and incorporated into their own files.[20]

It was Bladier who informed Déricourt that someone by the name of Karl Boemelburg was the head of the SD in Paris. The date of their reunion is uncertain, but it was sometime before the end of 1940. Karl Braun, Boemelburg's driver, recalled that Déricourt had been sitting in a café one morning when Boemelburg, himself and one other had turned up for coffee; Déricourt had noticed a large American limousine pull up outside and seemed to recognize Boemelburg as he stepped out. When they entered the restaurant, Déricourt stood up to greet him. There was a moment's hesitation from Boemelburg and then a smile of recognition. He greeted Déricourt politely but not warmly. He was, after all, the head of countersabotage and counter-subversion for all France.

With Boemelburg and Braun on this occasion was SS-Untersturmfuhrer Josef Kieffer, Boemelburg's immediate subordinate. Kieffer took no interest in the conversation and went to his table. Boemelburg and Déricourt reminisced about the summer of 1938 and then the SD man got very excited about showing off his new car. It was the armour-plated Cadillac that had belonged to the head of the French Communist Party. Braun watched as his chief went over the controls for Déricourt's benefit, then rapped the armour-plating with his knuckles as though he were a salesman for Cadillac. Braun was a simple man who found his chief's enthusiasms childish.[21]

Following this encounter, Déricourt met with Boemelburg on a number of occasions, but there is no evidence that he was involved in any work for the Germans at that stage. Although he became relatively well known in black-market circles, Déricourt had no particular cachet; there was nothing about him or his situation that might have been of any use or value to someone like Boemelburg, who was at that time engaged in a massive operation against the Russians.

It is often forgotten that during the 1940s the Germans in effect fought two wars at the same time, and that the one in the west was by far the smaller of the two. Just as German military commanders' careers were often split between the eastern and western fronts, so too were those of counter-intelligence operatives. Boemelburg's career is a perfect example of an SD officer who began by pursuing Russian agents in Germany and concluded by pursuing British agents in France.

By the end of 1940, the Nazis had learnt of an extensive Soviet intelligence network (the *Rote Kapelle* or Red Orchestra), that was operating deep in the heart of Germany and which, by 1941, extended into Western Europe. The man responsible for the campaign against the Communists was Reichskriminaldirektor Heinrich Muller, or Gestapo Muller, as he became known. Around him, Muller had collected a number of like-minded souls, like Horst Kopkow, who was head of counter-intelligence and counter-sabotage and who also had responsibility for the forging of political documents. Kopkow's representative in France was Boemelburg. For the better part of 1941 and early 1942, Boemelburg's preoccupation would be the hunting down and arrest of leaders of the Red Orchestra in France, the so-called '*Grand Chef*' and '*Petit Chef*'.[22]

In July 1941 Boemelburg sent word to Déricourt that a new airline was starting up and was looking for experienced pilots. Pétain's government had set up shop in the little spa town of Vichy, in what was hoped would be temporary accommodation. A year later, this arrangement still existed, and the Vichy government decided to put together an airline that would ease their communications problem. The *Service Civil des Liaison Aeriennes de la Métrople* (SCLAM) was essentially an airline for government use only, and although it had 'Civil' in its title there were rarely any fare-paying passengers. It flew to the large towns in the unoccupied zone, to the colonies in North Africa and to a few cities in Italy. Déricourt flew the old Goeland, a standard transport aircraft that could take up to six passengers. These tended to be Vichy government or military officials and sometimes German representatives.[23] Although he was flying again, Déricourt didn't feel comfortable with the Vichy authorities and he made his feelings known to many of the pilots at Marignon. As the occupation and the war began to take on a look of permanence, Déricourt started to look for ways out.

IV

Organization

Nicholas Bodington arrived in London just as the Germans were entering Paris. He had found a post with a semi-clandestine organization at Electra House, called the Political Intelligence Department.[1] Its function at that stage was to monitor and collect foreign radio and press reports, produce a digest and circulate it within interested government departments. It was also responsible for the first tentative steps in the production of subversive propaganda aimed at the enemy. It was not MI6, but it would do for the present.

The summer of 1940 saw many radical changes in Britain's attitude to the war, and much of that change of heart was due to one man. Unlike France, which in times of crises seemed always to turn to heroes from its past, Britain turned to a man who was, to most people, an unknown quantity. When Winston Churchill became Prime Minister and Minister of Defence on 7 May he brought a wholly new and aggressive approach to the prosecution of the war – and at a time when the opportunity for aggression was extremely limited. The most significant change Churchill brought about was an obsessive interest in the work of the secret services. From his youthful days in Britain's late colonial wars, he had developed a fascination for the work of spies and continued that fascination when in government. Even when he was not in government, Churchill maintained secret contacts with MI6 and MI5, which provided him with invaluable material with which to attack the Labour Government. He saw the secret services as a legitimate means by which influence might be exercised.

The secret services, however, viewed Churchill in 1940 as something of a double-edged sword. While on the one hand he secured for them more money than they had ever seen before, at the same time he tried to involve himself as much as possible with what they were up to. This degree of interest was something quite new to the men at Broadway Buildings, for here was a man who wanted to sit up with the engine driver, not with the guard. He criticized them for giving him digests or break-downs of reports. 'Authentic documents ... in their original form,'[2] he demanded – and received. Even then his voracious appetite for paperwork remained remarkably unsatisfied. Churchill also cherished a childlike fascination for the secret agents themselves and often insisted on meeting them before they departed on a mission, causing all kinds of headaches.

In the middle of May, just as Churchill was forming his wartime Cabinet, the Chiefs of Staff were preparing a report drawn up in the light of what seemed like the inevitable collapse of France. This report suggested that in the event of German victory in Western Europe, 'The creation of widespread revolt in Germany's conquered territories would become a major British strategic objective. For this a special organization would be needed, and in [our] view ought to be set up promptly.'[3]

Lord Hankey, operating on Churchill's instructions, looked into this report and concluded that, '…the burden of propaganda and subversion activities at Electra House should be joined with a special section within MI6, devoted to sabotage behind enemy lines, called Section D, led by Colonel Grand.'[4]

The idea had immense appeal to the new PM who, after just a few weeks in the job, had had to contend with the British Army's ignominious retreat from the shores of Dunkirk. If Britons could return to Europe, even clandestinely, well then, this was better than sitting at home licking their wounds.

At a meeting at the Foreign Office on 1 July, at which the new Head of MI6, Stewart Menzies, was present, it was agreed that this new service would be established without delay. As it would operate abroad and under cover, Menzies naturally assumed that it would come under the wing of MI6 and the Foreign Office. However, that assumption did not take account of coalition politics. Churchill's wartime National Government contained representatives from every political party. A somewhat paranoid Labour Party made it a condition of their joining the National Government that they must be given responsibility for one of the secret services. Labour had assumed this would be MI5. The Conservatives were reluctant to agree, but the creation of a new secret service presented Churchill with the solution. The Labour intellectual, Hugh Dalton, was made Minister for Economic Warfare and given responsibility for the new organization.

When news of this arrangement reached Claude Dansey he threw up his hands and declared, 'It's a disaster.'[5] He urged Menzies to try to halt the arrangement before it was too late, but Menzies, a little more attuned to the politics of the situation, knew how impossible that would be. Nevertheless, he sympathized with Dansey. A new secret service, not only completely separate from MI6, but not even under the umbrella of the same ministry, operating clandestine networks of agents behind enemy lines – it contradicted the most fundamental principles upon which MI6 was founded.

Even though the new service would not be responsible for intelligence matters, the very fact of its existence behind enemy lines meant that it would inevitably collect some secret information from the Continent. *Two* sources of foreign intelligence: it conjured up spectres of some of the intelligence disasters of the last war.

As Menzies had predicted, Churchill was not easily diverted from his course, and at a meeting on 22 July 'C' agreed with the proposed arrangement. His only compensation was an assurance that all intelligence, no matter what its source, would have to be channelled through MI6, who would digest it and be responsible for its distribution. Unfortunately, one major consequence for MI6 had escaped Menzies' attention. The original plan was to create this new organization out of an amalgamation of the subversion and propaganda outfit at Electra House, Military Intelligence (Research) and MI6's own Section D (Sabotage). Lord Halifax, the then Foreign Secretary, had agreed with Hugh Dalton that Section D was to be shifted across, in toto. Although Dansey knew what was going on, for some reason Menzies did not. It wasn't until 5 September that he learnt that an entire department of his empire was no longer there. No one had thought to tell him…[6]

Now Menzies had both personal and professional reasons for disliking this new outfit. He, however, was forced to accept the situation. Dansey was not. Section D was full of men Dansey knew well. Though they were all professionals to a man, how could anyone expect an officer to be loyal to MI6 on Friday, and then loyal to completely new masters on Monday?

This new organization was, of course, the Special Operations Executive – the SOE. It began as a unit made up of three main sections: Subversion, Sabotage and Research. The core of the organization took over Section D's old premises in St Ermin's Hotel, close to MI6 at Broadway Buildings. In October it moved to its famous address at 64 Baker Street. Eventually the Subversion section was hived off and formed into another separate organization, the Political Warfare Executive, and the Research section seemed to atrophy through inactivity. That left the area of expertise for which SOE is historically famous, Sabotage.

Dansey made certain from the beginning that he would exert as much influence as possible, without actually being on the staff. The first and most important area to be dealt with was recruitment. Dansey wanted to get as many of his people as possible inside before they got down to work. Hugh Dalton, the Labour Minister responsible for SOE, made it absolutely clear he wanted no one from MI6 in the top ranks of SOE. Nevertheless he was perfectly happy to seek Menzies' advice about the post of Director. Dansey and Menzies thought hard about this question and finally came up with Sir Frank Nelson, at that time a Conservative back-bencher. Menzies' recommendation went with the advice that he would find it impossible to co-operate with a Director of the SOE who had not had some earlier experience in clandestine work.[7] Dalton agreed, Nelson got the job and Dansey was delighted. Sir

Frank Nelson had been his 'Z man' in Basle before the war, and the two men understood each other perfectly.

Dansey never disguised his dislike for the SOE. Its existence was an interference with the business at hand. 'Sabotage isn't going to win the war,' he said, 'but intelligence will.' Dansey's hostility towards SOE was built on sound MI6 logic. Apart from the ludicrous situation of two organizations both having their own separate networks of agents, side by side in occupied territory, with the threat that one might inadvertently give the other away, there was the insurmountable problem that their separate objectives were mutually incompatible. SOE was charged with the job of establishing and training secret armies able to rise up on command from London, to blow up power stations, derail trains or create road blocks. MI6's objective was to establish networks of anonymous individuals who could supply, down a reliable line of communication, information about enemy activity, or planned activity. The best lubricant for intelligence work was absolute silence. The prospect of another secret network in the area, blowing up bridges in the middle of a well-planned intelligence operation, sent shivers down Dansey's spine. More importantly, SOE was a rival for precious resources, both human and material. Radio sets, weapons, aircraft, cash – and personnel. Both organizations were recruiting from the same groups of people with, broadly speaking, the same qualifications. But for Dansey it was more than just another service to compete with for valuable resources, it was a personal challenge to his monopoly, it was a rival empire.

Nevertheless, at the beginning, the relationship between SOE and Dansey was a cordial one, essentially because it was largely on Dansey's own terms. He demanded, and was given, an office at SOE headquarters in Baker Street, and as recruits began turning up to fill key positions in the field he insisted on interviewing each one personally.[8] Even given that SOE were starting from nowhere, Dansey took some strong proprietorial liberties with the fledgling secret service.

At these interviews he made it clear what he was going to allow the would-be agents to do. J. G. Beevor, who was sent to neutral Portugal, recalls how he was instructed, 'to make contact with the MI6 man in Lisbon, and liaise with him before I did any recruiting'.[9] As SOE began establishing networks in the occupied countries, it was made abundantly clear that no action of a paramilitary nature should be taken without clearing it first with MI6. In short, Dansey wanted SOE to 'do nothing'. The principle of 'No bangs without Foreign Office [MI6] say-so' was maintained for more than a year. But Dansey knew it couldn't and wouldn't last. As SOE developed, it naturally began to see things from its own perspective, and inevitably the relationship with Dansey became soured. He would refer to them as 'those amateurs' or 'the boys from Baker Street', and when SOE expanded its establishment in Britain, acquiring a number of old country properties in which they housed training schools,[10] Dansey rechristened SOE the 'Stately 'Omes of England'.[11]

Dansey knew that SOE's growing independence would make his enquiries into their operations more intrusive, so he ensured from the outset that he would be able to get 'intelligence' about their activities from other sources. Apart from Sir Frank Nelson, the head of SOE, who was always very amenable, and a clutch of other 'MI6 spies', the surest form of intelligence Dansey ever received came from SOE's 'signals'. As their networks expanded they naturally required wireless communications. Dansey argued successfully that SOE should use MI6's communications networks, which were already proven to be secure. From the beginning, right up until the spring of 1942, Claude Dansey received a copy of every single message, incoming or outgoing, to every single SOE radio operator in the field.[12] There wasn't a thing SOE were doing that Dansey didn't know about.

Put in perspective, the creation of SOE during the summer of 1940 was really no more than an unwelcome irritant for Dansey, at a time when his entire empire was virtually crumbling before him. From May until the French armistice, the storm that had swept through Western Europe also swept MI6's networks from the scene. Their original battle plan was to operate a number of networks from forward centres in Paris and Switzerland, which would collate and digest the raw intelligence before passing it on to London and the British Military Command in Europe. The Blitzkrieg came as such a shock that Dansey's networks were all over-run, communications were cut, contingency plans were dropped on a daily basis and one by one station chiefs and their staff made their way back to Britain.

As soon as it was possible to see the situation clearly, it was obvious to all the military planners that if and when a return to Europe was possible, it would be through France. For MI6 the situation in France was not good – but not hopeless. There were some whispers of information getting through, initially from the Americans. Britain had established an unofficial intelligence exchange with the United States in 1939 and by May 1940 a formal link was forged and William Stephenson, one of Dansey's Z men since 1936, became the official liaison officer in New York.

Following the armistice, the Americans, who were in principle still neutral, moved their consular headquarters from Paris down to Vichy, where the US Ambassador, Admiral Leahy, established a strong relationship with Pétain. The American 'intelligence service' as such barely existed. There was the Central Office of Information (later known as the OSS), which in May 1940 was very much a proto-intelligence service, with no networks and a skeleton staff of untrained agents. Such intelligence as was gathered was of a piecemeal nature from informal contacts made by their staff in Vichy and Marseilles.

MI6's other source in France was through their traditional links with the Deuxième Bureau, which despite the occupation maintained contact with London. Unfortunately, the Deuxième Bureau was not well spread in the northern occupied zone. But a real gift for Dansey came in the way of a self-made Polish network created by two Military Intelligence officers, Captain Roman Czerniawski and Colonel Vincent Zarembski. These two men, one in Paris, the other in Toulouse, linked up to create a network that stretched from Marseilles, across France and deep into the occupied zone. The network, known as INTERALLIÉ, made formal links with the exiled Polish court in London, in November 1940. Dansey came to an understanding with the Poles that INTERALLIÉ should work directly to him, and by January 1941 that link was formally made. Dansey had a network in France.

A problem that quickly became apparent once France had fallen was the growing number of British servicemen trapped behind enemy lines. This led to the creation of another network. An escape and evasion service, called

MI9, was set up to operate secret routes out of occupied Europe for British personnel. Claude Dansey was not going to allow the situation that had occurred with SOE to be repeated with MI9. A great deal of MI9's traffic was going to pass through Vichy France, which ideally meant Marseilles. Dansey had the contacts and the resources to set up a top-level escape service from Marseilles, which he offered to do and then put it at MI9's disposal. In return, MI9 had to accept Dansey's remote control, which he effected through his representative, the ex-Coldstream Guardsman James Langley. This arrangement had two distinct advantages for Dansey. First, it ensured he enjoyed full control over another of those wartime secret services; second, it gave him a good reliable service through which he could transport his own agents out of occupied Europe. It also provided him with another source of intelligence, albeit fairly raw intelligence. Everyone on his escape line would pass through his people along the way and so cut out the sometimes endless wait at the reception centres in Britain. He sent out Donald Darling (codenamed SUNDAY) to set up the escape lines.

Darling eventually made his headquarters at the MI6 station in Gibraltar and would be Dansey's filter through which all escapees had to pass. The next link in the chain would be James Langley (MONDAY) – and then Dansey himself. The man on the spot in Marseilles who actually got the line going was Ian Garrow, and when he was captured it passed to a remarkable Belgian military physician named Dr Albert Guerisse. He chose the codename 'Pat O'Leary', and in due course the Marseilles escape service became known as the 'Pat Line'.[13]

During that hectic summer of 1940, Bodington was wasting his days at Electra House with the Political Intelligence Department, what had become the Subversion branch of SOE. At this stage of the war, Bodington was composing uplifting messages for the French population, fabricating stories about the invincibility of the British and the corruption of the Germans, later dropped as leaflets over France. It wasn't his scene, it was too much like working for Reuters. In July 1940, after a long and tedious process of string-pulling, Bodington succeeded in getting another interview with MI6.

After the war, he would boast of having been seen by 'someone high up' over lunch at the Savoy (Dansey's haunt). It seems more likely that he was interviewed at St Ermin's Hotel, where MI6 were seeing hundreds of prospective candidates during 1940–1.

There is no record of the details of his interview, so we have no way of knowing how he might have recommended himself. One must assume he mentioned his experience in France, and possibly the kind of contacts he enjoyed there, though MI6 sources suggest that he did not make any mention of his contacts with a particular German intelligence officer in Paris. Perhaps MI6 already knew it. We will never know. But like most good gentlemen's clubs, MI6 had certain standards. They preferred candidates 'who were not over-burdened with brains and had plenty of solid irony between the ears'.[14] His intellectual qualifications apart, MI6 were not keen on his manners.

Bodington had an unfortunate reputation as a heavy drinker who had a somewhat irregular relationship with money. If Bodington had any money, he spent it so quickly he was never long from his natural state, which was broke.

He would borrow from people, two or three times over, neglecting to clear his debts first and sometimes never at all. Even Déricourt, who was always prepared to cut a few corners, drew the line at unpaid bills. On his visits to Paris in the autumn of 1940, Déricourt discovered a trail of Bodington's debts stretching right across town.

MI6 did not give any specific reason for turning down his application (they never do), but in due course he was informed that 'no opening could be found for his services'.[15]

However, by any definition, MI6 is a very unorthodox organization. Just because an individual had been refused a position did not mean he would not be employed (or used) at some later date. MI6's arrangements in this area were extremely grey. There was the establishment of 'officers', a position somewhere between a military and civil service rank, and then there were those whom MI6 paid for services rendered. People who were employed on the latter basis were usually engaged in non-attributable work.

Following his unsuccessful interview with MI6, Bodington's name was passed to L. A. Humphries at SOE. Leslie Humphries was one of the officers from MI6's Section D who had been moved across to SOE. Prior to the collapse of France, he had been the Section D representative in Paris. Whether he was acquainted with Bodington in those days is not known, but he was well known to Dansey. Humphries was SOE's first Head of French Section, and was engaged in building the department that would, at least theoretically, have the most crucial role to play in the war. Bodington moved across to SOE in December 1940.[16]

V

To England

By November 1941, Déricourt was flying regularly from Marseilles to Vichy and back for the government airline SCLAM. Life with Jeannot had settled into something of a routine; he picked up a little extra cash now and then on the black market and he was back in the company of pilots.[1] Air France had shifted the centre of its operations down to Marseilles and was trying to keep open just a few remaining routes to the closest and most secure French colonies. One evening, at a bar the pilots shared, Déricourt listened to a fantastic story being told by one of the Air France pilots. Léon Doulet claimed that he'd been in touch with the British, who were going to get him out of France so that he could fly for the RAF. At first Déricourt couldn't believe him, but then Doulet told his story.[2]

He had been caught up in one of the bitterest and most unlikely conflicts of the war, the Syrian campaign. Unlikely, because it involved French fighting French. In a gesture to the Nazis, the Vichy government had volunteered a large French force to assist the Germans in an attempt to capture the Persian oilfields. In Syria and the Lebanon, that force was met and defeated in June 1941 by a combined contingent made up of British, Australian and

Free French units. They were some of the toughest and most bitterly fought engagements of the war and led one observer to remark, 'If the French had fought like that in France, in May 1940, then perhaps...' – but that wasn't part of the pilot's story.

Léon Doulet was at that time flying the route from Marseilles to Athens and Aleppo. At Aleppo he and a group of colleagues from Air France were overrun by British forces. Representing Air Intelligence at that time was Wing Commander Arthur Forbes, Lord Granar, the man involved with transporting aircraft during the Spanish Civil War. He was summoned to Aleppo, with Robert Maxwell of BOAC, to see if they could recruit any of the AF pilots.[3] Lord Granar made the formal approach, but his appeal fell on stony ground. All the Vichy French personnel in the Middle East at that time felt very much under the influence of the commander of Vichy forces, who made it clear that anyone who crossed over to the British would be guilty of treason.

One pilot out of the whole group did indicate an interest in going to Britain. That was Doulet, who recognized Forbes from the 'planes for Spain' deal. Forbes explained to him that BOAC were trying to staff up a new route to Stockholm, but when it came to it Doulet hedged a bit, saying he first had to return to Marseilles to settle things with his family. Forbes understood. He then gave Doulet the name of a contact in Marseilles who was in touch with London and would make the arrangements. The contact was someone at the US Consulate.[4]

Déricourt listened with great interest. It sounded so fantastic, but it also sounded very exciting. They talked the thing through late into the night and after a few days, when Doulet was satisfied Déricourt was sincere, he agreed to take him to the American contact. The following day Déricourt and Doulet called on Mr H. M. Donaldson of the Visa Division at the US Consulate. With immense charm and conviction Déricourt trotted out his lie. He explained that he was an Air France pilot, that he had recently returned from Syria, where he had been approached by 'Forbes', and he wanted to 'go to England to fly for the Allies'.[5]

H. M. Donaldson was a functionary of the US State Department and, at the same time, a tiny link in MI6's intelligence chain. He had a secure line of communication with London, through Washington, plus local links with what he referred to as 'the British underground', meaning Dansey's escape service in Marseilles.[6] Donaldson believed everything Déricourt told him and sent his name on to London. He then sent Déricourt up to Vichy to call on Commander A. C. J. Savalot.[7]

Abel Savalot was the US Naval Attaché and Ambassador Leahy's assistant. Savalot's own deputy, Thomas G. Cassidy, was the COI station chief (US intelligence). Between the two of them, Savalot and Cassidy co-ordinated American intelligence operations in Vichy. Savalot's office on the third floor of the embassy building was right next door to the cipher room, which had direct communications with Washington and MI6 in London. Admiral Leahy, the American Ambassador, had a rather old-world view of all the intrigue and secrecy that went on in Vichy. He could barely tolerate the presence of intelligence agents in his own Diplomatic Staff, but the nightly comings and goings of the French were just about the limit.

> A number of Frenchmen who were escaping
> came to the Embassy to tell me what they

61

needed. Of course, this was done very quietly. Some had received their escape from occupied France by purchase or influence, and were trying to get away. I did not supply them with any false credentials, they would of course get the papers elsewhere! They may have obtained forged papers. I don't know. I did not want to know.[8]

Savalot was interested in Déricourt's position with SCLAM and encouraged him to pay a regular visit to his office during his trips to Vichy. In the course of their conversations, he asked Déricourt about the routes he flew and the aircraft he saw on the ground at various airports, a description of their markings etc. – very general intelligence. Occasionally he gave Déricourt a package to take down to Donaldson in Marseilles, and Donaldson did likewise.[9] Déricourt was back in the courier business. He didn't mind, the Americans were a new experience and his contacts with them increased his prestige. He had no choice really; the British seemed in no hurry to get him out of France.

On 7 December the Japanese attacked the US Seventh Fleet at Pearl Harbor, and three days later Germany and Italy declared war on the United States. Savalot's office in Vichy acquired a new strategic importance. The Germans, who had been incensed by the US presence in France, decided to open their own consulate in Vichy to counter what they claimed were America's 'intolerable espionage activities in France'. In fact, the creation of a German Consulate seemed only to increase the number of SD men in the southern zone and for the next twelve months they did nothing overt to hinder the Americans.

Déricourt was now in the unique position of having secret contacts with both German and American intelligence officers. Whether either side was able to exploit that situation is open to speculation. There is no evidence of it in the archives. Déricourt, on the other hand, certainly made the best of his situation. He occasionally visited a brothel in Toulouse that was operated by the SD and he made regular trips up to Paris, where he was seen in restaurants in the company of Germans. Meanwhile, his black-marketeering flourished.

Déricourt's relationship with the Americans had settled into a pattern, too. Each week he would turn up to see Savalot to hear if there was any news from the British, each week they would shake their heads. He became such a familiar face at the Embassy in Avenue Thermale that the staff began to call him Henry.[10] Déricourt had an iron in every fire, for apart from the occasional piece of courier work for the Americans, he also delivered material for his old friend in the Deuxième Bureau, André Borrie. Borrie, like a lot of Bureau officers, was secretly in touch with MI6 – until about April 1942, when he died in mysterious circumstances. From 1940 to 1943, Marseilles was infested with espionage agents of every nationality. It would have been very difficult for someone like Henri not to have worked for both sides of the fence.

Perhaps in an attempt to introduce some order into his life, Déricourt asked Jeannot to marry him. They had lived together at 50 Rue Curiol, in Marseilles, ever since the Armistice. In November Jeannot's divorce finally came through, and they were married on 13 December. He did not tell her anything about his trips to the US Consulate, nor did he mention that he had recently asked them to try to smuggle him out of the country.

During the spring of 1942, Déricourt began flying to destinations outside Metropolitan France. He flew to Tunis, Algiers, Istanbul and, occasionally, Turin and Milan.[11] From French North Africa he would report regularly to the Americans on the numbers of German aircraft he saw, the kind of shore artillery and anti-aircraft defences. North Africa had recently become important because of Allied plans for an operation in that area.

Since the Americans had entered the war, they had been involved in a long and sometimes tedious debate with the British over what their first common objective should be. In June and July of 1942, that debate warmed up dramatically, as the Americans insisted on an invasion of France as soon as possible. For them, the war in Europe was hopefully going to be a swift affair, so they could concentrate on the Pacific and the Japanese. The British, unfortunately, did not see it that way. With the memories of Dunkirk still fresh, they felt in no way ready for any kind of assault on France. However, an attack on French North Africa seemed far more realistic and feasible. The British argument eventually prevailed and Allied intelligence-gathering in North Africa intensified.

Meanwhile, Déricourt's name had been circulated amongst Claude Dansey's contacts in Marseilles. Ian Garrow, who established the escape line from Marseilles, was also a link with the local agents of the Deuxième Bureau. In May 1942, Garrow paid a surprise visit to Déricourt to ask him if he knew the whereabouts of André Borrie. Déricourt told Garrow he'd heard that Borrie was dead. Garrow already knew that and asked if he knew anything about some documents Borrie had been carrying at the time of his death. Déricourt knew nothing. Garrow was aware that Déricourt did a lot of courier work for the Americans and for the Deuxième Bureau and perhaps for that reason had no qualms about revealing that he was an MI6 man. He asked Déricourt if he knew the address the documents had been sent to. Déricourt shook his head; he didn't even know Borrie had been working for the British. He took the opportunity to ask Garrow to help him get to Britain and went through the whole Syrian story for his benefit. Garrow listened but said nothing, thanked him and then left.[12]

By this stage, London was very familiar with the names Déricourt and Doulet – and their story about Syria.[13] However, the Americans could not get their requests any further than James Langley at MI9, because as a rule aliens were not put onto British escape lines unless they were already working for a British service. It was not an operation run for refugees, it was a top-grade service for British agents and officers. However, it says a lot for Déricourt's and Doulet's persistence that they kept up their visits to the Americans in Marseilles and Vichy for well over nine months. The Americans pointed out the sort of courier work Déricourt had done and Garrow reported his connections with the Deuxième Bureau. Finally Langley relented and in what he described as a 'quid-pro-quo for help the Americans had given us' agreed to put Déricourt and Doulet on the escape line.[14]

In early July, Savalot and Donaldson each received signals saying the Frenchmen had been accepted. A week later Langley sent a personal message to 'Pat O'Leary' in Marseilles.[15] The message gave him the names of Déricourt and Doulet with the instruction that 'they were to be sent to London by the quickest possible means'. O'Leary thought the message very strange, given that the men concerned were French, but he didn't question it.[16]

Tom Cassidy, the American intelligence Station Chief, also informed London of some of the work Déricourt had been doing for them.[17] In recent weeks, this had taken an important new turn. Reports had been received that some squadrons of the Italian Air Force were preparing to depart for North Africa as reinforcements for Rommel. Déricourt was due for a few weeks' leave and was looking forward to a rest. On 24 June he took what he thought would be his last flight to Vichy and naturally paid a visit to Savalot and Cassidy. Following his meeting with the Americans, Déricourt arranged for a change in his flying schedule that would put him on a route to Turin for the next two weeks.[18]

Then, during the first week of August, Pat O'Leary called on Doulet to give him the details of their planned escape. Doulet in turn contacted Déricourt. It was a moment of some anxiety. Déricourt had almost given up hope of getting out, and now that the moment had come he was unnerved. His greatest anxiety was for Jeannot, who knew nothing about any of these plans. On 6 August he flew another trip to Turin, stayed overnight and returned to Marseilles the next day. He made a final delivery of notes to Donaldson in Marseilles and then, on the 15th, told Jeannot he would be going away for a while.

At first she had no idea how serious this would be. He had turned up at the Hotel Noailles, something he rarely did, to tell her he'd left some money in their room and that she wasn't to worry, he would be safe. Jeannot was used to him being away a day, three days, even a week, but it wasn't until she returned home that evening that she began to believe she might never see him again.[19]

Déricourt arrived at the Gare St Charles for his rendezvous with Doulet and together they waited for their contact. Suddenly Doulet was taken completely by surprise. Déricourt had burst into tears. Here was a man renowned within his little clique for his effortless and often callous sexual exploits, now crying over a woman none of them would have looked at twice. This scene introduced an element of drama into what had been a cold decision to leave France. There was no mistaking the depth of Déricourt's feelings for Jeannot at that moment, on the platform at the Gare St Charles. It was a revelation for Doulet.[20]

By the time the train pulled out of the station, they had been joined by a Canadian airman, an RAF fighter pilot and Pat O'Leary himself. They travelled to the little fishing town of Narbonne, where they spent the night. At first light they walked down to the shore and, at a pre-arranged spot, waited for a signal from a fishing trawler. In the grey morning light they gradually picked out the dark shape of a craft about half a mile out to sea and a small pinprick of light, which flashed a series of letters in Morse code.

Clutching their bundles of belongings, they climbed into a rowing boat that had been sent ashore. There were ten of them now, a navigator from a Wellington bomber, a Yugoslavian couple, two Belgian intelligence officers and an Englishman, whom Déricourt took to be from MI6. The trawler was of course the famous *Tarana*, one of MI6's fleet of cunningly disguised small craft. Beneath its livery of fishing nets and winches was hidden an anti-aircraft gun and heavy machine guns. For the next few days they cruised back and forth, dropping bundles of weapons and radios at anonymous points along the coast. Déricourt watched all this activity with keen interest, conscious that he too was being watched and would have to mind what he said.[21]

Doulet marvelled at how Déricourt could remember precisely what he had told to whom. He ran his story over and over again in his head, recalling pieces of it that even Doulet had forgotten. They both felt the man from MI6 was listening to every word they said. So far, the story about Syria had been his ticket and fare; he couldn't afford to blow it now.

While this party of clandestine mariners cruised along the Riviera, up on the northern coast of France a small but bloody episode of the war was unfolding. The Dieppe raid has significance for this story for two reasons. First, for the way in which the decision to attempt it was made, and second, for the way in which the result haunted later planning. Although the British had convinced American defence planners that North Africa should come first, there were some Americans who doubted British wisdom. As a sop to those doubting Thomases, Churchill agreed to a large-scale raid on the northern French coast to test German defences, and to attempt to draw the Luftwaffe into battle with the RAF. Dieppe was chosen because it had been argued up to that date that the capture of a major port would have to be the first stage of a major invasion. On 19 August, 4921 Canadians, supported by 1057 British Commandos, escorted by eight destroyers and thirty-nine coastal craft, attempted to seize the old French port. The German defences were prepared; their infantry had been on the alert since the beginning of the month. By eleven in the morning the action was aborted and what remained of the Allied force was evacuated. The Canadians had lost 3363 men, the Commandos 247; the Royal Navy lost 550 men, one destroyer and thirty-three landing craft; and the

RAF's new Supermarine Spitfire had been outmatched by the Focke-Wulf 190, losing 106 aircraft and 190 men. Churchill, the eternal optimist, wrote, 'It was a costly but not unfruitful reconnaissance-in-force. Tactically it was a mine of experience. It shed revealing light on many short-comings in our outlook.' The exercise had the desired effect. American doubts vanished and attention was properly focused on French North Africa.

Five days after leaving Narbonne the crew of the *Tarana* repainted the ship in battleship grey, hoisted the Union Jack and sailed her into Gibraltar harbour. The passengers were taken to the MI6 debriefing station, where they were met by SUNDAY. Donald Darling put each of them through a preliminary interrogation. He then sent a signal to Dansey in London: 'Request priority on two Frenchmen, Déricourt and Doulet.'

At his office in Broadway Buildings, Dansey ran through the list of names that had arrived from the Gibraltar station. He was more than a little surprised to see a pair of Frenchmen on his escape line. He sent a signal to MI6 in Gibraltar: 'Who are Déricourt and Doulet?' Gibraltar replied: 'Air France pilots. Recruited in Syria to fly for BOAC.' Dansey smelt a rat: 'Contact Forbes. Check their stories with him.'[22]

Wing Commander Arthur Forbes (Lord Granar) received a signal from MI6 Gibraltar, enquiring about the two pilots from Syria. He confirmed that he had recruited Doulet in Syria. 'The name Doulet was of course familiar, but the name Déricourt was not. Have no recollection whatsoever of having met Déricourt at any time, and certainly not in Syria.'[23] The message was relayed to Dansey and he replied to Gibraltar's original question: 'No priority Déricourt and Doulet.'

Well then, who was this man Déricourt? What did anybody know about him? What was he doing on the Pat Line? Dansey spoke to Langley about the two pilots and was told about Déricourt's work for the Americans and the Deuxième Bureau. Whether MI6 knew at that stage about Déricourt's contacts with Boemelburg is not known, but they very soon found out. Henri Déricourt, the man who had fancied himself as the great survivor, who was an occasional associate of the Corsican mafia, a functionary of the Vichy establishment, on nodding terms with the SD in Paris and an agreeable operative for American intelligence, was at that stage sailing towards a confrontation with the most dangerous man in the British secret services.

The secret cargo of passengers had been put on board a tramp steamer that joined a vast convoy of ships on its way to Liverpool and points north. Déricourt had no idea what to expect in Britain; he'd heard the cities had all been razed to the ground by German bombers and that the country was starving and on the verge of revolt. Of course, the other thing preoccupying him was how he would cope with the situation if the 'Intelligence Service' uncovered his lies. He was philosophical about it; he was there, so what could they do about it?

They docked on 7 September, at Greenock near Glasgow. Immediately two Special Branch officers came on board, sought out the Frenchmen, separated them from the rest of the passengers and discouraged any further contact.[24]

Déricourt was quite shaken by the experience. Whether he knew it or not, he was at serious risk of being interned. Before there was any chance of the information being used against him, Déricourt immediately declared that he had contacts with German intelligence.[25] The Special Branch showed no particular interest, but they noted his comments. The name Boemelburg would not have been unfamiliar to Dansey.

Déricourt and Doulet were put onto a train and escorted down to St Pancras. From there, they were driven to a magnificent Victorian Gothic pile in Battersea that gloried in the title of Royal Victorian Patriotic Asylum for the Orphaned Daughters of the Soldiers and Sailors Killed in the Crimean War – more commonly referred to as the Royal Patriotic School (RPS) and officially as the London Reception Centre (LRC). It was one of a number of alien reception centres that had been established at various points in the country and operated jointly by MI9 and the Security Service, MI5. It was MI5 who supplied the officers skilled in interrogating newly arrived aliens, for the purpose of winkling out German agents that were trying to enter the country. They were very successful.

The two Frenchmen were immediately checked by medical officers for any infectious diseases, parasites and other physical ailments. Then each was issued with an Alien Registration Card and a number, and a file was opened. Déricourt was RPS 9435/E.1a(USA). 'USA' referred to the fact that he was sponsored by the Americans. Déricourt's interrogation would have begun immediately. From the RPS perspective all aliens were German agents unless they could prove otherwise. Déricourt managed to give a thoroughly convincing performance and the RPS gave him a favourable report. His file was sent to MI5 proper, and it was then that the first doubts arose.

MI5 was extremely suspicious about both the men, but about Déricourt in particular. In October the MI5 officer responsible for liaison with the Americans, Peter Ramsbotham, wrote to the US State Department asking them to corroborate Déricourt's story.

> We have in this country two French airmen, whose story is rather curious, and whose names are Henri Alfred DÉRICOURT and Léon Jean DOULET … They both had been working for Air France in Metropolitan France and the Near East, and when the Allies occupied Syria they were promised by the Air Ministry that jobs would be provided for them with British Overseas Airways if they would join the Allies.

Déricourt was still sticking to his story about having worked for Air France. For some reason, MI5 neglected to try to get corroboration from Wing Commander Forbes, who would have told them precisely what he had told MI6. Anyway, MI5 made enquiries with the MI9 people who had brought him in, just to confirm that the story he had told the RPS in Battersea was the same he told MI6 in Gibraltar. Claude Dansey would not sanction MI9 saying anything more to MI5 than the old story about Syria. He told them nothing about his own private enquiries which would have revealed that Déricourt was a fraud. Dansey was a great believer in the right hand not letting the left hand know anything. Nor was it the last time Dansey withheld critical information about Déricourt from those who should have had it.

But why? What possible reason could Claude Dansey have had for withholding this information from the Security Service? The fact that Déricourt had fraudulently got himself to Britain should have alerted Dansey to the possibility that the man was a German agent. MI5 certainly suspected as much. Ramsbotham, in the same letter to the Americans, stated:

> ...and while their interrogations produced no suspicious evidence, we do not feel that they can be cleared from a security point of view, since, with the promises they were given to join the British Overseas Airways, they would have been likely subjects for German attention in France.

A perfectly logical conclusion – and MI5 knew only half the story. Ramsbotham goes on to ask Mr Donaldson (the contact at the US Consulate in Marseilles):

> ...if he could make a statement as to what he knows of these men, and whether he is satisfied that they could not have been sent to this country as German agents.

H. M. Donaldson, clearly alarmed that he might have been accused of allowing a couple of German agents to get by him, answered as any public servant would:

> ...I may say that, while as a result of my numerous conversations with them I was unable to detect anything of a suspicious nature, *I did not in any way recommend them*, but merely passed their names ... to the British.[26] (Author's italics.)

He then goes on to say that they were also in touch with Savalot in Vichy and that it was Savalot who had sent their names to London. In any case, MI5 received no positive reassurance from the Americans. Within a few months, they were satisfied as to Doulet's bona fides, but were never convinced about Déricourt's reliability.

Soon after their arrival in Britain, a very strange thing occurred. Normally an alien who turned up at the RPS and who was unattached to any British service would have been detained for two or three weeks, sometimes longer. Déricourt and Doulet were in and out of the place in four days. They were taken to a hotel in Victoria, and a short time later they were separated. Doulet was given a room in a bed-and-breakfast establishment, while Déricourt – disappeared...[27]

VI

Prosper

Since the summer of 1940, the Special Operations Executive had grown into a world-wide organization. It had developed networks of agents as far afield as Burma and Malaya and throughout most of occupied Europe. But the country where SOE expended most resources and where they experienced the most frustration was of course France. Operations in that country had been complicated from the very beginning by the presence in England of an obscure French General named Charles de Gaulle, the self-declared head of the Free-French. SOE found it necessary to have two separate country sections operating in France: RF Section, which was linked to de Gaulle's secret service – the BCRA, and an independent French Section, or F Section, which operated mostly British agents exclusively under British command. De Gaulle never countenanced Britain's right to operate their own agents in his country and consequently he never recognized F Section. On the other hand, many in SOE were equally exasperated by de Gaulle, who had succeeded in establishing his own networks in France early on, but then did nothing with them. As Colin Gubbins wrote, 'De Gaulle is busy furthering his political ends... and [his] agents do not appear to be making any attempt to fulfil their primary role of executing an active sabotage and subversion policy.'[1] It became apparent to SOE that if they were to play any significant role in the liberation of France, then it would have to be done through F Section.

French Section had been launched during the summer of 1940, by Leslie Humphries, late of MI6's erstwhile Section D. Humphries was already engaged in this work at a time when the head of MI6, Stewart Menzies, was still unaware Section D was no longer his. Dansey, on the other hand, did have his finger on the pulse, both in London and in France. Because his operations had been pushed back across the Channel, future work in France would rely heavily on recruiting from the native resistance groups that were springing up – the same pool of resources from which SOE would seek personnel. Dansey was greatly disappointed when his man in F Section, Humphries, was transferred before the end of the year to establish a new section. His replacement, H. L. Marriott, who had been the Courtaulds representative in Paris, lasted less than ten months. The man who succeeded him was the irrepressible Colonel Maurice Buckmaster.

It was Buckmaster and Buckmaster's personality that became synonymous with F Section. It is his name that is recalled in the histories and memoirs of those who went to France for the SOE. In 1941 he was a tall, bluff-looking man, with an invariably beaming countenance that was too often darkened with each setback in the field. He was already older than most of his contemporaries and beginning to thin out on top. That and his boundless enthusiasm gave him, for many, the air of a father figure. There were many who admired him, and equally as many who did not.

Buckmaster's problem, if one might call it that, lay in the deep-rooted attachment he felt for most of his agents, an attachment that many felt was soft and could sometimes cloud his judgement.[2] In the end Buckmaster was responsible for sending nearly four hundred men and women into France, each with their own false identities, codenames and operations. The intense concentration of facts and names that were compressed into those four extraordinary years often meant that after the war, old pre-war friends and acquaintances had become complete strangers to him.

When Buckmaster succeeded as Head of French Section, he inherited a young man who had risen through the ranks to be Deputy Head. Nicholas Bodington had been an outside candidate for the post of 'F', but unfortunately all the worst habits that had been manifest in Paris also surfaced at Baker Street, and though there was no doubting his extraordinary courage and remarkably dexterous mind, there wasn't one officer in F Section who would have followed Bodington anywhere. The relationship between these two men was not good; it could not have been otherwise. Bodington's swift and cutting intellect was bound to clash with that of the generously spirited father figure.

The other personality whose influence was felt just as strongly as Buckmaster's was that of Vera Atkins. Flying Officer Atkins of the WAAF joined SOE in 1941 and surfaced in the role of Intelligence Officer. She was responsible for collecting all the intelligence that came into the place, either from returning agents or from the bits and pieces that trickled through from MI6, and turning it into practical information that could be used by agents in the field. Atkins' powerful memory and sharp analytical mind earned her considerable respect and an authority that belied her official rank. She too felt a deep attachment for the agents who went to France, though her feelings were always well below the surface. Atkins was of much tougher stock.

Gradually, Dansey's few remaining appointees began drifting from their original positions and his access to SOE's operations had to become more serpentine. The simple fact was that SOE was expanding and absorbing people who had no prior MI6 or Dansey connection. Probably the most significant personality within the entire organization was a Scot who had moved across from Military Intelligence. Brigadier Colin Gubbins wrote most of the Army's manuals on guerrilla warfare, and it was his vision and his authority that eventually became the driving spirit behind SOE. He became Head of Operations in November 1940 and succeeded as Head of SOE in 1943. His tough, independent mind inevitably brought SOE into deeper conflict with the man they called 'Uncle Claude'.

1941 had been a year of training, organizing and of immense frustration. F Section struggled to get any kind of presence established in France, a struggle made more difficult by Dansey. F Section got so little intelligence about conditions in France that by the end of the year they still couldn't put together a list of strategic targets.[3] Most of that information came from MI6, and Dansey just would not pass it on.

1942 was a different story. After a great deal of criticism for foot-dragging, F Section finally began to see some action down in the southern, so-called Free Zone. In fact, the summer and autumn of 1942 saw an unprecedented whirl of clandestine activity all along the Mediterranean coast. Not just by SOE. Everyone seemed to be there.

At the time when Déricourt was still shuttling back and forth between Marseilles and Vichy, there was a quickly expanding network of American agents, part of the newly named Office of Strategic Services – OSS (the precursor to the CIA); there was MI6's new network expanding from the south, ALLIANCE, run by Marie Madelaine Foucarde; there was the Soviet Red Orchestra, whose second in command was operating from Marseilles; and, of course, in addition to all that, the SD was everywhere. Somehow, superimposed over what now seems like an entire espionage industry, SOE were trying to construct a network that would eventually reach north into the occupied zone.

Like the proverbial two ships passing in the night, Bodington came to the South of France just as Déricourt was preparing to leave for Britain. On 15 July 1942, Bodington flew to Gibraltar with one of the first women agents SOE ever sent into the field, Yvonne Rudellat. When they were landed by felucca near Antibes on 20 July, Déricourt was in Vichy. By the time he had returned to Marseilles, Bodington had moved to Cannes where he stayed until early September. Then, while the latter was lying low in Cannes, Déricourt was engaged in the last series of flights from Marseilles to Turin. Though they were just a few hours apart, they did not meet.

Bodington had arrived to make contact with a number of Resistance groups which had indicated they would work with the British. From SOE's point of view, they needed to find a leader who could unite the various groups and act as a liaison with London. In time, liaison would come to mean 'take orders from'. SOE required someone who could instil in the disparate groups a proper sense of discipline, forge reliable channels of communication, and ensure that everyone operated to a single, clearly understood strategy. In return, SOE were prepared to supply *materiel*: Sten guns, Bren guns, pistols, ammunition, explosives and the training to use them. SOE would also provide wireless equipment and the operators who would maintain contact with London.

F Section thought they had found just such a figure in André Girard (codenamed CARTE), who had set the pulses quickening at Baker Street with tales of a Resistance army of the most prodigious size. After so much frustration and procrastination, SOE hoped they were about to make the leap into the big time. The first reports about CARTE's 'legions' dated from January 1942. Since then, precious little had happened. Bodington went out to meet him because time was running out and SOE needed to know for certain if CARTE was really the answer to their prayers. CARTE claimed there were already detailed plans for sabotage teams and that he had organized a private army of no less than 300,000 men ready to rise up and throw the Germans out. CARTE was no fool. He meant what he said. He was a very intelligent and persuasive man whose loyalties were unimpeachable. He was anti-Hitler, anti-Pétain and anti-de Gaulle. But by the time Bodington returned to London, CARTE had delivered nothing more than the very best of intentions. There was no army. CARTE had been a false messiah.

Even before the truth was known, SOE were already preparing to send in their own man. The woman who had travelled out with Bodington, Yvonne Rudellat, had been sent out to help provide the reception for someone who was at that time still completing his training in Britain. She moved from Antibes and settled herself in Tours to wait. There she made contact with a fugitive from the

SD, Pierre Culioli. In the Battle for France in May 1940, he had been taken prisoner but was released after he became seriously ill. He attempted to get to Britain to join General de Gaulle and to this end enlisted the help of the US Consul in Marseilles, but without success. He was involved with a small Resistance group who were helping RAF pilots get across the Spanish border when he had his first run-in with the SD. After his meeting with Rudellat he decided to join her and work for SOE. In mid-September they received instructions from London to prepare a reception for some incoming agents. Among them was another of SOE's distinguished women agents, Andrée Borrel (DENISE), who arrived by parachute on the 25th. Borrel too had been sent to prepare the way for the one who was coming.

Like most SOE agents, Francis Anthony Suttill had been put through an exhaustive training course at various establishments up and down the country. At Warnborough Manor, south-west of Guildford, he was given rudimentary training with Sten guns and pistols, taught how to read a map, and learnt a little of conditions in occupied France. At the Airsaig schools in Scotland he was taught paramilitary skills; to live off the land, to use explosives, to strip, clean and repair every likely firearm an agent might encounter in Europe, from the common Sten to the Schmeisser MG38. And he was taught how to kill – with his hands, with a pistol, with wire, even with poison. Finally, at Beaulieu he learnt how to live under a false identity. He was taught to become someone else – someone with a history, an occupation and the necessary papers that would enable him to slip silently into French society. While all this was going on, psychologists watched him to see how he coped with the pressures of a clandestine existence.

From the middle of the year Suttill had been marked down to take on a critical role in F Section's plans. His departure had been scheduled for the early autumn but had been postponed a number of times. It was almost as though F Section had been caught by a bout of stage bright. By September, the fog that had shrouded Allied strategy had begun to lift. A major Allied operation in North Africa was imminent. It was expected that the Germans would react by occupying the southern zone, and so before German control became too extensive F Section concluded that they should immediately establish a significant presence in Paris and northern France.

Suttill was driven out to Tangmere airbase, with an accompanying officer who checked him for the umpteenth time to ensure he had the correct papers and other pieces of paraphernalia a Frenchman would be carrying in the autumn of 1942. Around ten p.m. on 1 October, laden with parachute, weapons and maps, he clambered into a Hudson. Three hours later, nearly two thousand feet above the town of Vendôme, a tiny pinprick of light from Andrée Borrel's torch signalled to the pilot the presence of a reception committee. Once the pilot was satisfied that he was correctly positioned above the drop zone, he switched on the green light in the bay and Suttill heaved himself through the trap in the belly of the aircraft – and into the French night air.

Yvonne Rudellat, Pierre Culioli and Andrée Borrel were all there to receive Suttill. He stayed briefly with Culioli and Rudellat and arranged for them to provide another reception for his deputy, due to arrive in a week or so. Eventually Culioli and Rudellat established a new sub-circuit in the Tours area, linked to Suttill in Paris. Borrel had already found him a little pied-à-terre on the Left Bank to use as his initial base, and from that humble beginning his influence spread throughout northern France.

Suttill had been born in Lille in 1910 of a French mother and an English father. He spent his early childhood in France, was schooled at Stoneyhurst in England, studied law in both countries and was called to the Bar in 1936. During the last few months before his departure for France, Suttill was asked to think of a codename by which he would be identified. He chose the name of a fifth-century Christian theologian, Prosper of Aquitaine, who preached Grace and Predestination. If ever a man's fate had been predestined, it was PROSPER's. He had arrived with a particular message and with a particular role to fulfil – and with the ambition to succeed. It was immediately obvious he had been invested with considerable authority. He and Andrée Borrel set out on a lightning tour of known Resistance centres, made contact with the local leaders and invited them to join their groups to his and create one vast single network. From Paris they went to Chartres, Melun, Orléans, Blois, Ramorantin and then north to Beauvais, Compiègne and St Quentin. And so the network grew.[4] A few of these initial contacts had been known to the great CARTE spectre, including two sisters, Genevieve and Madelaine Tambour. Genevieve Tambour introduced Jacques Bureau.

Jacques Bureau was not a major figure in the network, but he does provide an excellent illustration of the way Suttill's charisma drew hundreds of French men and women under his influence. Bureau's attraction for Suttill was his expertise in radio technology. He had been a committed jazz fan since his university days, which led him eventually to become a broadcaster on French radio, then a technician – and so developed a unique marriage of jazz and electronics. In 1940 he was attached to a branch of French Military Intelligence based in the Middle East, where he was employed as a wireless expert to eavesdrop on Italian military signals. After the Armistice he returned to Metropolitan France and finally arrived back in his native Paris at the end of 1941. He became loosely associated with the CARTE organization, but was greatly disheartened by endless meetings and interminable talk. Bureau was a great lion of a man, bursting with enthusiasm and courage, and, like thousands of others, he had been waiting for Suttill's irresistible message.

> CARTE was a group of amateurs, we didn't believe anything he told us. With PROSPER's arrival we felt we would at last be of some use and this was so exciting. We were not just working for the Resistance, we now worked for a purpose, for a date, for a reason – for a military goal. *The invasion.*[5]

PROSPER's mission was to establish a network that would have but one goal, to be a fundamental part of the invasion and the liberation of France. All operations would be carefully planned to form part of some greater strategic objective. The immediate priority would be slowly to build a secret army, disciplined, well trained, well armed and supplied to do the job, which would rise up on the eve of D-Day. PROSPER would be the avant-garde of the invasion.

London was not prepared for the response that followed PROSPER's call. It was something that surprised not only the SOE but also the Allied commanders, de Gaulle and Claude Dansey. Somehow the mood in France had been miscalculated. The anti-British feeling that had erupted after May 1940 was presumed to be still there. But that was not the case. Two years of occupation had changed a great many hearts in France. The fact that Britain had not capitulated in the autumn of 1940 had given many people hope of defeating the invader. But mostly it was to do with the realities of the occupation. When the Vichy Government agreed to send vast numbers of Frenchmen to the east to work in German factories in return for French POWs, the tide began to change. Obligatory Work Service was one telling fact that led to the growth of the Resistance, but it wasn't the only reason.

Since May 1941 French police had agreed to assist in the internment of foreign Jews. Then, at the turn of the year, Hitler decided to proceed with what became known as the 'final solution'. From May 1942 all Jews were required to wear a yellow star and with the assistance of the French police, systematic deportations became a reality. On 11 June Himmler presented the French with a quota of 100,000 Jews to be deported by the end of the year. On 16 June, '*La Grande Rafle*', the big round-up by the Paris gendarmes of 13,000 Jews into the Velodrome d'Hiver, resulted in over 100 suicides in the first few days.

The gendarmes took their captives to a large unfinished housing estate in the suburb of Dransey, and from there they were driven in convoy to the railway station at Bobigny and there herded into cattle trucks for the journey to the east. The almost daily sight of the deportation of fellow Frenchmen brought home to the masses the reality of collaboration.[6] The invader was a tyrant of unspeakable brutality. However close anti-Semitism floated under the surface of French society, it was not part of the French character to contemplate genocide. To a growing number of Frenchmen, Britain and the Allies seemed to offer the promise of liberation, and for those who were prepared to take up arms PROSPER had arrived with what they wanted to hear. Here was the true Messiah.

Within three months Suttill had established control over a single network of some sixty sub-circuits that stretched from the Ardennes to the Atlantic coast, from as far north as the Belgian border down to the Loire. As 1942 drew to a close, Buckmaster and his colleagues could stare at the map and only marvel at the extent of their influence in France, concentrated in the person of one man in Paris.

Suttill's Paris organization had grown to cope with the business of communication and supply. His deputy and radio operator, Gilbert Norman (codenamed ARCHAMBAUD), had arrived exactly one month after Suttill; and at the end of December another radio operator, Jack Agazarian (MARCEL), joined them too.

As lines of communication improved with the groups in the country, Suttill began to receive emissaries to be taught the skills of guerilla warfare. Bureau's connections with the famous centre of French jazz, the Hot Club de France, provided the ideal sanctuary for some of these meetings. Upstairs in a tiny room, above the ear-splitting cacophony produced by the bands, Suttill or Norman would demonstrate the use of the Sten gun – how to strip it, clean it, load it and so on. It was a perfect location, noisy, central and – most importantly – never discovered.[7] Suttill was extremely security conscious. Very few contacts knew more than two or three others: Bureau knew Suttill, Gilbert Norman and Madelaine Tambour. As the network grew it became more difficult to maintain these standards, but it was a subject Suttill laboured again and again.

The PROSPER network attracted a certain amount of apprehension in London. There was particular anxiety about Suttill's success in recruiting a large number of the communist groups in the industrial towns and in the northern suburbs of Paris, the so-called 'Red Belt'. By the end of November, Moscow's influence in France had been largely expunged and many of the French communist groups that existed at the fringes of the Red Orchestra were more than happy to accept support from London. De Gaulle was particularly enraged that communist guerilla armies were being armed and trained by London. He saw it as a blatantly devious British act to thwart his own political ambitions and 'plant Albion in France again'. SOE's priorities were more straightforward; as far as they were concerned they would arm anyone who was prepared to kill Germans. Antelme, one of PROSPER's colleagues, wrote in a report to London in early 1943, 'Germans are killed daily in the streets of Paris, and ninety per cent of these are made with arms provided by us, e.g. to the Communists.'

Suttill's relationship with the Communists was a strictly personal one. No one in the network knew much about them and no one had any idea of the quantity of arms and equipment that was delivered to them. The Foreign Office was concerned about the lack of any political guidance at SOE and there were many within MI6 who worried about the post-war legacy of this policy. Claude Dansey was more worried about the inevitable increase in German counter-espionage activity and the consequences for his own networks in a country where SOE seemed to be giving a weapon to anyone who would fire it.

Dansey was right. PROSPER could not have gone unnoticed for very long. The SD had begun to put together a vague outline of something significant from about the middle of October. During November and December a number of radio operators were 'identified' by the German radio detection centre in the Boulevard Suchet.[8] Gradually intelligence had begun to come in to Boemelburg of a lot of movement by certain key figures around the country. There was nothing specific they could pinpoint, except that the status quo had recently altered.

The Abwehr, who were also conducting counter-espionage work, were not so well served as the SD. They were still pursuing CARTE long after Suttill had arrived. In November, André Marsac, a courier in the CARTE organization, was followed onto a train in Marseilles by an Abwehr agent. Marsac carried with him a comprehensive list of agents connected with CARTE. During the journey he fell asleep and awoke to discover that the contents of his briefcase had been stolen. Most of the names on that list were redundant. However, a few might lead to some people on the fringes of PROSPER's network. Though the Abwehr and the SD were on the same side, there was precious little active co-operation between the military and Nazi Party intelligence services.

The arrival of PROSPER couldn't have come at a better time for Boemelburg. He was coming to the end of a long campaign against the 'Red Orchestra' and was about to cap it off with something of a coup. On 7 November the Allies landed in French North Africa; on the 11th Germany responded by occupying the rest of

Metropolitan France down to the Riviera coast. On the same day Boemelburg and his colleague Kieffer drove down to Marseilles in the armour-plated Cadillac to arrest the Petit-Chef of the Red Orchestra. Boemelburg even stopped to have his photograph taken along the way.[9] It marked the end of a long campaign and the beginning of a new one. From that day he turned his full attention from the Soviets to the British.

VII

The Trojan Horse

The autumn and winter months of 1942–3 were unexpectedly lonely for Léon Doulet, the Air France pilot who had travelled to Britain with Déricourt. In September, after a week in a scruffy hotel near Victoria Station, he and Déricourt were separated from each other. Doulet was moved to an even scruffier bed-and-breakfast establishment, where he lived on his own in the strange city for the next four months. He had no idea of Déricourt's whereabouts. Doulet had presumed they were both under the authority of the Air Ministry, but neither they nor anyone else could or would tell him anything about Déricourt. Doulet found British indifference very depressing. Having come all this way to fly he couldn't fathom why he was being ignored.[1] On three occasions, twice in October and again in November, Déricourt contacted Doulet by telephone and arranged a rendezvous at Piccadilly Circus. At their first meeting they had a drink at a nearby pub and Doulet railed about his abandoned state. Déricourt listened to him sympathetically but there was nothing he could do. In contrast to Doulet, Déricourt seemed to have found some occupation, though he wouldn't reveal what that was or where he was staying. Finally, when Doulet pressed him on this, Déricourt hinted that he was staying with an ex-girlfriend. There was, of course, no girlfriend and Doulet knew it, but he left it at that. He mentioned that no one at BOAC seemed to know anything about Déricourt, but Henri made no comment.[2]

It was remarkable that Déricourt was able to walk the streets with impunity, when everything that was known about him at the time should have been sufficient to ensure he was interned for the duration.[3] He was a known black-marketeer with associates in the so-called Corsican mafia (Doulet at least knew that, as did the Americans in Marseilles); MI5 received reports by the end of the year that Déricourt had been seen in the company of Germans in the occupied zone[4] (this too would have come to Dansey's attention); and, as Dansey knew himself after his own enquiries, Déricourt was not the person he claimed to be, and was in fact a most accomplished liar. To put it simply, he had all the hallmarks of the kind of person the Germans would have slipped onto the Pat Line for espionage purposes. (It has been speculated that this was actually the case. But German archives contradict that view.[5]) Far from being interned, however, Déricourt was already gainfully employed.

The next time Doulet met Déricourt, Henri led him to a luxurious flat that was shared by the two Belgians with whom they had sailed on board the *Tarana*. They were joined by 'an English intelligence officer called FRANCIS, who was very brilliant'. FRANCIS asked Doulet if he had ever been up to Paris since the occupation. 'Of course,' he replied, 'many times.' He was then asked if he was prepared to do some secret work. Doulet declined. He had come to Britain to fly and that was all he wanted to do. The meeting ended amicably and Doulet departed. It was immediately obvious to him that

Déricourt was somehow involved with 'British intelligence', and was probably going to return to France. They met on one other occasion, at which Déricourt warned him to keep silent about the meeting with FRANCIS and his return to France.[6]

Déricourt had been working with MI6 for nearly a month. Once he had emerged from the Royal Patriotic School and been separated from Doulet, he was taken to MI6 Section IV – the Air Intelligence branch, where he answered questions about the aircraft he'd flown as a test pilot in Marseilles, gave what information he knew concerning the French aircraft industry's involvement with German manufacturers, made detailed lists of the names of French pilots and their current employment (Déricourt had been a minor official of the French airline pilots' union), and described the intelligence he had passed to the Americans during the summer.[7] Déricourt also repeated the somewhat startling revelation that he was acquainted with a high-ranking officer in German intelligence, based in Paris.[8]

That kind of information was of little interest to Section IV, but it was something that interested Dansey. Once again, this important piece of intelligence was not communicated to MI5. Déricourt had been put up at a secret address in London, known only to Dansey or one of his contacts, and kept there in isolation until the right opportunity arose to use him.

Everything that Dansey did was cloaked in impenetrable secrecy, the whys and the wherefores often unfathomable at the time, but later revealing a cold logic. As the Deputy Head of MI6, he had the freedom to run his own private operations, answering to no one but Stewart Menzies, and then not always with complete frankness. His manner, both charming and terrifyingly vitriolic, ensured there were no prying enquiries into the precise nature of his work. He garnered new agents at an alarming rate and was reputed in the more mundane levels of the service to be running his own private army – at least, judging by his legendary expenses claims.[9] Dansey enjoyed a singularly close relationship with all his agents, which was another thing that set him apart from his colleagues. 'Uncle Claude' made his agents feel that they belonged to an extremely exclusive community, which was deeply appreciative of their invaluable work. Dansey had a deep and genuine affection for his agents.[10]

He was not enamoured of the more technical forms of intelligence-gathering like aerial photography. He preferred the man on the spot, the agent, the human operative – with all the attendant virtues and vices. For many younger men in the service this obsession with the 'agent' seemed positively archaic, but it took a lot to convince him that there was a better way of doing things.[11]

It must be remembered that Claude Dansey was a man of 66, who had seen service in the last of the colonial wars, had worked in both MI5 and MI6 during the Great War and who had founded the Z Organization. He had seen it all and knew it backwards – and there were few who would contradict him. Certainly not his chief. Dansey had a talent for attracting the very best, the most unsavoury and often the downright criminal into his world of espionage, and also for extracting absolute loyalty from those he employed.[12]

He also possessed a gift for having the right man in the right spot, someone whose unique position could be exploited with the very minimum of manipulation. He had a particular interest in people who were well known to the enemy. Individuals who had worked for the foe or were currently working for them were an extremely valuable commodity, Dansey recognizing that someone who had already established his credentials had far more value back in the system than locked away and at the mercies of the Special Branch.[13] Déricourt had precisely those qualifications, with the added distinction that his contacts were with the ubiquitous Nazi spectre, the Sicherheitsdienst.

At the end of 1941 the British codebreakers at the Government Code and Cipher School (GC&CS) had broken the Abwehr ENIGMA codes, the German military intelligence secret codes.[14] Since then they had been successfully reading the Abwehr's signals communications, a far greater prize than anything Dansey's agents could deliver. The British had also broken the German Army, Air Force and Navy ENIGMA codes. The information that was extracted from ENIGMA codes, known as ULTRA, was the single most important British intelligence advantage of the war. Perhaps the most valuable ULTRA material concerned German intelligence operations in Britain and counter-intelligence operations against British agents in Europe – not just MI6 agents, but *any* British agent. But this intelligence, invaluable though it was, only concerned operations conducted by the Abwehr. The one and only ENIGMA code that defied Britain's de-crypters throughout the war was that used by the Sicherheitsdienst – Key TGD, known, somewhat misleadingly, as the 'Gestapo Enigma'.[15] This ruthless and extraordinarily successful Nazi intelligence organization had defied all British attempts at penetration – its dark internal workings were a complete mystery. Déricourt, if he was exploited carefully, could be a key to unlock some of the SD's secrets.

It's worth digressing for a moment to reflect on the price of ULTRA. British intelligence chiefs quickly appreciated how invaluable ULTRA would be to the British war effort, and for that reason great efforts were made to protect that advantage. No operation was ever undertaken that might have signalled to the enemy that his communications were being monitored. Consequently the manipulation of ULTRA was very critical; access to it was highly restricted and virtually at the discretion of 'C'. SOE's access to ULTRA material was, like any other operational organization's, strictly on its 'need to know'. The question one might ask is: whose needs were greater – SOE's or MI6's?

But in the autumn months of 1942, SOE's access to ULTRA was the least of their problems. Their major preoccupation was their relationship with the RAF. The transport of agents in and out of occupied Europe was most successfully achieved by aircraft, and for this purpose the RAF had established the 'Special Duties' squadrons. In 1940 a single flight (419) had been established for MI6's purposes. Then in 1941 this was reformed into 161 Squadron and later joined by 138 Squadron. They were equipped with Hudsons, Halifaxes, Oxfords, the occasional Beaufighter and of course the remarkable Lysander. The Hudson and the Lysander were designed to land on short rough strips, usually a meadow in some foreign field, where agents could be put down and others collected and returned safely home. MI6 had always expressed a preference for the Lysander pick-up where SOE preferred drops. However, by 1942, SOE had come round to the idea of the pick-up, even though the operation was far more involved.

It was necessary to have someone with knowledge of the right kind of fields for these aircraft to land, to communicate the correct map co-ordinates to London, to organize and transport the homeward-bound agents to the field, to correctly lay out a flare path safe from trees and bogs, and then to get the incoming agents away.

As SOE were expanding in northern France they pressured the RAF for more flights. But as the number of failed operations mounted, the strain began to show in the RAF's sarcastic memos.

> It is most unfortunate that attempts by the pilots of No. 138 Squadron to carry out this operation have been frustrated by the absence of a reception committee. The operation was asked for in all good faith in the belief that the committee would be waiting to receive personnel and stores...
>
> ...it is hoped that [in future] the Air Ministry and the officer commanding RAF Station Tempsford will have sufficient confidence in the organization [SOE] to believe that if we are putting the operation on there is a reasonable chance of the reception committee playing its part.[16]

The RAF threatened, and not for the last time, to cancel all flights for SOE. And then, with miraculously good timing, the solution to SOE's problems in France came to hand.

During the third week of November, the name Henri Déricourt was brought to their attention. By the end of the week, it had been sent to Maurice Buckmaster, head of SOE's French Section.[17] Buckmaster liked the look of what he saw on paper and put a trace out to MI5, whose reply was received on 23 November. In the meantime, Déricourt was invited to the Northumberland Hotel to be interviewed by Selwyn Jepson, one of F Section's recruitment officers. Déricourt had the most fabulous qualifications: he had good first-hand knowledge of aircraft similar to the Lysander and had landed them countless times on very rudimentary country strips; he knew the countryside around the Loire well; and he knew Paris extremely well. But Jepson was there to learn about the individual's character as well as his qualifications, and there was an arrogance about Déricourt that was somewhat disquieting.[18] When Buckmaster received the MI5 file on Déricourt it was a great disappointment – not what he wanted to see at all. It stated that although the RPS had given him a clean bill of health, they (MI5) would *not* recommend him.

Although MI5 were still under the false impression that he had been an Air France pilot in Syria – a story he maintained even long after the war – their suspicions were based on the assumption that Déricourt had passed through France before coming to Britain, and that fact alone made him a doubtful risk. For if the Germans knew he was bound for Britain, '[Déricourt] would have been a likely subject for German attention... [and therefore]... we do not feel [he] can be cleared from a security point of view'.[19]

There is no doubt that if MI5 had learnt what Dansey already knew, that his entire story was a complete fabrication, then Déricourt's name would not have got anywhere near SOE. As it was, they already felt he was untrustworthy. Was Dansey simply being derelict in not passing on what he knew about the Frenchman, or was there some other reason for his silence?

Then someone spoke up on Déricourt's behalf. Nicholas Bodington had learnt that his old Paris friend was being considered for work within his section. He immediately declared that he knew the man personally and wouldn't hesitate to employ him. 'Déricourt is first class material!' Bodington's extremely timely recommendation went a long way towards suppressing any qualms.[20]

But Déricourt's qualifications were in fact so irresistible that there hadn't really been any serious doubt about employing him. Buckmaster and his senior colleagues, Gerry Morel, Bourne Patterson and of course Bodington, were of one mind – Déricourt was the answer to their prayers. However, those feelings were not by any means universal. Vera Atkins, whose opinion was always greatly valued, was asked to go and see Déricourt and then report.

> When I saw him, my heart sank because I felt that he wasn't a man that I could trust. Why I had that impression I don't know, but I suppose one does sum up people in one's own way. Possibly it was his slightly mocking attitude, perhaps it was that he didn't seem to look one very straight in the face; but I came back and said that I didn't like him, and that I wouldn't trust him.[21]

Unfortunately on this occasion Atkins's 'instincts' were disregarded. Déricourt joined the SOE on 1 December and began an extremely specific and condensed training programme.

Déricourt's arrival at SOE was, however, far more involved than appears from the account above – in fact there is a great deal of opacity in the official record concerning his recruitment. It was generally held that the individual who brought Déricourt's name to SOE's attention was '…probably André Simon'.[22] Simon was a logical guess, since he was responsible for liaison between SOE's F Section and the branch of Air Intelligence concerned with organizing flights of the Special Duties squadrons. Déricourt encouraged this view by later claiming that he'd been in the RAF, flying with the Special Duties squadron when he was 'talent spotted' by Simon. Déricourt even fabricated his flight log to support that story. In France, a pilot who deliberately made false entries in his flight log faced a strong risk of losing his licence. Clearly, Déricourt felt it was a risk worth taking. When he left Marseilles in August, the Vichy authorities had just certified his log, which stood at 3658 hours daylight flying and 94.5 hours night flying. Then, a page or two later, commencing on 6 November 1942, Déricourt filled twenty pages of his log adding no less than 150 day-time flights, a total of 1243 hours, and sixty-eight night flights totalling 192 hours; all apparently with the RAF's 161 Squadron. Not one of those flights actually took place. It was an invention of staggering proportions.[23]

In fact, Déricourt *was* officially in the RAF. On 1 December, the day he was enlisted with the SOE, he was given an honorary commission as a Flying Officer in the Admin and Special Duties Branch of the RAF Volunteer Reserves.[24] It was a technical requirement of the SOE that all its officers had to have an official rank in some other British service. But Déricourt never flew a single mission for the RAF, and André Simon was not the man who brought him to the attention of the SOE. Despite what the SOE archives state, senior SOE officers recall that Déricourt's name arrived at Baker Street at a much higher level.

In mid-November, Air Commodore Archie Boyle handed a slim file to his immediate superior (by then Major General) Colin Gubbins, with the briefest summary of Déricourt's details. Once Gubbins had read it, he passed it to his deputy, Harry Sporborg, who let it gravitate down to F Section.[25] Who, one might ask, brought Déricourt's name to Archie Boyle's attention in the first place?

Air Commodore Boyle's background was Air Intelligence. After the outbreak of war, he became associated with MI5's B Division, the section responsible for all counter-espionage work in the United Kingdom. By the end of 1939, B Division had succeeded in 'turning' a number of Abwehr agents and making them work for Britain. To operate double agents successfully, B Division needed a good supply of secret or highly confidential information that the 'turned' agent could affordably pass to the enemy, along with bogus or misleading material, so that he was not suspected. This genuine material had to be of a pretty high quality and would have to withstand the probability of being checked. Boyle became fascinated with the work of B Division and volunteered, without any official authority, a selection of genuine intelligence from his domain at the Air Ministry.

By 1940 the work of running double agents had grown more complicated. Not only were there more agents to run, but a number of these were operating abroad and foreign operations were technically the responsibility of MI6. It became necessary to establish a new section that would co-ordinate operations between MI5 and MI6 and provide a proper control over the material that was being passed to the enemy. In July 1940 the Wireless Board was created, a lofty panel of senior intelligence officers which consisted of Guy Liddell from MI5 (who was also the Director of B Division), Stewart Menzies (and sometimes Claude Dansey) from MI6, John Godfrey the Director of Naval Intelligence, the Director of Military Intelligence, and Archie Boyle. During this period, Boyle got on very close terms with Menzies and Dansey and although he never cared for 'Uncle Claude', he nonetheless admired his acumen.

In June 1941, Boyle became the SOE's Director of Intelligence and Security and was a magnificent asset to the organization in that role. He used his good relations within the intelligence community to effect a high level of liaison with MI6 and the Security Service. It was from MI6 that Boyle received the name Déricourt.[26]

Boyle was a shrewd and extremely intelligent man, and there is no evidence that he would have given a potentially unsuitable candidate like Déricourt his recommendation, unless, like MI5, he too had been misled. There were no more than three officers inside MI6 who even knew of Déricourt's existence; one was in Gibraltar, another was Kenneth Cohen and the other was, of course, Claude Dansey. Dansey not only succeeded in slipping Déricourt into SOE, but in doing so he also managed to disguise his own hand.

Before he came anywhere near SOE, Déricourt was told that he would be sent to a section of MI6 that specialized in sabotage operations, called 'special operations'. In a sworn statement to the DST in 1946, Déricourt wrote:

> I was transferred to SOE, a unit specially concerned with sabotage. This service, like

all Allied services at the time, was controlled
by SIS (MI6). I entered into an additional
commitment, through André Simon, about
the secrecy of my work.

In a revised version of this statement, made in 1947, he
circumspectly removed the reference to MI6.

It would seem, from other evidence too, that André
Simon was aware of Déricourt's links with MI6. Although
his name sounds French, Simon was utterly English and,
indeed, spoke French very badly. He was the son of the
famous wine merchant and had a fairly comfortable life-
style, with a place in the country where his wife lived and
a flat in town where he tended to be for twelve months
of the year. Sharing the flat with him was another woman
whom he kept secret from his wife, but apparently not
from his colleagues at SOE.[27]

During the weeks before Henri was sent to France, he
and Simon became good friends. In fact there was a trio
of bon-viveurs who would congregate at Simon's flat in
Harley Street to sample his excellent collection of pre-war
vintages, the other member being Nicholas Bodington.
Bodington, better than anyone, knew about Déricourt's
connection with German intelligence, since he was the
man who had introduced him to Boemelburg in the first
place. In conversation, Déricourt and Bodington always
referred to Boemelburg not by name but by the sobri-
quet '*notre ami*'.[28] Bodington was also privy to Déricourt's
secret connection with MI6 – and he was the only one to
suffer for it.

There was someone else in SOE who suspected a relationship with MI6. Gubbins's deputy, Harry Sporborg,
had been a solicitor with the city firm of Slaughter and

May and had initially been involved with SOE's operations in Scandinavia. He later became head of SOE's London Group, the directorate responsible for all operations in northern Europe, and he was also the principal private secretary for SOE's affairs to the Minister. Sporborg was Gubbins's deputy while he was Head of Operations and then later when he became Head of SOE. The initial details about Déricourt that Boyle brought into Gubbins's office were of no immediate concern. However, when Sporborg read a transcript of one of Déricourt's initial interviews he heard the very first faint ring of alarm bells. Déricourt, under the impression that he was talking to another MI6 officer, once again declared his contacts in German intelligence. According to Sporborg,

> It emerged during the initial questioning before he was engaged. I think he'd put it forward as an advantage, as something he could contribute, as a plus-point, you see. That he'd be able to get information for us whereas others couldn't. That was knocked on the head and he was told that he would not be expected to do anything of that sort.[29]

At first Sporborg simply doubted the suitability of the man for a sensitive role such as F Section had in mind. Later, however, his doubts were replaced with a dark suspicion that Déricourt had other allegiances. Sporborg's account of Déricourt's declaration has consistently been denied by those who hold the records.[30]

These declarations of Déricourt's would seem to indicate that he was not as self-assured as reports have made him appear. At least, not in the company of very senior officers. He repeated this detail about his German contacts on at least three occasions (upon his arrival, to Air Intelligence, and then to SOE), assuming, as so many Frenchmen did, that there was simply one great amorphous conglomerate called 'British Intelligence'. (It never occurred to either the French or the Germans that SOE and MI6 were separate entities.) When he arrived in Britain, Déricourt knew he faced probable internment (no doubt Dansey even threatened him with it), but he also knew that a personal acquaintanceship with figures in German intelligence was currency he could bargain with. Being passed from one senior British officer to another, Déricourt never knew to whom he was talking at any one time. Eventually, he would learn to be more circumspect.

Claude Dansey had plucked Déricourt out of the stream of unsavoury life that inevitably washed up on Britain's shores during times of war. He then disguised the truth of the man's origins from MI5 and proffered his services to an organization that he knew was too naive and trusting to spot a 'wrong 'un' when it saw one, but at the same time was not so naive that it wouldn't have been suspicious of a gift from Dansey. Consequently, and with Déricourt's connivance, he carefully disguised his own hand in the transaction.

Why was there so much deception between the British secret services? Why had F Section officers like Bodington and Simon not reported to their superiors in SOE what they knew about Déricourt? Did they feel responsible to some higher authority?

Vera Atkins was the only F Section officer who expressed any reservations about Déricourt and, just to add grist to her mill, Déricourt made the irregular request to be given a few diamonds to supplement his planned operations in France. Diamonds, he assured her, were currently at a premium in occupied Paris. Atkins realized this was the bare-faced try-on of a hardened black-marketeer. When she protested to Buckmaster and company her objections were overruled and Déricourt got his diamonds.[31] F Section just couldn't wait to get him in the field.

On 5 December he was driven down to RAF Tempsford to be introduced to some of the pilots who would be flying operations out to him in France. One of these was the young Hugh Verity. He had just been transferred from Fighter Command HQ to 161 Squadron and was himself learning about the Lysander. In time Verity would become Squadron Leader and, later, Group Captain, but during that very damp December he was still a 24-year-old Flight Lieutenant, Oxford graduate, fluent in Spanish and French, with a few weeks' training in Lysanders. He and Déricourt immediately hit it off. For Déricourt, RAF Tempsford was like a home away from home. The society of pilots, dozens of strange new aircraft to explore, even the scent of aviation fuel made a welcome change from all the pressures in London. Déricourt began to relax and a little of his old congenial charm resurfaced. For Verity, Déricourt was a figure of some fascination. He was ten years older than himself and clearly an extremely experienced pilot. But as well as his obvious experience, there was also an air of intrigue about him.

Déricourt told Verity some pretty tall stories. For instance, that he used to earn £300 a week as a stunt pilot with an aerobatic team, whereas in fact in the days of the flying circus he barely ever had enough money to pay for fuel. He claimed to have a flat in Paris, which he did not; that he was the mayor of a small town in France; and that he had escaped from France by trekking across the Pyrenees.[32] Well, the lads in 161 Squadron certainly took to him. He wasn't one of your typical 'joes' (the term they used for agents), he was really one of them, someone who had a genuine appreciation of the dangers involved in their work. His taciturn humour belied a sense of careful responsibility and dependability. Tales of the flying circus, or of his 'adventures' in the Spanish Civil War, regularly earned him drinks in the officers' mess – hallowed ground to an outsider.

Déricourt quickly learnt the routine for laying out flare paths for the Lysanders and Hudsons, the rudiments of parachuting at Ringway airbase, and basic security procedures at one of the SOE's training centres. On the night of 22 December, barely three weeks after joining, he was kitted out in a suit of French clothes, given a set of false papers for a Maurice Fabre (the new persona he was expected to adopt in France), the codename GILBERT, and a parting gift of a pair of gold cufflinks from Buckmaster. He sat and waited to be driven out to the Hudson, but by midnight the weather had closed in and the operation was aborted. Depressingly, the weather settled into a pattern for the rest of the week and the mission was cancelled until the next moon period, in January. Déricourt did not get home for Christmas.

He had about a month to kill before the next moon and spent some of that time back in London. On 11 January, Verity took him up in an Oxford bomber and gave him dual instruction. The same afternoon he was allowed to take a Lysander up and do a couple of circuits of the field; and that was the sum total of the flying he ever did for the RAF. At 10.30 p.m. on 22 January 1943, Operation OCTO took Déricourt and another SOE agent named Jean Worms in a Halifax across the Channel into occupied France. Worms jumped first, to a reception prepared by Andrée Borrel and Francis Suttill in a field near Chartres. Worms was the leader of an all-Jewish '*reseaux*' (network) called ROBIN that would establish itself in the Marne district and become another sub-circuit of the PROSPER network. Déricourt preferred to be dropped 'blind', coming down twenty minutes later in a large field north of the Orléans Canal, near Pithiviers.

VIII

The Rules of the Game

During the early morning hours, Déricourt walked across the frozen open fields towards the little spur line that runs out of Orléans to Poitiers. He caught one of the early morning milk trains that rolled slowly into Gare d'Orsay around mid-morning. His first priority was to get warm and get some sleep. He turned up at JuJu's flat near the Place des Ternes, knocked but got no reply. His old flame, Julienne Aisner, had become quite serious about the young lawyer Charles Besnard. Besnard's own flat was not far, in the Avenue Malakoff, but Déricourt decided not to disturb them.[1] He took the Metro to the Gare de l'Est and bought a ticket for Reims.

Sometime that afternoon he arrived at the little village of Coulognes-en-Tardenois. He waited in the small bar until his mother returned home from work before knocking on the door. He slept most of the day and woke about ten that night to talk. His mother knew from experience not to believe much of what her son told her; his father said nothing to him at all. Sitting by the fire in the large armchair, the even larger frame of Alfred Déricourt seemed to his son to expand with every breath. Henri, on departing, left his mother a large wad of notes from the cash the SOE had given him.[2]

By midday on the following day he was outside JuJu's flat again in the Place des Ternes. When she opened the door she had to catch her breath. After another of his characteristic disappearances there he was, as large as life. She would never get used to his unpredictability. He explained crudely that he was working for the British, which of course she didn't believe, and that he was going down to Marseilles to collect his wife and bring her up to Paris. Could she find them somewhere to stay? JuJu said she'd try.[3] He then left her some of his SOE cash and took the train to Marseilles.

Rémy Clément had been stood down from Air France when that company was forced to cancel its few remaining routes. He got employment in the office of the La Bourne company in Marseilles and was sitting at his desk, his mind a long way from his work, when the phone rang. It was Jeannot. She was nearly incoherent with joy, but the gist of her message was that Rémy should come round to her flat on his way home that evening. She said nothing else, but Rémy was in no doubt, Henri was back. Déricourt opened the door and ushered Rémy into the small room at 50 Rue Curiol. There was much embracing and nods and winks as Déricourt began to reveal his purpose. He wanted Rémy to come up to Paris with him, to help in a secret operation for the British. Secret agents were flown in and out of France late at night and they needed someone to organize the flights, discover the right fields, lay out flight paths – gradually Déricourt went into the whole operation for the SOE in great detail. Rémy was extremely tempted but at the same time very wary. Déricourt was such an outrageous adventurer.

> I had a good job, but it had no future. I felt
> up against a wall and with the occupation I

> felt trapped. He was offering me something
> I was craving for. To be involved with flying
> again.[4]

Against this Rémy had to weigh up two things. He didn't like the idea of having anything to do with secret agents, and he was terrified of being caught by the Germans. He asked for some time to think it over. Déricourt explained that he and Jeannot were taking the first train in the morning. He would have to know Rémy's answer before they left.

At five-thirty the next morning Clément slowly climbed the steep hill of Boulevard d'Athenes to the Gare St Charles. At the station he told Déricourt he would come but needed some time. He was not restrained by doubt but by bureaucracy. In a few weeks he would be due his holiday pay and didn't want to forfeit the cash. In three weeks he and his wife should be in Paris. His only condition was that he would never be expected to have anything to do with agents. Déricourt didn't have much choice; he agreed. Sometime during the journey to Paris, Déricourt decided to dispose of the bogus identity papers SOE had given him. He was too well known, he could never pass himself off as 'Maurice Fabre', so he sensibly remained Henri Déricourt.

In Paris he and Jeannot stayed the first few nights with JuJu, sleeping on the bare boards. His wife knew all about Henri's relationship with the other woman, but seemed to cope with the temporary discomfort with no complaints. However, it was clear the arrangement could not last.[5]

Sometime within the first three days, Déricourt contacted Sturmbannfuhrer Karl Boemelburg. He was collected somewhere in the Bois de Boulogne by a black

Citroën and driven around the maze of small roads that weave through the Bois. Naturally, there is no transcript of the conversation that took place, but it has come down through 'Gestapo folklore' (absurd but true) that Déricourt managed to convince Boemelburg of his strong political feelings. The conversation went on the following lines.

Déricourt described, in minute detail, the process by which he'd been transported out of France via the Pat Line, to Gibraltar. This satisfied Boemelburg that the black-marketeer probably had been in touch with 'British intelligence'.[6] Then Déricourt embarked on a vivid description of a Britain on the verge of mass revolt, where the government was riddled with Socialists and Communists, and where the ordinary Briton felt no sympathy for Churchill's warlike policies. Because of his own special qualifications, Déricourt had been recruited to organize the transport of secret agents in and out of France. However, sickened by the sight of rampant Bolshevism, he had determined to offer his services to the only people who knew who the real enemy was and how to fight it – the Nazis.[7]

Whether or not Boemelburg believed Déricourt doesn't come down with the rest of the story. The old Nazi was a highly suspicious man and would have required a great deal more than mere tokens of political empathy to convince him. One thing that would have impressed him, indeed always did impress him, was Déricourt's remarkable calm and self-assurance. There was something about his quiet, careful speech that radiated confidence, and it was Boemelburg's confidence he wanted. They arranged to meet again before the end of the day. At that second meeting Déricourt emerged with a valuable envelope in his coat pocket. Henri's and Jeannot's accommodation problems had been solved.

On their third day in Paris, Jeannot and Henri packed up their belongings and strolled down the Rue du Faubourg St Honoré, to the Hotel Bristol, where he presented the man on the desk with Boemelburg's letter of authorization.[8] The Hotel Bristol was a German-controlled hotel. It was not occupied by Germans but by their guests, civilians mostly; Vichy officials, bankers and industrialists. It was a discreet and convenient meeting-place where private enterprise could meet and be entertained by the Nazi authorities. It was almost the most expensive and certainly the most exclusive hotel in Paris. Highly polished marble floors reflected jet-black jack-boots and the glittering lights of the crystal chandeliers. For Jeannot it was an experience she never forgot. Having lived in Marseilles and away from the more obvious manifestations of the occupation, the sight of so many German uniforms absolutely terrified her. She couldn't bear to eat in the restaurant because the sight of so much black and grey made her uncontrollably nervous. She had no idea of the significance of the place and knew nothing of her husband's arrangements with the Germans. All she knew was that she didn't like it. Henri, on the other hand, revelled in it.

Of course, living at the Bristol was an extraordinary risk to take, if only because he might have been seen by a future contact from PROSPER's network. There was a convenient back door to the hotel which opened onto a small lane that led to the Rue de Penthièvre. Henri and Jeannot would slip out to eat at a small black-market rendezvous they called La Conte where they met up with JuJu and others, JuJu hadn't told Besnard about

Henri for fear the respectable lawyer might disapprove of the black-marketeering pilot. He would certainly have disapproved of her having anything to do with the Resistance. Déricourt convinced JuJu that his work in Paris was serious and that he needed someone else to work with him, to be his courier. She was at first incredulous, but was eventually intrigued by the prospect and agreed to help. JuJu never found out where Henri and Jeannot were staying – nor, of course, about his contacts with Boemelburg.

The arrangement at the Bristol couldn't last. Three weeks later, JuJu mentioned to Déricourt that his black-market contact Bladier had a flat for sale in the 16th Arrondissement, not far from the Avenue Foch.[9] The simple two-room apartment on the third floor of 58 Rue Pergolese suited them perfectly, but there was a great deal of work to be done before it would be habitable. Meanwhile Henri and Jeannot moved into a room at a hotel in the Avenue Colonel Moll until the accommodation in the Rue Pergolese was ready. Déricourt was absolutely tickled at the prospect of owning an apartment in that area. There was a small black-market restaurant 100 metres from his door and less than ten minutes away, around the corner, was Boemelburg's headquarters at 82–84 Avenue Foch.

Towards the end of February, Rémy Clément and his wife arrived and settled into a wonderful artist's studio flat in Montmartre, with a view of Sacre Coeur from the window. Déricourt's little group was now gathered. It was codenamed FARRIER. They were contacted by some PROSPER people; Andrée Borrel, who would share courier duties with JuJu, and Jack Agazarian, who would provide radio communications with London. Déricourt and Clément created a simple telephone bell code. Two rings: meet me at La Conte; three rings: meet at Chez Tutulle; one ring and then two: news from abroad, and so on. Almost immediately Rémy was despatched down to the Vienne to make a survey of possible fields to use as landing strips. But before these arrangements had been made, Déricourt had already entered into his understanding with the SD. There were a great many lives at stake already, and the game hadn't even started.

During the last week of February he was contacted by Lise de Baissac, who wanted help to get some people back to London. One of these was her brother Claude, the organizer of another extensive network that stretched along the Atlantic coast, called SCIENTIST. The SCIENTIST and PROSPER networks were linked both geographically and strategically, Lise de Baissac being the conduit through which most information flowed between Claude de Baissac in Bordeaux and Francis Suttill in Paris. These two great men had a great deal in common, but the most critical element they shared, along with innumerable other networks in France, was their reliance on the SOE's Air Movements Officer, Déricourt.

Déricourt's first operation, which they called TRAINER, was planned for the next full moon in mid-March. It would be a double Lysander; two aircraft landing, one after the other. The Lysander could carry three adults in the rear cockpit – or, at a pinch, two adults and two children. It was a single-crew operation, no navigator or gunner. With his maps spread out across his lap, the pilot would fly out to the given co-ordinates and then, by the light of the moon, be guided by the rivers or railways to the field where the reception committee was waiting.

On 17 March, four men bought tickets for Poitiers at the Gare d'Orsay and, having made visual contact with Déricourt, boarded the train and sat themselves at intervals along its length. At Poitiers they all went separate ways, having arranged to rendezvous after curfew at a spot on the outskirts of the town, where Déricourt waited with half a dozen bicycles. They pedalled in single file, Déricourt – with the only lamp – in the lead. He was taking them to a field SOE had given him in London. Already tried and tested, it had been coded B/19.

Throughout France over eighty such fields had been identified as being suitable for clandestine use. Those used for MI6 operations were classified RED and carefully segregated from SOE fields, which were classified BLUE. Officially pilots were not supposed to know either the identity of the people they carried or the service for which they were working, but by noting whether he was flying out to R/12 or B/31 a pilot could deduce whether it was an MI6 operation or one for SOE. When the coded references were translated into soil and trees, one begins to appreciate the extraordinary courage of the men who brought aircraft down into the French countryside in the dead of night.

Déricourt left his passengers in a small gully shrouded by trees at the top end of the field and ran off to lay out the flare path. It was vital that the pilot had a clear approach to the field, so that he knew he could descend comfortably without fear of clipping the top of a tree or electricity cables. The precise direction of the strip depended on the direction of the wind, which was faintly from the northeast that night. A hard frost had created a firm crust on the soil – in theory, it should go well. The entire field had to be at least half a kilometre long, within which the flare path, some 150 metres long and 50 metres wide, was marked out with torches in the shape of an inverted L. The top end of the inverted L gave the pilot the width of his strip; two, sometimes three lights set into the wind gave him the length.

Back in the gully, sweating and breathing great plumes of steam, Déricourt rejoined his passengers. With an hour or so before the aircraft would be due, they took out some coffee and bread and tried to keep warm. Amongst the four passengers were three important SOE officers. The SCIENTIST organizer Claude de Baissac had been in France since June 1942, and was returning to London for a rest and re-briefing. With him was France Anthelme, the organizer of the parallel but much smaller circuit to Suttill's, called BRICKLAYER. Come D-Day, BRICK-LAYER would be responsible for creating secret supply lines of food and finance for the invading army. He too was closely associated with Suttill. With him was a wireless operator, not identified. The fourth, Raymond Flower, was the organizer of the MONKEYPUZZLE circuit, based around Tours. He had been in France since June the year before, but his little group had never got off the ground and he was returning to London, although he didn't know it at that stage, to take up a liaison post.

Soon after midnight, the sound of the Rolls-Royce Mercury engine could be heard drifting in and out of the wind. Déricourt told them to stay hidden until his signal and then made a dash to the torches, turning each one on and then standing at the command point with his own torch in hand. As he made visual contact he would flash in Morse the identification letter 'D'. The Lysander would respond with the same letter. Flying Officer 'Bunny' Rymills banked his aircraft and descended to about 300 feet, flying over the row of lights, re-orientated, and made another approach. Then, coming down quite low, he made another pass, getting the feel of the wind. His final approach was perfect and he put the aircraft down at 12.30 a.m.

Déricourt flashed the signal to the men in the trees, who scrambled up the slope and across to the Lysander. Out of the rear cockpit, where a gunner used to be positioned, three men gingerly made their way down the ladder. He picked out three of his four passengers to go on the first aircraft and ordered the newcomers to help them on board with their luggage. Seven minutes later, Rymills pulled the throttle back, released the brakes and let the plane roll down the bumpy strip until she gained enough velocity to be lifted, almost vertically, into the air. Meanwhile Déricourt and the three newcomers plus Anthelme walked back to the gully to wait. Normally on a 'double', the second aircraft was just a couple of minutes away. On that occasion he was nearly half an hour behind his leader. As the new arrivals waited, the rush of adrenalin had begun to dilute and the first anxieties about being dropped into enemy-occupied territory were diminishing. Déricourt always kept a flask of cognac to loosen up the tenseness.

At about ten to one, the sound of Vaughan-Fowler's Lysander drifted slowly into earshot, and Déricourt clapped Anthelme on the back, as if to say, you aren't going to be left behind after all. Vaughan-Fowler's pick-up didn't run quite as smoothly as that of Rymills. The ground was particularly bumpy, which shook the Lysander badly and caused the engine to ignite. He taxied to a halt with flames licking the engine cowling. Déricourt climbed up the wing struts until his face was virtually inside the cockpit, where there followed a brief conversation, conducted at the top of their lungs. Out of the rear cockpit clambered Madame Agazarian, the radio operator's wife. Once she was down, Déricourt leapt up the ladder, grabbed a spare Mae West (an inflatable life-preserver) and stuffed it into the engine exhaust, which had the effect of suffocating the flames. Meanwhile Anthelme, terrified that the whole aircraft would blow up, stood motionless at the foot of the ladder. Déricourt made a swift jerk with his thumb and Anthelme scrambled on board. A signal to Vaughan-Fowler and the engine was throttled up. He was off the ground by 1 a.m.[10]

Back in the gully with his torches, Déricourt began to sort out the new arrivals. The first few hours that incoming agents spent in France were often the most gruelling. Having flown through a freezing black night into a foreign field, they needed that first contact with a friend in hostile territory. They were also hungry for news, for an assessment of their situation, any trivial little thing that they might need to know which London had neglected to pass on. Déricourt abandoned his usual mute efficiency and chatted to the agents, apparently just to put them at their ease. But in the cold light of the morning after, many of these agents reflected on Déricourt's inquisitiveness.[11] He made it his business to learn as much as he possibly could about everyone who passed through his hands. He had a prodigious memory and soon built up a mental record of who worked with whom. Apart from Madame Agazarian, who had come to work beside her husband, there was John Goldsmith, who had had a brief and unprofitable career with CARTE in the south but was now working with the Paris-based networks; Henri Lejeune, who was with the Gaullist section (RF) but who seemed to have links with F Section networks; and Roland Dowlen, a radio operator for a small network in Paris, separate from but in communication with PROSPER, called CHESTNUT. Hardly key figures at the centre of the northern networks, yet all with one single common factor; all had links with PROSPER. This in itself was of no great significance, but it did impress upon Déricourt that apart from a common link, there may also be a common purpose. At that stage he knew very little about PROSPER's stategic significance, but he did know that it could not be long before he met the man at the centre of the great network.

The party pedalled in single file down the pitch-black lanes towards Poitiers. Their security procedures had been well rehearsed in London. Each had his own cover story, false identity papers, the return stubs of pre-purchased train tickets and so on. At Poitiers they separated, filling in the hours until dawn, when they converged on the railway station. On the platform, where they waited for the train for Paris, they mingled inconspicuously with the early morning crowds, avoiding the impulse to glance at each other. Though their paths would doubtless cross again, for the moment they were on their own.

Déricourt had to remain to deal with the bicycles and took a later train that got him into Paris after lunch. From his point of view, Operation TRAINER had been a success.[12] He found the agents were on the whole fairly at ease with him. His professionalism seemed to create a sense of confidence and in that mood many of them were very talkative. In fact the whole operation had been quite exhilarating. It seemed as though the business might have its moments. Back at the 'Coll Moll', the hotel in Avenue

Colonel Moll, Déricourt collapsed on his bed and slept through until the following morning.

Within days of the March operation, there was another meeting with Boemelburg – a kind of re-appraisal, with a view to formalizing the situation. At that meeting Déricourt provided Boemelburg with a detailed description of everyone who had travelled in on the Lysanders. Boemelburg asked him if he knew anything about PROSPER, to which Déricourt replied that he had heard it had something to do with the invasion.[13]

The relationship that developed between these two men was one of the great partnerships of the secret war. From the beginning it had all the hallmarks of something that would endure, and it was significant not for what it involved but for what it did not involve. It was the experience of most senior officers at the Avenue Foch, and Boemelburg especially, that coercion was not an enduring basis for any intelligence contract. It built up resentment and threatened the security of everyone involved. Coercion was fine for the short term when immediate results were the essence of the contract, but it did not hold any promise for the future. Money had traditionally been essential to these arrangements and it was well known that the SD had almost unlimited resources. But here, too, Boemelburg was remarkably circumspect. He did not trust anyone whose motives were purely profit. Like Dansey in London, he knew not only the value of money but also its worth. If every man had his price, then it was extremely unwise to base an understanding on the vagaries of the free market.[14] On the other hand, the SD were also extraordinarily correct and they would have been equally suspicious of anyone who would not accept any money at all. SD archives reveal that, unlike most of their informers, Déricourt did not receive a regular salary, though of course he did accept the odd bit of largesse that came his way. (There is a massive archive of signed receipts which the SD extracted from all their informers, which now rests in the vaults of the French DST in Rue Saussier. It is guarded as though it were a national secret – which it probably is.)

Déricourt was officially identified as BOE/48 – Boemelburg's 48th agent. Soon after that meeting, Boemelburg introduced the name GILBERT (synonymous with BOE/48) to a few of his colleagues at Avenue Foch, most notably to his immediate subordinate, Josef Kieffer. Boemelburg had already placed GILBERT within the larger context of the expanding phenomenon known as PROSPER. Déricourt's confirmation of PROSPER's strategic position guaranteed the relationship would proceed from first stages. But here lay a fundamental flaw in the way the Germans operated their double agents. The man who made the initial contact always became the controller – it was a matter of some personal pride. But it was also a critical error, for the controller then lacked the objectivity to run his agent wisely and his judgement was often biased when analysing the intelligence he received. In Britain, it had long been appreciated that 'doubles' were a volatile species and were passed on by those who had made the first contact to professional controllers who were more dispassionate. In Déricourt's case there was the prospect, for Boemelburg, of information that would be immediately verifiable. So upon that basis their mutual trust grew.

What, then, was Déricourt's role? Why was he there and what was he doing? German and French archives confirm that he entered into an arrangement with the Sicherheitsdienst in February 1943. Before examining motives, it is worth making one small point here about the issue of money. British authorities have always claimed that Déricourt did what he did for financial reward. He was paid by SOE to organize Lysander operations and was paid again by the Germans for delivering intelligence on those operations. Of course he was a 'Déricourist', as his friend Clément once described him, but if he went into the arrangement with the SD just for money, then he didn't do particularly well by it. Taken over the course of his entire mission, the money Déricourt earned from the SD didn't amount to much more than any typical black-marketeer earned during the course of the war. In fact, it was a matter of some resentment with Déricourt that he didn't do a good deal better.

Whatever Déricourt's private motives may have been, his approach to the SD was, in fact, carried out on instructions from Claude Dansey. Karl Boemelburg was the highest-ranking SD officer in France. (Above him was the SS officer Standartenfuhrer Dr Helmut Knochen, who reported directly to Himmler.) Boemelburg reported directly to the head of counter-espionage and counter-sabotage at the RSHA in Berlin, Horst Kopkow. Boemelburg was the most important counter-espionage officer in France. If it were possible to win the hearts and minds of the SD in Paris, then it would be a tremendous advantage to Dansey's own intelligence operations. If Déricourt could get an insight into the SD's operations, it would be a coup comparable to deciphering their ENIGMA codes.

But how would Déricourt get any information out of Boemelburg? Surely the SD weren't going to sit down with Déricourt and discuss their operations. Of course not. The basis for Déricourt's operation rested upon the old maxim that questions are far more revealing than answers. Dansey's real objective was to *discover what Boemelburg wanted to know*. It was a classic double-agent operation. First a British agent approaches the Germans and offers to pass them information about British operations, and then gives them material that could be quickly verified and evaluated. Once that had occurred, their expectations would begin to rise. 'If he can deliver information about X, perhaps he may know something about Y.' As their confidence grows, coupled with their appetite for information, their questions become more expansive, more greedy – more direct: 'Have you heard anything about a wireless operator who was travelling down to the Jura?' 'Do you know anything about a group up near Compiègne?' 'Can you find out something about a certain doctor in Toulouse?' 'Do you know of any contacts of the Abbé in Tulle?'

Like the French, the Germans never imagined SOE and MI6 to be two separate organizations. They were simply seen as different departments of something called 'British Intelligence'. Boemelburg's pre-eminence in the SD's counter-espionage operations meant that his enquiries covered a wide range of networks, some of them Dansey's. Déricourt would make a careful note of all Boemelburg's questions and send it to one of Dansey's contacts. In London, a patient process of listing, collating and cross-referencing those questions would gradually reveal what the enemy already knew, what he needed to know, what were his preoccupations and, most importantly, what were his priorities.

A steady stream of this material would enable London to create an extremely clear picture of the

SD's operations in France.[15] Of course there was a price for this information. Just as with ULTRA, Dansey's freedom to act on this intelligence was restricted by the risk that such action might compromise its source. For example, an enquiry about a group near Rennes would reveal that an operation was being conducted against the SOE's PARSON reseaux. Whether Dansey alerted SOE to that fact depended upon the result of his weighing up the value of saving PARSON against the risk of compromising his source. For if Boemelburg decided to arrest PARSON and found they were no longer there, he would naturally conclude there had been a leak and eventually Déricourt would no longer be trusted. The same calculation would also have to be made if the intelligence concerned one of Dansey's own groups. Intelligence about the enemy's counter-espionage operations always presents the dilemma of how to use it. Do you take evasive action – or somehow exploit the situation? There was of course another price to pay for this operation: Déricourt's answers. The more Boemelburg's expectations rose, the more answers BOE/48 would have to deliver. Some of these answers could be deceptions, others would have to be verifiable.

How did Déricourt communicate with Dansey? There were at least two routes. The first was through a particular bank teller at a branch of the Credit Lyonnaise in the Rue Caumartin. He was a 'mail drop' left over from the Z Organization. The second was through PAUL, the barman at the Bar Lorraine in the Place des Ternes, who came on the scene in 1942.[16]

But was it really possible that a senior British intelligence officer would feel it was worthwhile jeopardizing the lives of other British officers for the sake of an intelligence advantage? Harry Sporborg, the deputy head of SOE, was in no doubt: 'Make no mistake about it, MI6 would never have hesitated to use us or our agencies to advance their schemes, even if that meant the sacrifice of some of our people.'[17] It was common practice in war for a commander to sacrifice some of his men to gain some strategic advantage. At Dunkirk the British Army took over 68,000 casualties in rearguard actions while nearly 340,000 men made it safely off the beaches. However, Dansey's game actually threatened an entire operation. Would that have been worth the sacrifice?

Trying to make sense of a personality as complex as Dansey's is all the more difficult because he entrusted so little to paper. At the beginning of 1943 it probably made sense to his vindictive way of thinking that it was worth giving a little SOE information away in return for some insight into the SD's operations in France. The problem was, and Dansey must have been aware of it, how to restrict that information when Déricourt was operating on his own over 150 miles from London. There is good evidence from the German side that for some time the information Déricourt gave away was pretty insubstantial and that it was the *promise* of what he might give that made him so attractive. It is the *modus operandi* of all double agents to provide thin material to begin with, coupled with an undertaking to deliver the earth tomorrow.

But that was the problem with this operation. It was Boemelburg who was asking the questions and it would be he who effectively set the stakes. On the other hand, Dansey had no qualms about exploiting an organization he absolutely despised. If Déricourt was going to be any good to Dansey, then he needed to win Boemelburg's absolute confidence. That would be bought with first-rate, verifiable information – and the only information Déricourt had that was worth anything was what he knew about SOE operations.

As far as MI6 were concerned, this particular operation was one of Dansey's private enterprises, probably known to no more than two of his most trusted associates. But despite his obsession with secrecy, a thin trickle of information about his activities would occasionally leak out and inevitably appal the new breed of young intellectuals that hovered about the dingy corridors at Broadway. One of those wartime recruits from the academic world, Hugh Trevor Roper, now Lord Dacre, described Claude Dansey as 'an utter shit; corrupt, incompetent, but with a certain low cunning'. Malcolm Muggeridge, equally damning of him, added, however: 'He was the only true professional in MI6. The others at the top were all second-rate minds.'

Unfortunately for SOE, they had few friends at court. Most MI6 officers still considered them a bunch of undisciplined amateurs who were more a danger to themselves than to the enemy. Added to which, everyone was terrified of Dansey and would never have dared blowing one of his operations. Now that the fuse was lit, they would just have to wait and see.

IX

An Eastern Influence

The war was not fought in separate isolated corners but on a wide canvas where events at one end had a direct effect on events at the other. Déricourt was originally planted amongst SOE's French networks just to provide intelligence on the SD, but soon he would be involved in a different operation. The game in Paris was about to be altered by the changing circumstances some 1600 miles to the east. There the real war, the war that had occupied the lives of tens of millions of people, was being fought on the frozen fields of Russia. Along a 600-mile front, 200 German divisions faced more than 300 Russian divisions. Over 5 million men waged war on a scale that defied the imagination. By that second winter, the Russian army had lost nearly 8 million men and the civilian population had suffered almost as badly. That was where the war was being fought and lost.

In 1942, Hitler redoubled his efforts in a bid for total victory. Each month, his armies brought him closer to that goal; in the Kerch Peninsula, the Crimea, Sevastopol, the Donets Basin, Rostov, the Kuban granaries, then turning in the direction of the Caucasus the Germans seized the Maykep oilfields. The roll call of Russian defeats sent signals of doom to the strategic planners in Whitehall. If the Russians capitulated, the Germans would have nearly 200 divisions to deploy in the west, making an Allied return to France a very distant prospect. Allied strategy to date had been to put as much strain as possible on German resources, in the hope that the enemy would outstretch his lines of supply.

In the west, the German Commander in Chief, Von Runstedt, had over 50 divisions at his disposal which, unless there was a real threat of an Allied invasion, could easily be re-deployed to the eastern front. Fifty extra divisions on the Russian Front would have made the difference between victory and defeat. Stalin appreciated the situation as well as anyone, and had peppered Churchill throughout the year with the persistent and ever more desperate demand, 'When will you open up the Second Front?'

In August 1942, immediately following the Dieppe débâcle, Churchill promised Stalin that a proper cross-Channel invasion would materialize in 1943.[1] For most of the Combined Chiefs, both British and American, the bloodletting that had taken place during the Dieppe raid had left them sober and cautious about 1943. As planning progressed for the first major Allied operation of the war, the invasion of French North Africa, it became apparent that an invasion of Europe was unlikely to take place before 1944. A week after the North African landings had taken place Churchill wrote, 'We have pulled in our horns [plans for 1943] to the most remarkable extent and I cannot imagine what the Russians will do or say when they realize it.'[2] He was worried that the Russians might conclude that without a second front their situation was hopeless and capitulate or sue for peace. In January 1943, with the North African campaign well under way, the political leaders and military commanders of Britain, America and the Free French met at Casablanca to hammer out the strategic programme for the new year.

Like all conferences, it was partly to do with business and partly to do with the business of being seen to be doing business. President Roosevelt was driven past ranks of GIs in an open-top Jeep, pausing for the cameramen to get shots of him being spontaneously mobbed by the common soldier, while the British Prime Minister provided his own brand of theatre by displaying a remarkable variety of dress. On the first day he appeared in his tropical suit and topi to take the salute amid the thrashing sails of palm leaves that shrouded all the state buildings. On another day he appeared as Admiral of the Fleet and towards the end, in his double-breasted woollen navy pinstripe and Homburg, looking every bit the Chicago gangster. It was important for domestic morale that the Western leaders emerged with a solid, unified strategy that could be communicated in three-inch headlines.

On 19 January the Allied commanders and the political leaders announced they had come to just such an agreement. 'Germany will be defeated in 1943.' As Churchill sat in the Moroccan sunshine, gangster-like and aggressive, surrounded by the ranks of the Combined Chiefs, he reaffirmed the common view, 'The Allies are determined to enforce Hitler's unconditional surrender!', and then he extemporized about 'an invasion of Europe within nine months'.[3] Churchill had done it. He had managed to extract from the Combined Chiefs a commitment towards a number of small-scale cross-Channel operations. Within the top-secret plans was the provision for 'Amphibious raids that would hopefully provoke air battles. A landing to seize and hold a bridgehead on the Cotentin Peninsula [in France], targeted for 1 August, and – in the event of a German disintegration – a return to Europe.'[4] Arrayed around Churchill and Roosevelt, the Combined Chiefs gritted their teeth behind enthusiastic smiles. They knew perfectly well how impossible a return to Europe would be within the next nine months. Nevertheless, back in London they set about trying to put this commitment into practice.

20 March was an historic day for SOE. They received a directive from the Combined Chiefs that formalized the organization's role and official position with regard to the future operations in Europe, as set out on 19 January:

> You are the authority responsible for co-ordinating sabotage and other subversive activities including the organization of the Resistance Groups, and for providing advice and liaison in all matters in connection with Patriotic Forces up to the time of their embodiment into regular forces.[5]

The exiled governments could no longer argue about SOE's right to carry out its clandestine operations in their countries; it was of course a directive aimed at de Gaulle and his people.

It went on to say that SOE should concentrate its efforts to support the Allied strategy for the war, which was to defeat Germany in 1943. The mainstays of the strategy were the invasion of Sicily, an uncompromising bomber offensive on Germany's war effort and, 'such limited offensive operations as may be practicable with the amphibious forces available'.

At Baker Street they began to roll up their sleeves and spit on their hands. This directive came as the clearest signal yet that 1943 would at last be the year of the return to Europe. More to the point, the Whitehall mandarins had finally displayed a confidence in the SOE and acknowledged they had a legitimate role to play in the plans for victory. As the first signs of spring began to appear on the trees in Regents Park, an unmistakeable frisson swept down the corridors of Baker Street. But although the Combined Chiefs of the regular services had acknowledged that SOE had a role to play, within the cloistered environment of the intelligence community they were still regarded as an amateur secret service.

—

Since the invasion of North Africa, Allied strategic planning had made provision for simultaneous 'deception plans' that would be operated before and alongside the real military operation to encourage confusion in the enemy and disguise the true objective. If there was one aspect of military planning at which the British were pre-eminent, it was in the inventiveness of these masterpieces of strategic deception. So elaborate were these plans, that to some American strategists, it seemed the British were 'preoccupied with theatrical shows of force, in preference to the real thing'.

The Allies' joint headquarters were established at Norfolk House in St James's Square under the stewardship of the genial General Frederick Morgan, officially titled Chief of Staff (to the future) Supreme Allied Commander; COSSAC. His initial priority was the invasion of France in 1943. At COSSAC (Morgan's title was also used to describe his headquarters) a sub-section of Operations Department, Ops B, was responsible for the administration of deception plans. Downstream from Ops B were a number of organizations that were responsible for inventing and then executing the plans. The man most closely associated with these deception plans was John (Johnny) Bevan, the Controlling Officer of Deception, who led a committee of highly inventive individuals called the London Controlling Section. The LCS, created in April 1941, was another of Churchill's brainchildren. An organization that would invent vast games of illusion and deception for which Churchill himself was often the greatest inspiration and which, like the pugnacious Prime Minister, was required to steel its heart to all the dark iniquities that such deception entailed.

Bevan had not been the first choice. Colonel Oliver Stanley, the first Controlling Officer, had resigned at the time of the Dieppe raid rather than be involved with deception plans to shroud that raid – an operation that he felt was suicidal and would serve no greater strategic purpose than to keep alive German expectations of an Allied invasion of France in 1942. The particular principle over which he felt so strongly was a suggestion that the SOE should be asked to deliberately misinform its agents in France to expect an imminent invasion. It was the kind of deception for which Stanley had no stomach. Colonel John Bevan on the other hand, a stockbroker with ancestral ties to the City, was a man much closer to the heart of 'the great game'.

From LCS, the ideas for deceiving the Germans were channelled through various agencies – MI6, MI5 and the XX (Double Cross) Committee, by what was known as 'Special Means', i.e. controlled leakage. The most commonly used vectors were the 'controlled' German agents that were operated by the XX Committee. But they also planted false stories in the press or through the BBC, and even forged letters to POWs laced with false information for the benefit of the German censors. They were extraordinarily inventive and ultimately extremely successful. But like ULTRA, the running of deception plans was regarded as a secret of the highest classification. Even to the present day the British Government is in two minds about what should and what should not be published about World War Two strategic deception. It can be no surprise that SOE were kept well out of the picture when it came to the details of deception plans. In the view of one of the members of the Double Cross Committee: 'They were regarded as horribly insecure. They weren't brought in on any of the really secret stuff. They were simply regarded as being terribly amateurish.'[6] However, in the view of John Bevan, SOE did have a role to play in strategic deception – an unwitting role. Just as the press and the BBC were exploited as channels through which disinformation could be passed the SOE was regarded, 'as a legitimate organization for exploitation at the disposal of the London Controlling Officer'.[7] In other words their very amateurish qualities were exploitable.

–

One of the few things that went according to plan during the Allied invasion of North Africa was the deception plan. Following that success, deception became all the rage in London and the Prime Minister was among its most ardent advocates. The danger with using SOE as a channel for deception was that it threatened to destroy a precious and non-renewable asset, the French willingness to resist.

X

Down to Business

At Norfolk House, General Frederick Morgan and his COSSAC team had worried over the problem of the planned invasion of France. Their major priority had always been the invasion of Sicily and as the plans for that operation crystallized, it became more and more obvious that the invasion of France was not going to be possible in 1943. The cross-Channel operation was doomed because of limited resources and imprecise objectives, but that argument wasn't going to go far with Churchill. The issue was left for as long as possible – in fact, until the first week of April when the Chiefs of Staff presented Churchill with some cold hard figures. The Allies had enough landing craft for the Sicily landing, but not for France as well. If Sicily came first, and it would, then it would take four months to transport and make ready the same craft for the cross-Channel operation. That meant it would not be possible to mount the operation before winter, which was out of the question.[1] Churchill's commitment to the Russians was at stake. He took these painfully hard details away and lived with them for a week. Then finally, on 10 April, he notified the Chiefs of Staff that he concurred with their view but that 'these facts should not become widely known' – and that at the earliest opportunity 'an elaborate camouflage and cover operation' should be mounted to conceal them.[2]

All he had to do now was break the news to Stalin.

—

Meanwhile, on 26 April, General Morgan was informed that the real invasion of France would now take place in the spring of 1944 and that the original operation to seize and hold a bridgehead on the French coast had given way to a deception plan. He had been given full command of Churchill's 'camouflage and cover operation', entitled Operation COCKADE. The Prime Minister's views were made clear: the absence of a real operation must be completely disguised from the enemy and all measures should be explored to ensure success.

But already there was a flaw, a critical flaw that would only become apparent long after the dust had settled. The virtue of a deception plan was that it was a cloak cast round a real operation to disguise from the enemy the actual objective. Here there was no 'real operation' to disguise, it was a cloak cast round nothing at all.[3]

On 30 April, the Chiefs of Staff delivered a report that formalized the Prime Minister's wishes and pride of place was given to Operation COCKADE, 'a vast scheme of cover and deception' to keep alive the expectation of an invasion of France and so pin the German forces in the west. The target date for this phantom invasion had to be set late enough to give them enough time to set it up, but not so late in the year that it stretched credulity. The first week in September was judged the latest possible date.[4] It had not escaped their notice that this had been the month the Germans had planned to invade Britain in 1940. The only spot along the coast that could accommodate an invasion force of any size was Calais – which became the geographical focus of all their plans. The Allies' first Commander in Chief was not destined to orchestrate the return of Allied troops to French soil, but instead to direct a rather elaborate piece of amateur dramatics, on a scale that would have satisfied Cecil B. de Mille.

At Baker Street, SOE received no indication that the grand strategic plan had been altered. Quite the contrary. SOE, and F Section in particular, were encouraged to believe the invasion of France was imminent. Drops of arms and equipment to the networks in France had, after a brief hiatus during December because of bad weather, resumed and remained steady. Then suddenly, in April, there was a massive leap of more than two thousand per cent. The total number of Sten guns, incendiaries, pistols and grenades that the networks had received in the previous five months was doubled in the month of April alone. The build-up was staggering. From 32 Stens in March to 644 in April; 34 grenades in March to 421 in April; 162 kilos of high explosives delivered in March, 2508 kilos in April. In May, the figures doubled again, and more than doubled again in June.[5]

During that April, the PROSPER network received over 20 containers of arms, by far the lion's share of material sent to France. An infectious mood of expectation spread throughout the twelve Départementes the network covered. Local sub-circuits were thrown into an unprecedented level of activity. Pierre Culioli and Yvonne Rudellat were out nearly three times a week with their teams, laying flare paths and then rushing to gather up the containers dropped from what seemed like a continuous relay of Halifaxes. All over their area, well supplied armouries were being secreted in barns, in chicken houses, anywhere. Francis Suttill now stood at the head of the largest SOE network in Europe. From the Ardennes to the Atlantic coast, thousands of Frenchmen had been drawn into his embrace. He felt, with the arrival of spring, a step closer to the point and purpose of his mission, to what he saw as his destiny.

Déricourt and Suttill had actually met in March. They developed the habit of occasionally lunching at the restaurant Chez Tutulle, near the Place des Ternes. Then in early April, Suttill felt it was worth introducing GILBERT to a wider circle of the group. He collected Déricourt and JuJu in his car and drove them south-west towards Versailles. At the famous agricultureal research establishment, the École Nationale d'Agriculture in the town of Grignon, Suttill had perhaps the largest and most picturesque of safe-houses; the home of the principal, Professor Maurice Vanderwynckt. He, his family and some of the staff secretly worked for Suttill. The college became a kind of out-of-town headquarters and was extensively used for meetings and planning sessions. Suttill gathered round him an eclectic group of solid practical foot-soldiers and intellectuals. He could, on the one hand, convince a young farmer that he should allow them to use one of his fields for parachute drops, then, on the other, conduct a philosophical examination of the nature of fear with the young students from Paris. At Grignon he gathered quite a colony of farmers and philosophers.

It wasn't quite what Déricourt expected to find in the headquarters of a great secret army. Instead of a martial atmosphere, there was a distinct 'on campus' feel about the place. Suttill enjoyed nothing better than a stroll with two or three friends amongst the groves of fruit trees that embraced the college buildings. Jean Cocteau often came there, as did Octave Simon the sculptor (organizer of the SATIRIST group) and the Irish writer Samuel Beckett who was a member of a small Paris-based group of intellectuals organized by Armel Guerne. Colleagues of Vanderwynckt, the distinguished biologist Professor Balachowsky and his wife, also organized a small sub-circuit in the Versailles area from the town of Viroflay.

Déricourt found Suttill's coterie of intellectuals, artists and academics a little hard to swallow. He never doubted the man's greatness and was certainly attracted to him, as most people were, but he also felt that he looked completely wrong for the part. 'Prosper was magnificent, strong, young, courageous and decisive, a kind of Ivanhoe; but he should have been a cavalry officer, not a spy.'[6] But if Déricourt saw him as a cavalry officer, Suttill was also a man whose courage matched his ambitions. He was not *just* an intellectual, he was also a trained killer and a born leader of killers. A killer with the diplomatic skills to win the trust and support of the Communists, which automatically increased the price on his head.

Between March and April Déricourt got to know those at the core of Suttill's organization, namely Gilbert Norman, Suttill's deputy; Andrée Borrel; Agazarian, the radio operator; and Jean Worms, the man with whom he had flown into France. Borrel was one who did not take to Henri, possibly because his masculine charms were of little consequence to someone who was otherwise persuaded, but more likely because, like Vera Atkins, she knew insincerity when she saw it. Borrel aside, everyone else trusted him and came to depend on his Lysander operations. In fact the meeting at Grignon was called in order to discuss the increase in Lysander traffic that was anticipated during the next few weeks. In London there was a growing queue of agents waiting to get back into France and prepare for the invasion.

Soon after the visit to Grignon, Déricourt and Clément met to scour some maps of the Loiret for suitable fields. As they chatted into the night Déricourt paused – then suddenly declared that the job had become too much for him. He needed help. Henri was deadly serious. He looked tired and drawn, the weight of some hidden responsibility had begun to drag him down.

What Clément didn't know was that Déricourt had begun to worry about the consequences of his secret arrangement with the Germans. Once he'd actually met PROSPER and the others, people he found it impossible not to admire, there was no mistaking a change in his attitude. Slowly it had dawned on him that his operation for Dansey was not only dangerous but also exceedingly sinister. But he couldn't get out of it. Nor could he explain anything to Clément. He simply had to convince Rémy that he had to have assistance with the actual operations. Rémy asked him to describe in minute detail precisely how the March operation had proceeded, which Déricourt did with obvious relish. Clément, typically cautious, thought about it for a day, and then agreed.[7]

Déricourt was grateful, for Boemelburg was about to increase the stakes. During March and April there had been a five-fold increase in the radio traffic between the Paris-based networks and London, mostly concerned with arrangements for arms drops or Lysander operations. From the Boulevard Suchet, the SD had monitored this increase and reported it to Kopkow in Berlin. The Fuhrer himself had taken an interest in PROSPER, ever since reports from Boemelburg claimed he would play a vital part in the Allies' invasion plans.[8] These latest reports provoked a new set of priorities from Kopkow. Henceforth all attention must be focused on PROSPER and discovering the date of the projected invasion.

Boemelburg had asked Josef Kieffer to secure a couple of apartments for his meetings with GILBERT. Kieffer was not impressed with this development, and sceptical about GILBERT. He had a polite but not warm relationship with his chief, who was twenty years his senior and about three ranks above him. Born in the German border state of Saarland in 1907, Kieffer had been a civil policeman in that district during the time it was administered by the French after the Great War. He had learnt his trade amongst professionals whereas Boemelburg was a product of the Party. Having joined the SS and been transferred into the SD, Kieffer was sent to Paris because the SS assumed from his record that he would have some knowledge of the French. In fact, like most Saarlanders, Kieffer didn't speak a word of French.[9] For someone who was a relative newcommer to the SS he was considerably less tolerant than Boemelburg, less appreciative of the well-played 'double agent'. He considered intellectuals highly suspect and believed that Boemelburg could be too easily led. In one aspect, however, Kieffer and Boemelburg were very similar. They were both extremely ambitious. Despite their differences, Kieffer rarely quarrelled with his chief, and despite his scepticism about GILBERT he was prepared to wait and see.[10]

Déricourt was summoned to his next meeting with Boemelburg. Instead of being picked up by car, he was told to rendezvous at an apartment – a worrying precedent. Boemelburg sent him a pair of keys, one for a flat in the Boulevard Malesherbes, up near the Metro St Augustin, the other closer to the Champs-Élysées, near Madeleine. Both apartments had been confiscated from Jewish families. The meeting took place at the flat near the Champs-Élysées. There was a long corridor leading from the front door, at the end of which was a small table and chair. On the table sat a telephone and some writing paper. To the right, a single door led into the living room which had been stripped of everything of value. Leading from the living room there was a bath-room, kitchen and bedroom. As a precaution, Kieffer had microphones placed in the lamps and the telephone, but they were rarely used.[11]

This meeting marked the start of a steady increase in the quantity and quality of information Déricourt delivered. Mere information about who had come and gone was not enough. In future Boemelburg wanted the date and place of each operation *beforehand*, so that he could arrange to have the new agents followed.

It was at this stage that they worked out a finely balanced arrangement that promised to keep the game going indefinitely. Boemelburg wanted to be able to trace everyone London was sending into France. Déricourt needed to preserve his integrity. In return for receiving notice of all the Lysander operations in advance, Boemel-burg guaranteed there would be no arrests. It looked like the ideal arrangement. Boemelburg needed to get a complete picture of the PROSPER network and, if possible, to discover the date of the expected invasion. From experience they knew that any premature arrests would only result in the creation of a new series of networks out of the remains of the old. This time he wanted total victory.

Déricourt's terms were clear. No one, absolutely no one, should come anywhere near the landing field. Once he had relinquished responsibility for the incoming agents, Boemelburg's men could then begin their surveillance. Most importantly, under no circumstances must there ever be an arrest. The British must never be given any reason to question his integrity. There was very little argument[12] – the old Nazi appreciated the advantages of the arrangement, for the more the British came to trust and rely on GILBERT, the more valuable he would be to Boemelburg. Déricourt's only other concern was for Rémy and JuJu. They had to be protected from all eventualities. If it worked, FARRIER would be safe and Boemelburg would become a hero.

There were many solemn promises and declarations, 'Even if Germany loses this war, we'll take care of you. We'll get you a new identity, take you to some neutral country, see that you have enough money to start a new life.'[13] Déricourt, however, preferred to look after his own future.

On 14 April, Déricourt was at the Gare d'Austerlitz for a rendezvous with a radio operator called Maurice Clech. Déricourt told him to buy a ticket and then meet with him again, outside the station at Amboise. From there they walked to a small restaurant where Clément was waiting. Clément went ahead to set up the flare path, the others would follow in an hour. It was another double Lysander operation, bringing in four important organizers and their assistants. Déricourt and Clech collected bicycles Rémy had secreted outside the town and rode to a small field near the tiny hamlet of Pocé-sur-Cisse. Déricourt did not know for certain whether or not they were being observed. He had given their location to Boemelburg and had his assurances. They now had to wait and see.

For Rémy, that first operation was one of the most exciting moments of his life. The first few notes of the Mercury engine, drifting out of the thick night sky, sent shivers of excitement down his spine. Down came Flying Officer Vaughan-Fowler, Déricourt flashed the recognition signal and the Lysander acknowledged. Rémy dashed out to the aircraft and up to the ladder. Down came Henri Frager (PAUL), after him came Dubois (HERCULE). Meanwhile Déricourt had leapt up on the wing-struts towards the pilot's cockpit and passed over the mail Suttill had given him. With the passengers clear, the thumbs-up was given and Vaughan-Fowler took the Lysander down the Amboise field.

In the air, circling the field in another Lysander, was Flying Officer McCairns and two passengers. Once Vaughan-Fowler was airborne and at a safe distance Déricourt signalled to the other pilot that he could begin his approach. McCairns began his descent too soon, much further from the field than was safe. Rémy could tell something was wrong and asked Déricourt, 'Why don't they put on their landing lights?' Déricourt shrugged. The pilots were reluctant to turn their lights on until they were on the ground, for fear of being seen. But the sound of the huge Rolls-Royce engine could be heard for miles and everyone in the neighbourhood knew when an aircraft was in the area. Then crack!

On the ground it sounded like heavy timber snapping; in the cockpit, it was the sound of splintering and tearing material. There had been a collision with a small tree. The aircraft rose up then the engine was heard to throttle back and the aircraft descended like a stone, crashing and shaking itself to a halt near Déricourt's torch. McCairns was furious. He and Déricourt bellowed at each other above the engine noise as Rémy helped the two passengers down.

There was nothing Déricourt could say that could explain the situation; McCairns was convinced it was the reception committee's error and he would say so in his report. At Tangmere they found the propeller badly damaged, the extra fuel tank gashed and the tailplane hanging by a single bracket. The pilot was lucky to have made it back to base under the circumstances. He had been doubly lucky. First there was the fire in the plane's engine back in March, now this. It was a black mark for the SOE and Déricourt's credibility was about to take a plunge.

Back on the field at Amboise another complication was developing that would also affect the future of Déricourt's operation. It started as a simple argument with one of the new arrivals. Beneath the small grove of trees where the bicycles had been stored, Rémy had been trying to organize the next stage, transporting four passengers and nine packages of equipment. Phillipe Liewer and his assistant, a French Canadian named J. C. Chartrand, were heading north to Rouen, where they were to set up a new group codenamed SALESMAN. The other couple, Henri Frager and his wireless operator A. Dubois, had arrived to establish the network DONKEYMAN in the Yonne district, north of the Loire. Frager had only been out of the country for three weeks and had returned to pick up the threads of what had already been a long tour of duty. He and Suttill had developed close ties and these would continue, though the DONKEYMAN and PROSPER networks were not formally linked.

Déricourt had planned to take them as far as the little town of Amboise, a few kilometres away, where they could take a quiet local train to Orléans or wherever. Frager had other ideas. He had no interest in Amboise, he preferred to go straight on to the city of Tours and catch a train from there.[14] The idea seemed absurd to Déricourt, Tours was over 30 kilometres away. Still a little shaken after his row with the RAF, Déricourt was in no mood for an argument. In fact there was more than a little tension on both sides. Frager, not the calmest of individuals at the best of times, was prepared to make an issue of it right there under the trees.

At the back of Déricourt's mind sat the quiet dark figure of doubt about his arrangement with Boemelburg. With the noise of the Lysander just a memory and the merest whisper now seeming to travel to the other side of the field, he just did not know whether or not they were being observed. It was quite possible his arrangement with Boemelburg would be worth nothing and the SD had decided to take advantage of the situation. In which case, all he wanted was to be rid of these four marked men. But Frager would not be charmed into submission. There was no alternative; they mounted their bicycles and set off for Tours.

It was about 3.30 in the morning when Dubois led them to a small schoolhouse at Tours, where his mother-in-law, Madame Menon, was the headmistress. They all went inside for a rest and something to eat. At about 7.30, the party at the schoolhouse were disturbed at their break-fast by an early-morning visit from the SD. The Germans apologized for the intrusion and, demonstrating every courtesy, explained that they were part of a commission that was obliged to inspect the school's library for works the occupying authorities felt might be incompatible with the Nazi view of history. Having browsed through the library for some thirty minutes, the gentlemen from the SD thanked Madame Menon for her assistance and departed.

Everyone let out a great sigh of relief. It had been one of those remarkable accidents of fate which were bound to happen in an occupied country. They were all secretly proud of themselves for having kept so calm and collected. All except Henri Frager. He found the experience deeply unsettling and was immediately suspicious.[15] He worried at it, like a dog with a bone, suspecting that somehow Déricourt was responsible. But his was a lone voice; these visiting commissions were a fairly common event. Though it must be said, it was not work the SD were usually concerned with. Normally it was one of those tedious tasks left to the Feldgendarmerie led by a representative of the German occupation authority. Frager's instincts were probably correct, the men who called at the schoolhouse probably were Kieffer's. Though Boemelburg's orders were clear enough, it was more than likely that on this first operation for which they had details of time and place, Kieffer just couldn't resist putting his people on the spot.[16]

Déricourt was just as surprised by the visit as everyone else. Clearly, the arrangement needed a lot more refinement before it could be said to be working properly. For that reason, he hadn't told the SD anything about the operation he was to conduct the following night. Déricourt and Clément took leave of the others, took the train up to Vendôme and then travelled cross country to the tiny village of Pont-de-Braye, about mid-way between Vendôme and Le Mans. There they rendezvoused with

JuJu who was on her way to London. If she was going to be in constant touch with PROSPER's people, then SOE insisted she be put through a training course and be properly established. The day before, there had been a nervous little scene at Charles Besnard's flat in Rue Malakoff. Julienne (he never called her JuJu) had anounced that she was going away for some time: 'A tour of duty in the provinces.' Besnard suspected she had something to do with the Resistance, but didn't press her on it. The evening had ended in silence and Julienne left before he woke the next morning.

At Pont-de-Braye, Squadron Leader Hugh Verity brought his Lysander ('J' Jiminy Cricket) down and badly damaged his tail wheel on what must have been a cart track across the flare path. He knew nothing about it until his return, when it went down in the book. He off-loaded two agents from the Gaullist section who had no need of Déricourt's assistance and departed the scene. Meanwhile the young JuJu climbed half-way up the ladder, gave Henri a big hug, and was sent on her way.

With the arrangement now fairly neatly poised, though perhaps still needing a few refinements, there developed an unnecessary complication – a political problem that threatened to jeopardize Boemelburg's operation unless it was nipped in the bud. The problem, at this stage a mere ripple flowing out from Berlin, had been caused by the hostility that raged between the Nazi Party security machine, the Sicherheitsdienst and German military intelligence, the Abwehr. The head of the Abwehr, Admiral Canaris, was not only unsympathetic to Nazi ambitions, he was downright hostile. This mercurial doyen of the German intelligence community was secretly engaged in a plot to remove Hitler and attempt to negotiate peace with the Western Allies. Since Churchill's declaration at Casablanca that the Allies wanted nothing less than Germany's complete surrender, that idea had run into sand. Nevertheless there were a great many young turks in the SD who harboured the darkest suspicions about Canaris and the Abwehr in general. One in particular, Horst Kopkow, had made it his personal ambition to destroy Canaris. Consequently, the Abwehr were engaged in a life-and-death struggle for control of German intelligence and counter-espionage operations.

Whereas in the past, the division of labour between the Nazi security police and the Abwehr's own counter-intelligence departments had proved very effective, by the turn of 1943 that spirit of co-operation was dead. The SD demanded complete responsibility for what they referred to as 'war winning intelligence operations'.[17] Kopkow had ordered that the SD's operations in France were to have absolute priority over anything the Abwehr was engaged in, and that there should be no interference whatsoever in those operations. His wishes had been communicated before the end of 1942 and had recently been re-affirmed in the light of Boemelburg's reports on PROSPER.

Unfortunately, Kopkow's threats of fire and brimstone were made a long way away, in Berlin. In Paris, the Abwehr felt that the SD's methods, though they produced results, were crude and distasteful. At the headquarters in the Hotel Lutetia, Colonel Reile held command over a young and brilliant group of officers, none more audacious than Sergeant Hugo Bleicher, who was engaged upon an operation that would allow him to penetrate right into the centre of the PROSPER organization – and into direct conflict with the Avenue Foch. The Abwehr were aware of the development of a new network in the north and their reports indicated it had some significant strategic importance. At that stage, however, no one – not even the SD – had the vaguest inkling of its true size.

Unlike Boemelburg, the Abwehr had no easy entrée into this new network, but Bleicher did have an asset ready to exploit – the list of names they had stolen months before from a member of the CARTE network. In November the previous year André Marsac, one of the CARTE couriers, had been followed onto a train to Paris by an Abwehr agent and while he was asleep the contents of his briefcase, a list of co-conspirators, was removed. Bleicher had presumed that CARTE's legions and PROSPER were one and the same – a fair assumption. In fact, his first use of the list led him not to Suttill, but to Henri Frager.

Through various deceptions Bleicher made contact with a number of people in what was the DONKEYMAN network. One of these was a Roger Bardet whom Bleicher had succeeded in recruiting to work for him. Bardet, apart from being a key figure in DONKEYMAN, was also Frager's lover. By the time Frager had returned from London, Bardet had become Bleicher's agent. The young Hugo had also got control of a number of SOE wireless sets down in the Yonne and was using them in what was known as a *Funkspiele* or radio game. Essentially, when a set was captured, preferably with the correct codes, then a skilled operator could play that set back to London leading the British to believe their agent was still free, and that way feed them a lot of false intelligence. In essence it was the reverse of what the British XX Committee were doing with German agents sent to Britain, though without the co-operation of the operator.

Through the radio monitoring centre at Boulevard Suchet, the SD discovered Bleicher's radio game and mistakenly presumed that the 'little sergeant' from the Hotel Lutetia had already penetrated the PROSPER network.[18] Boemelburg was furious. Slamming his hand down onto his desk he demanded Bleicher be stopped. No one had any right to PROSPER but himself. Kieffer was given the added responsibility of keeping the Abwehr out of the game. Soon after they had learnt of the radio game, Kieffer kept an appointment with Colonel Reile at Abwehr headquarters, where he gave the Colonel the full benefit of SS Sturmbannfuhrer Kopkow's views regarding PROSPER. By that stage, Reile (and his ace, Sergeant Bleicher) knew they hadn't yet penetrated PROSPER, but a group they called 'the St Jorioz Terrorists' – Frager's group DONKEYMAN. He reassured Kieffer they had no knowledge of PROSPER.[19] Kieffer did not believe him.

In the meantime, a very sophisticated operational structure was created at Avenue Foch to deal with the GILBERT operations. Dr Josef Götz, an interpreter and linguist, was given administrative responsibility for building up the surveillance teams. Josef Placke organized recruitment. It was decided to draw upon the infamous Bony-LaFont gang, a gangster-like outfit created by Inspector Pierre Bony and Henri LaFont, largely out of crooked ex-policemen and criminals. Götz went through long and detailed briefings, explaining how important it was to select the right people for each operation, where they should hide themselves, how to remain inconspicuous on a country railway platform and so on. The whole operation took on the look of a well-planned military manoeuvre.

The next meeting between Déricourt and Boemelburg occurred sometime during the third week of April, following JuJu's departure. The most important subject under discussion was the fact that Déricourt had been ordered back to Britain at the end of the week. Flying Officer McCairns' report had placed the blame for the near-disaster at Amboise squarely on Déricourt's shoulders. Squadron Leader Verily felt that Déricourt was getting somewhat over-confident and that 'perhaps he needed a strip torn off him'.[20] At least he should come back for a week or two for a rest. It was not something Déricourt could avoid, he had been ordered back and that was that. Boemelburg wasn't happy at all. Déricourt had become his key man and he didn't like the thought of losing him – even for a few weeks. It was an awkward moment. There was even the outside possibility that he might not come back at all!

Déricourt's answer was that he wouldn't abandon his wife and Clément. Boemelburg didn't have a great deal of choice in the matter. Clément's and his wife's safety was a guarantee for both sides. Before they parted Boemelburg gave Déricourt a warning not to involve himself with Frager or any of his contacts. They had been penetrated by the Abwehr and for that reason were highly dangerous.

Leaving Jeannot on her own in Paris was very difficult. Doubly so as he had left her, in a sense, as surety. In their little room in the 'Col Moll', Déricourt and Jeannot had found a kind of peace and security since moving to Paris. Though he found it impossible to be faithful, he was utterly devoted to her, as she was to him. She was not a co-conspirator, she was his sanctuary and he would do almost anything to preserve that state of affairs.

On the other hand, he was relieved to be returning to Britain. He desperately needed to talk to Dansey. The situation with the SD was escalating each week and he no longer felt in control. He was also beginning to have certain moral qualms about what he was doing, especially after having met Suttill. These feelings needed to be assuaged, along with a lot of doubts and uncertainties about his own security.

On Thursday the 22nd, the day before Good Friday, Déricourt bought a ticket for Le Mans and then visited one of his restaurant meeting places to wait for the evening train. Before he departed, news arrived of a disaster. Earlier that day two elderly sisters, Germaine and Madelaine Tambour, had been arrested by the Abwehr. The news streaked around the PROSPER meeting places like lightning. Alarm bells were going off everywhere – especially at Avenue Foch. Germaine Tambour was an associate of Suttill's. In fact she knew a great number of people. Bleicher had finally stumbled into PROSPER, probably through the list of old CARTE associates that had been stolen in November for, long before Suttill had arrived in France, Germaine Tambour had worked for CARTE.[21]

At first none of this was clear. Arrests had been made and for a while no one knew how or why. Déricourt tried to telephone Boemelburg but couldn't get through. At the Avenue Foch, Kieffer could be heard bellowing down the corridors at his subordinates. He was telling them what he was going to do with Reile. Before he boarded the train for Le Mans, Déricourt finally spoke with Boemelburg who tried to reassure him that it had nothing to do with the SD, it was the work of the Abwehr. Nothing would happen, it would be all right.[22]

Hardly reassured, Déricourt stood on the field at Pont-de-Braye with Rémy, waiting for that familiar sound of the Rolls-Royce engine. Out of the moonlit sky, Verity brought down 'Jiminy Cricket', while above them Flight Lieutenant Bridger circled in a second Lizzie. In six hours Déricourt would be sitting down to eggs and bacon in the mess at Tempsford, hundreds of miles away from the chaos in Paris.

XI

The Other Game

At Tempsford, Déricourt changed into an RAF uniform and formally received his honorary commission as Flight Lieutenant in the Special Duties Squadron. He was not required to wear the shoulder flash that identified a foreigner's country of origin; to all intents and purposes, he appeared British and was allowed the free run of the base. The dressing down he expected was, according to Verity, a pretty fierce affair and though Déricourt knew the incident with the tree had not been his fault, he was nonetheless suitably contrite. The refresher course wasn't too gruelling and for the most part his trip was an opportunity to relax and unwind. About two weeks later, Déricourt travelled up to London and stayed with Bodington and Simon. He reported to F Section at Baker Street and gave them a brief report of his operations to date. But as he was more or less in Britain at the RAF's behest, his time was pretty well his own. He also caught up with JuJu, who was coming to the end of her training course and was due to return to France in May. His most pressing priority, however, was to meet with Dansey.

-

Across the Channel, the Easter season marked the start of an extraordinary piece of 'theatre of the absurd', played to a select audience in Paris. Upon receipt of the news of the arrest of the Tambour sisters, Francis Suttill called a council of war. Germaine Tambour's flat had been used as a safe-house by a dangerously large number of people. Andrée Borrel and Gilbert Norman, Suttill's deputies, had used it for meetings. Suttill himself had used it as a mail-drop, as had Jean Amps, Peter Churchill, Agazarian and his wife, Ben Cowburn, Johnny Barrett and a radio operator called Staggs. A stunning cross-section of people from a variety of networks, all of whom needed to communicate with the networks in Paris. Borrel, Norman and Suttill used to sit and argue late into the night.

It was safe for them to assume that Germaine's address was now a worthless asset to the Abwehr (it would have been dropped by everyone the moment news of the arrest had circulated). The crucial concern was what she might know – and be forced to tell about them. Francis Suttill was seriously shaken. It had not been just bad luck – the Germans had gone straight to her door. He worried about trying to locate the leak in the network, while others argued that they should cut their losses, take the normal security procedures that would insulate them from the Tambours and then forget it. But Suttill would not. The incident seemed to provoke an uncharacteristic wave of anxiety – the beginning of an erosion of his self-confidence. Suttill became even more obsessed with the network's security, and with a misplaced sense of chivalry he advocated trying to spring the women from Fresnes Prison – either by force or by other means.

Another Paris-based sub-circuit of PROSPER, the exclusively Jewish network ROBIN, run by Jean Worms, contained a fascinating figure by the name of Jacques Weil. Weil, a Swiss merchant who traded in everything from oriental carpets to diamonds, was another of those well-placed entrepreneurs who had worked for Dansey's Z Organization. Following the occupation, he had maintained his connections with MI6, via a number of 'mail-drops' in the Paris business world, long after his colleague Worms had volunteered their network to the SOE. Weil's professional orbit led him inevitably to the SD, an organization that flourished on its links with every form of trade.

Weil had learnt that the sisters were in the custody of the Abwehr, and not with the SD. Nevertheless he claimed that his SD contacts might, with the application of some hard cash, be able to extract the Tambours from the Abwehr's grasp. Suttill was desperate enough to try it and authorized Weil to approach the SD. He finally struck a deal with two unknown SD officers, who claimed that in return for F250,000, they could deliver the Tambours to a rendezvous at the Château de Vincennes.

Unfortunately, the Abwehr were not prepared to release the sisters. Undaunted, the SD men seized the opportunity for a little private enterprise and sent a message to Weil to say that the women *would* be delivered. Weil handed over the money and on the appointed day, he and one of his colleagues turned up at the Château de Vincennes to wait. Suddenly, a black Citroën with the two SD men, pulled up and disgorged two elderly whores – substitutes for the Tambour sisters.

That kind of earthy humour didn't appeal to Boemelburg or Kieffer, though it did lighten the atmosphere down on the lower floors of Avenue Foch. Boemelburg was still furious with Riele for allowing the arrests to take place at all – especially after Berlin's instructions to keep off. He demanded that Kieffer deal with Colonel Reile and 'that swine Bleicher'.[1]

But the farce wasn't over yet. To the SD's immense surprise their contact, Weil, came back with another offer. This time he offered F2,000,000 in return for the Tambours. Finally Kieffer took a direct interest in the proceedings. He contacted Colonel Reile and demanded the women be released into his custody. He had no better luck with the Abwehr than before, but he did have some success with the other side. Kieffer had proposed that at the next rendzevous, PROSPER himself turn up to collect the women. Amazingly, Suttill agreed. Now even Boemelburg had begun to take an interest.

The rendezvous was an open restaurant, close to SD headquarters near Porte Maillot. Suttill and Norman arrived and sat at a table overlooking the actual rendezvous spot, drank their beers and waited. At various points of the compass a number of Suttill's well-armed men watched over the same ground. Without any warning, one of those ubiquitous black Citroëns pulled up at the kerb, the window came down and a man armed with a Leica leant out and started to snap their photographs.[2]

At first the unlikely subjects were simply confused, then stunned and finally, once they had overcome their paralysis, they bolted for the entrance to the nearest Metro. No one got out of the Citroën. Having accomplished their mission, the SD simply drove off. Suttill arrived at the safe-house to which he had intended bringing the sisters, slammed the door shut and cursed, 'We are lost. We've been photographed!'

Now Suttill really was shaken. It seems difficult to believe this was the same man who had toured France six months before, calling men to arms. His judgement and self-confidence were being eaten away. Of course, it was immediately clear to him that he'd been set up, that the SD were just playing with him. Nevertheless he still would not give up trying to free the Tambours. G. A. Cohen, the ROBIN wireless operator, informed London of the general picture and set off a torrent of anxious memoranda.

Kieffer handed Boemelburg a series of photographs of the man he felt certain was PROSPER. Boemelburg told him to keep them in his office safe until GILBERT returned from London. Kieffer's safe contained copies of all the reports from Déricourt, identified with a stamp – *von BOE/48* (from BOE/48). The file quickly expanded and the information in it became the hottest material at Avenue Foch.

By June, the name GILBERT was known to most of the SD in Paris. His fame had even spread to Berlin. Kopkow received weekly dispatches from Boemelburg, peppered with references to BOE/48. Despite GILBERT'S new admirers at SS Headquarters, Kieffer could not dispel his doubts about him. He felt his superior put far too much store in this single informer. But Boemelburg's faith was unshakeable. So long as PROSPER was not interfered with, 'We will make our careers with GILBERT. Through him we will get the date of the invasion.'[3]

When Déricourt had left Paris the first cracks in PROSPER's network had begun to appear, though he made no mention of it to anyone at Baker Street. Vera Atkins, one of the few F Section officers who saw

Déricourt during that trip, lunched with him at a little restaurant in Soho. By this time she had come round to the view Buckmaster and the others had shared from the start; that Déricourt was an exceptional asset to the section. Her only reservation was that during the course of their meal she was alarmed that he spoke, with scant regard for security, about people he'd just left in Paris. Atkins cautioned him to keep his voice down, but he ignored her. Though he talked freely about PROSPER and the others, he naturally never mentioned that the network was seriously compromised and in mortal danger. Nor in any conversation with Buckmaster did he mention anything that might have given cause for concern.[4]

Later, however, Déricourt reported PROSPER's situation in great detail to Claude Dansey at MI6. Long after the war, Déricourt described that trip to London. He explained that although he did operations for 'French Section', 'I reported to an officer of much higher rank [than Buckmaster], and I believe that Buckmaster did not know at that time.' This 'officer' was with 'another organization in London' which he claimed had 'authorized [him] to maintain contacts with the Germans'. Without actually spelling it out, he made it clear. 'It was not by French section I was authorized, but it was by London.' He continued, 'I reported on my visit in Easter to London, that the French Section was penetrated from a very early stage.' He supposed that his 'chiefs knew that and handled it in their own way' [sic]. He admitted that he was puzzled by his chief's indifference to news of PROSPER's perilous state.

'The ways of HQ are impenetrable,' he said. Then he speculated that perhaps the French Section networks had been 'written off', but had been allowed to continue to operate to distract German attention while something else was going on elsewhere. It was an intelligent guess – but that's all it was. He was never told anything more than was necessary for him to do what was required of him. He was certain, however, that the decision to exploit PROSPER and the other networks in France had not been taken by SOE but by '...people in another quarter [who] were animated by honest motives'.[5]

The most important intelligence that Déricourt reported at his meeting with Dansey was Boemelburg's obsession with discovering the date of the forthcoming invasion. The SD's expanding role in German intelligence and security operations was giving cause for concern not only because its secret communication code, the so-called 'Gestapo Enigma', was proving impenetrable, but because the Abwehr were being steadily shunted out of the picture. It had become obvious that the internecine war between the Abwehr and the SD would result in victory for the latter.

By the end of 1942, the British knew they had captured all of the Abwehr's agents in Britain, many of whom they had successfully 'turned' and these had become a tremendous asset for deception purposes. If then, when the Abwehr finally went under, the SD discarded the Abwehr's old agents, then all the XX Committee's hard work would have been for nothing, just when it was needed most – during the run-up to the real invasion.

Dansey's grip on the ear of the SD had become a potential 'ace' that might be used in another game – a game of deception. Naturally Dansey instructed Déricourt to maintain his contacts with Boemelburg, which is precisely what he did.

Around the middle of May, soon after Déricourt had returned to France, Gubbins and a select few of the staff at SOE were informed by MI6 of reliable intelligence that the major French Section network named PROSPER was penetrated and seriously compromised. Information about German penetration of their networks often came via MI6, so there was no reason to question it – or its source. The significance of the information was that it arrived under a heavily 'restricted' classification – not to be passed on to country section level. In fact, apart from Gubbins, his deputy Sporborg, the Director of Intelligence and Security, Archie Boyle, and perhaps one or two other senior officers, no one else in SOE heard a whisper of it.[6] The only reason anyone in SOE was informed at all was because a decision had been taken to exploit PROSPER's situation and this would require a certain amount of cooperation from SOE itself. No one who was informed of this had the slightest suspicion of anything untoward. It was just very hard not being able to inform F Section.

Meanwhile, on 30 April, while Déricourt was still in London, SOE received a report from MI5 that cast serious doubt on his reliability. This information, which MI5 received from de Gaulle's security service, seemed to date from before Déricourt had been sent into France in January. It made sobering reading. The report stated, 'Since the Armistice in France, Déricourt had started to frequent German circles in Paris...' and '...Later, he was often encountered in Toulouse, *frequentant des femmes de moeurs legères payées par les Allemands*.'[7] MI5 also mentioned that Déricourt had been overheard talking in London about returning to France 'on behalf of a British service'. MI5 commented with typical understatement,

'This seems to us dangerous.' Coupled with the fact that they would not recommend Déricourt for employment in the first place, the April report was the clearest warning SOE could have received that Déricourt was not someone they ought to trust in a sensitive position abroad. F Section never had a better opportunity to save themselves from disaster. It would have been very simple to eliminate him, while he was still in London. Instead Bodington came to the rescue, dismissing the report with the remark, 'This sounds like typical French back-biting.'[8] The report was ignored. Bodington seemed to make a career of protecting his friend's reputation. But even without Bodington's support, with the scent of invasion so strong in the air F Section would have been hard pressed to consider finding a replacement for Déricourt.

Rather than wait for the moon period and return by Lysander, Déricourt chose to parachute back into France on 5 May. Hugh Verity, being off-duty that night, came along for the ride and saw him off through the hatch in the belly of the Halifax. Déricourt was dropped 'blind' over a familiar field west of St Laurent-en-Gartinais, not far from Tours. He made a perfect landing; he touched the ground, bent his knees and stood up again. Then he stumbled into a ditch, ricked his back and was in pain for weeks.

His return to the 'Col Moll' and to Jeannot was more tearful than joyful. As he lay beside her during the early morning hours, she began hesitantly to tell him of a visit she'd had from the SD. She attempted to laugh it off as insignificant, but couldn't disguise her obvious terror. There could not have been a more sobering return to Paris.

Jeannot related that one afternoon, she had opened the door to two young and extremely handsome gentlemen wearing the grey uniform of the SD. One of these young Adonises held out in the palm of his hand, a button from his tunic. In his very best French and with all the grace he could muster, he asked whether Madame could help by sewing the button back on. Jeannot had been so terrified she could hardly speak. She could think of nothing else to say except yes. Somehow she managed to thread a needle while the younger man sat beside her in his shirtsleeves and the other, who didn't speak much French, paced about the room. They asked if her husband was at work and she replied that he was in the country on business. They were so grateful, so effusive as they stood in the doorway again, the younger one rebuttoning and rebuckling his uniform.[9]

The message was unmistakeable, 'We know where you live and we know your wife.' The thought of Jeannot being subjected to Boemelburg's surveillance frightened and infuriated Déricourt. The boundaries had begun to shrink – and his clever operation, played at the end of a very long and very loose piece of string, could with a single tug be ended. A peculiar dilemma had been created. In London he was protected by Bodington, and more distantly by Dansey. In Paris, that role was assumed by Boemelburg. London was London, this was Paris. Self-preservation dictated that his security depended upon Boemelburg's success against the British. He would have to prove to the old Nazi that he had his best interests at heart. At worst, he was no more than a puppet held by controllers on both sides of the Channel for their own separate ends. At best, he might escape with his life.

Boemelburg and Déricourt no longer met in the empty flat near the Champs-Élysées. In future, other less senior officers would come for the Lysander material. Boemelburg insisted on a far more secure location where they could meet and where Déricourt could deliver the really important material.

For some months Déricourt had been given dispatches of mail from the PROSPER network to be sent to London on board the Lysanders – written communications between the networks and London, messages too long and detailed to be entrusted to the wireless. Drawings, photographs, lists of agents' addresses, descriptions of sabotage plans, even letters to wives or sweethearts. Letters in minute copper-plate, sometimes typewritten on onion-skin that went on for pages, sometimes no bigger than a piece of cigarette paper. Material that would provide a picture of the inner structure of the greatest network of guerilla fighters that had ever been formed under one man. It would lead the SD to the heart of the machine – and, of course, to the date of the invasion.

Boemelburg was a creature of habit. He worked long, hard hours, rarely socialized with the rest of his colleagues, spent a weekend with his wife in Germany as regularly as possible, kept no mistress, and his movements to and from the Avenue Foch were as regular as clockwork. So it was to be expected that his meetings with Déricourt settled down into a regular pattern too.

At the appointed time Karl Braun, Boemelburg's driver, would collect Déricourt, usually from somewhere around the Boulevard Beausejour near the Jardin du Ranelagh, and then drive him through the Bois de Boulogne to Boemelburg's château in Neuilly. Braun would drive round to the side of the house, to a door used by tradesmen and which could not be seen by the neighbours. Déricourt, carrying the mail, would be met at the door by Boemelburg. The Frenchman was then entertained to dinner and a long evening of conversation followed.[10]

The next morning, the mail was passed to Kieffer who had it photographed and returned within 24 hours. Déricourt then slipped it onto the next plane back to London. It was not just PROSPER's mail. All the networks in touch with Déricourt passed him their mail for London. This was treachery on a massive scale; Boemelburg's appetite for intelligence was matched only by BOE/48's ability to deliver it. In return, Boemelburg's benevolence embraced the lives of Henri, his wife, Rémy and JuJu. They would need it.

During Déricourt's absence in London, the seeds of denunciation had been sown in France. Henri Frager, who had never forgotten the incident when the SD had disturbed them at the schoolhouse in Tours, began to complain to Suttill that in his opinion Déricourt was untrustworthy. Suttill was at first not convinced that GILBERT was a traitor, but as Frager persisted he began to have doubts. What really troubled him was a general lack of security in Déricourt's operations, his over-inquisitiveness with contacts. It wasn't much, no more than a tiny gnawing in a back tooth, but it contributed to Suttill's general uneasiness.[11]

During the first week of May, Déricourt met with Suttill to discuss the details of an operation that would take Suttill back to London. A signal had recently been received requesting PROSPER's return for an important briefing. The news had shot round the inner circle and of course raised everyone's expectations. Everything to date clearly pointed to the fact that the invasion was at hand. The work-load had built up to an extraordinary level while the great network had expanded to cope. April's massive increase in arms drops had already been dwarfed during the first two weeks of May. By the end of the month a total of 1006 Sten guns, 1877 incendiary bombs, 4489 grenades had been dropped. Judging from their work-load, PROSPER's inner group was confidently predicting a June invasion, July at the latest.

Suttill, of course, had been expecting the call to London and simply took it as though it were the most logical preliminary to the invasion. The only ripple on the surface was his deep anxiety about the security of the group. Could the great network hold out until July?

The SD could not miss the signals of an impending invasion either, and when Déricourt informed Boemelburg of PROSPER's planned return to London, the news was flashed to Berlin. On or about the 11th, Suttill purchased a return ticket to Amboise, where he rendezvoused with Déricourt and was taken to a safe-house he kept in that town.[12] That night they listened to the BBC for the 'personal message' that signalled the operation was on for that night. Bad weather forced the RAF to cancel the flight and there was no BBC message. There was no message the following evening either. As they did their best to fill up the time together Suttill was nervous and ill-at-ease.[13] What passed between them is long beyond reach.

On Wednesday the 13th, the BBC finally came through and they set off on their bicycles for a field downriver towards Tours. Verity's 'Jiminy Cricket' made a faultless approach, landed and disgorged two men. Francis Suttill climbed in, gave a thumbs-up to Déricourt and was gone. A few minutes later, Bunny Rymills' Lysander came in to land. The double operation brought in three agents with instructions to re-establish the INVENTOR circuit and operate alongside Frager's DONKEYMAN – Sydney Jones the organizer and liaison with Frager, Vera Leigh his courier, and Marcel Clech the radio operator. Last off the second Lysander was JuJu, now christened CLAIRE. A party of six pedalled off towards Amboise with the sound of Lysanders drifting away down the Loire, carrying PROSPER to his London rendezvous. At the station, even Déricourt was unaware of the silent group of Bony-LaFont men trailing behind them.

In Paris the following day, there was a touching reunion at a little bar in the Rue du Calisée, JuJu had telephoned her lover Besnard, 'Voilà, I'm back. Can I see you?' Any doubts she had about her feelings for him had been resolved in London. When finally they began to talk she completely surprised him, 'I've just returned from London.' Besnard took it in his stride and decided not to enquire. Two days later he met Déricourt who simply said to him, 'The less you know the less you can say.' Besnard had already come to the same conclusion. He liked Déricourt at first but as he came to know him better, he found he could not trust him. Julienne, he noticed, thought Henri was infallible.[14]

–

The decision to recall Suttill had been made at the very highest level, beneath the pavements of Westminster in the famous Cabinet War Rooms (CWR). Near where

Churchill had his command post, buried under four feet of concrete and steel, was a small conference room that was the meeting place of the London Controlling Section. In the Prime Minister's personal headquarters the LCS, a commission of seasoned strategists and scholars, would gather and create deceptive stratagems to leave the enemy 'puzzled as well as beaten'. Led by Colonel John Bevan, the LCS included such illuminati as Sir Ronald Wingate (deputy), Wing Commander Dennis Wheatley and Lieutenant Lady Jane Pleydell-Bouverie. Their single preoccupation during May 1943 was Operation COCKADE, a vast deception plan designed to convince the enemy the Allies would invade France in September 1943. Deception schemes were all the rage that summer and Churchill was their greatest advocate. He and the LCS were as one.

Up to nine regular members would meet round an ornately carved table, occasionally joined by representatives from MI6, MI5 and the American OSS. Dansey was a familiar face at the oak table. He had recently revealed intelligence that SOE's PROSPER was badly penetrated and living on borrowed time. Under the bleak stare of the perpetual electric light, the LCS had decided to exploit the situation. It was at that stage that SOE's top brass learnt of PROSPER's situation. Subsequently, Churchill had passed the word to Lord 'Top' Selbourne, then the Minister responsible for SOE, who passed it to Gubbins. From Gubbins it drifted down to Buckmaster; the PM wanted to see Francis Suttill – personally.

At COSSAC headquarters, a group of Army Intelligence officers were alarmed to learn of the LCS plan to exploit SOE's patriotic armies in France. To the practical-minded officers, who would at some later date rely heavily on loyal Resistance armies in France, it seemed suicidal to abuse their patriotism for the sake of a deception plan. On 28 May, soon after Suttill's return to London, they declared their concern:

> Public opinion in all countries probably expects an attempt to be made this summer to open a *Second Front* by the invasion of France. No account has been taken in the plan … for the repercussions this operation may have on public opinion…
>
> [They emphasized] … the repercussions in FRANCE might be such that patriots would no longer be prepared to play a part in future invasion operations.[15]

General Morgan was at that stage drafting the final report on COCKADE, which would explain precisely what it was expected to do. In the final planning, COCKADE had grown into a highly sophisticated scheme that was actually broken up into three main operations: COCKADE-STARKEY, meant to convince the Germans of an invasion at Pas-de-Calais; COCKADE-WADHAM, a fictitious landing by Americans at Brest Peninsula; and COCKADE–TINDALL, a fictitious landing in Norway. In his report, dated 3 June, Morgan acknowledged the Army Intelligence concern for '…undesirable political repercussions both in this country and abroad' that would result from raising hopes for an invasion and then dashing them. But, at that stage time was short. 'I recommend that this aspect *should not be allowed to influence or delay the necessary preparations* which must be put in hand now and at once.'[16]

The COCKADE–STARKEY fictitious D-Day was set for 7 September at Pas-de-Calais. The plan was immediately sent out to all the agencies responsible for putting it into effect.

–

Together, Lord Selbourne and Francis Suttill rode in the back of a large black staff car down Baker Street, across Oxford Street towards Whitehall. Turning off The Mall at Horse Guards Parade they drove past the edifice of the Foreign Office to the doors of the Cabinet War Room. At the entrance, guarded by Royal Marines in blue tunics with red tabs, they were identified and then ushered inside. After a long walk down a passage brightened by vividly painted plumbing, they were led into the reception room of a small flat. Off this was a dining room, a map room and a bedroom. Below them was the command HQ. A Marine brought them both a whisky and asked them to wait.

Churchill and 'Top' Selbourne were very close friends and saw eye to eye on most matters of importance. It was not uncommon for Churchill to ask 'Top' if he could see SOE agents before they returned to the field and it was the sort of request Baker Street was always keen to fulfil. Churchill's entourage, on the other hand, would try and discourage Selbourne from bringing any of Gubbins' ruffians round to the CWR because they said, 'It got the Prime Minister over excited and he tended to take his eye off the ball.' But on this occasion, there were no tales of derring-do to disturb his concentration.

Through a frosted-glass partition, Selbourne and Suttill could see the unmistakable shape of the Prime Minister loom towards them and then recede. A moment or two later they were ushered into the Cabinet Room where Churchill sat waiting. He rose to greet them.

If there were minutes taken at the meeting they have either been lost or remain classified. Churchill's diaries for the period were stolen some time ago and are still officially missing. There is no available record of precisely what words were used, what ideas were expounded, what visions were conjured; but when Francis Suttill emerged from the CWR he was a changed man. He had been charged with what he believed was the greatest secret of the war – the date of the invasion. Unfortunately, the news rather knocked him sideways. He was told the invasion would take place at Pas-de-Calais, on the northern coast of France, sometime during the first week of September. More than three months away.

If the full weight of the information entrusted to him was any burden then there was no trace of it on his face when he saw Buckmaster. He spoke to no one in F Section about his conversation with the Prime Minister. Security was now his utmost priority. A debilitating fear that plagued a great many SOE agents abroad, was that Britain was just as thickly covered with German agents as France was by the SOE. And the worst nightmare, the one that gave them the coldest sweats in the early morning hours, was that the Germans had spies right in the very heart of Baker Street. Suttill was one who believed that.

Perhaps only Dansey would have appreciated the irony in that. The other wicked irony, of course, was that the secret Suttill locked away in his conscience, was a lie.

It was about this time that Brigadier Gubbins and some of his officers were 'COCKADED' – the term used to describe whether an individual was privy to the fact that

COCKADE was a deception plan. Many people were involved in some element of COCKADE, thinking they were engaged in a training exercise or the like, but unless you were aware of the deception element of the operation, you were not 'COCKADED'.[17]

There existed a standing instruction (though SOE tended to think of it as more of an understanding) that when it was known that one of their networks had been penetrated, then the LCS had to be informed (usually through MI5), 'so that the network in question might be exploited as quickly as possible for deception purposes'. In this case the information had travelled in the opposite direction and the LCS was simply informing the SOE that the decision to exploit PROSPER had already been taken. Neither Colonel Buckmaster nor any of the other F Section officers was ever informed of this decision.[18] It was also part of the understanding that the relevant country section should also be subject to the same deception. In an organization that was regarded by many outsiders as hopelessly insecure, the country section level was thought to be the most sieve-like. In other words the SOE would sometimes have to deceive itself. This placed extraordinary internal stresses on an organization that was already hard pressed by the pressures created for it in the field.

Buckmaster was informed that Suttill had been given 'an alert signal, warning the whole circuit to stand by ... and to accelerate [F section's] preparations to support an invasion'. In 1957, Buckmaster published *They Fought Alone*, in which he recorded,

> In the middle of 1943 we had had a top secret
> message telling us that D-Day might be closer
> than we thought.

> This message had been tied up with international politics on a level far above our knowledge and we, of course, had acted upon it without question.

Clearly, by 1957 someone had told him something of what had been going on back in 1943, but equally clearly he was not told the whole truth. Even up to the time of the writing of this book, Buckmaster had only enough information to piece together a very imperfect explanation.

> Churchill told Suttill he wanted to increase the amount of sabotage operations and general unrest in the west of France so he could have some defence against Stalin's claim that we weren't doing enough to help him. Suttill was encouraged by Churchill to run enormous risks, to forget his security training and produce violent explosions in and around the Paris area, so that Churchill could turn to Stalin and say – now, look at what we're doing.[19]

Whether Churchill actually gave Suttill a lesson in war and geo-politics is perhaps unlikely. What is beyond doubt is that Suttill returned to France, convinced the invasion was coming in September. But before his departure he expressed to Buckmaster and others his very real anxieties about the network. It had grown too large, its boundaries stretched from the Belgian border round Sedan, down to the Loire and across to Nantes on the Atlantic coast. The Tambour sisters, though no longer a threat to their security, were still a source of anxiety and now Buck-master had a list an arm long of new people queuing up to be sent in. Suttill began to have nightmares about whether the great network could survive for another three months.

XII

In the Wilderness

The differences that existed between MI6 and the SOE paled into insignificance in comparison with the internecine rivalry between the two German intelligence services. In Paris, it threatened to blow Boemelburg's neat arrangement wide apart. Déricourt's – or BOE/48's – information had acquired a degree of status in Berlin that caused Boemelburg's own stock to rise to an all-time high. At RSHA headquarters in Prince Albert Strasse, from Himmler down to Kopkow, the SD were basking in the Fuhrer's unprecedented admiration. Meanwhile the SD were closing in on the anti-Hitler conspirators and Canaris' days were numbered.

But the senior service was not about to lay down all their good work without a struggle. The animosity that existed was not merely proprietorial. They each had a very real personal distaste for the other's methods. Canaris, the gentleman of the old school, head of the Abwehr since 1934, believed that intelligence work should be carried out according to the articles and rules of war. Not just for humane reasons, but for good solid practical reasons too. He opposed the execution of hostages because he was convinced it would throw the population into the hands of the Resistance.[1] In Paris, Colonel Reile claimed, 'The population was, if not overwhelmingly pro-German, at least disposed to do nothing if they were left alone.'[2]

Kopkow did not read the situation that way at all. His rise to power had been a struggle, quite literally from the beer halls and gutter brawls of the early 1930s. He was born in Ortelsburg, East Prussia, on 29 November 1910 and apprenticed as a chemist in 1928, at the Rathaus Drugstore in Allenstein. He joined the party in 1931 and the SS a year later (SS no. 45043). He first attracted the Fuhrer's attention as 'the sternest of guardians' by consistently being in the front rank of numerous beer-hall battles during the early 1930s. In 1938 he was seconded to the Gestapo headquarters at Prince Albert Strasse where he set up his own office to deal with communist saboteurs.[3] During 1942 he gained even greater recognition for the manner in which he conducted the interrogation of the Berlin leaders of the Soviet espionage network, the Rote Kapelle (Red Orchestra). In a celebrated coup, Kopkow agreed a deal with the leader, Schulze-Boysen, whereby in return for some much-heralded secret papers, he promised to postpone the expected death sentences on Schulze-Boysen and his colleagues – until after December 1943. (By which time, the Soviet agent was certain the war would be over.) Kopkow's assurance that he would preserve the lives of the Soviet agents even convinced his own staff. When the promise had extracted all that he needed to know, Kopkow stunned everyone with the coldness of his comment, 'I was not authorized to make such a promise.' He knew the execution squads would have ignored him anyway.[4]

Following their success with the Rote-Kapelle, the penetration of the PROSPER network seemed to make the SD invulnerable. Boemelburg, his 'crack criminal investigator', had assured him they as good as had the date of the projected invasion. Kopkow liked to boast about his men in Paris. 'Kieffer was meticulous, utterly dedicated and totally immersed in his work. Boemelburg, though not a political Nazi, was completely loyal and a committed anti-Communist.' Kopkow and Boemelburg were of like minds when it came to running double agents. 'Avoid the scoundrels who are only interested in money. Look for the intelligent and politically committed.' He was often heard to quote: 'I love treason; I despise traitors.'[5]

In the atmosphere Kopkow and his colleagues generated in Berlin, the Abwehr's opportunity to fight for its continued independence was extremely limited. But in the occupied territories its freedom of movement was still considerable. During May, Canaris gave his tacit approval to a little operation that was born in Colonel Reile's headquarters at the Hotel Lutetia in Paris – an operation to destroy BOE/48 – the extraordinary GILBERT.[6]

Like the SD, the Abwehr had their connections in the black market, where they had learnt something of GILBERT'S extra-curricular activities. (In fact Déricourt was not the only one. There was a flourishing little symbiotic trade in gold and diamonds between certain ranks of the SD and members of the Resistance, some of whom were SOE.) From the outset, Baker Street had been prepared to give Déricourt a small quantity of diamonds which he claimed he would use as a contingency fund. The SD always paid well above the street value[7] which, of course, bore no resemblance to their official value. Despite the success of his espionage arrangements with the SD, and despite Boemelburg's reassurance, Déricourt prudently sought to look after himself. Unfortunately he never actually laid hands on enough of the stuff to make the sort of killing that would provide the ideal pension.

The Abwehr had managed, through scraps of intelligence, to piece together enough information about GILBERT to neutralize him, either by spoiling him for the SD or discrediting him with Baker Street. However, to avoid incurring the wrath of Avenue Foch, the operation was set running from Holland.

Colonel Giskes, Reile's opposite number in Holland, had provided the springboard for the Abwehr's intrusion, with intelligence he had gathered from London. The SOE networks in Holland had been under the Abwehr's complete control since 1942. The most valuable product of that control had been the famous North Pole 'radio game', whereby the Abwehr played back captured SOE wireless sets to London and received a wealth of arms and equipment, which Baker Street assumed was going to its agents in Holland. In September, London sent instructions for one of their agents, 'Anton', to return home. The real Anton was in a German prison so Giskes stalled while he thought of a solution. Meanwhile London sent further instructions, giving 'Anton' an address in Paris where he could be put in touch with an escape route, run by a certain GILBERT. Giskes immediately saw the solution to two problems. How to respond to London about Anton and how to spike the SD's best informer. He notified London that 'Anton', accompanied by a Belgian guide, would be travelling down to Paris.

The two 'agents' who were dispatched were, of course, Abwehr men. Karl Bodens, who did not speak French, assumed the role of 'Anton', and his Belgian guide 'Arnaud' was played by another of those deceptive chameleons that turned up in the world of espionage,

Richard Christmann. Born in the town of Metz in 1905, at a time when it was part of Germany, Christmann had been his father's greatest hope, but had grown into his parent's 'sickly disappointment'.[8] He had served briefly with the French Foreign Legion, the Gestapo in Holland and eventually with the Abwehr. According to Giskes he was at once a strange product of some painful 'psychological problem', whose reports often stretched credibility, and a brilliant agent with a gift for insinuating himself into people's confidence.

In Paris, Colonel Riele had been a party to the 'Anton and Arnaud' scheme from the beginning and when the pair called at the Hotel Lutetia he made a point of meeting them both.[9] From Bleicher and others, Christmann received a further briefing about his target, GILBERT, including the address of one of the latter's favourite rendezvous. On 20 May Christmann posing as the Belgian 'Arnaud' called at Chez Tutulle in the Rue Troyon. There he asked the proprietor, Monsieur Touret, if he could be put in touch with GILBERT. Since March, Chez Tutulle had become a favourite meeting-place for PROSPER people, and for that reason Déricourt had begun to avoid it. Consequently, Touret thought this slim, fair-headed Belgian was asking for Gilbert Norman, Suttill's second in command. He told Christmann that Gilbert normally came in for lunch. 'But if it's urgent,' he glanced at his watch, 'you'll find him playing poker at 10 Square de Clignancourt.'

Near the Metro Jules Joffrin in the 18th Arrondissement, Alain Bussoz and his wife lived in a flat that overlooked the delightful Square de Clignancourt. The Bussozs, another couple who worked for PROSPER, allowed Suttill's people to meet there and these meetings had developed into a regular pattern, focused round a poker game. Not long before mid-day, Christmann and Bodens knocked at the door and presented themselves as two agents from Holland needing a Lysander to get to Britain. They said they'd been told to ask for GILBERT. Inside they found Jack Agazarian and his wife, Andrée Borrel, and of course Gilbert Norman. The confusion was soon cleared up and Agazarian, who knew more about Déricourt's operations than anyone else, offered to put them in touch with the real GILBERT. Agazarian knew there was no room available on any of the May Lysanders and that they would have to wait till the next moon period. A rendezvous was set up for 9 June at the Restaurant Capucines. Christmann wasn't aware of it at the time, but of course he had just stumbled into the very heart of the PROSPER organization. He reported all that had happened to Abwehr headquarters and then he and Bodens went to ground until June. Meanwhile Agazarian got in touch with Déricourt and told him about the pre-arranged rendezvous at Capucines.

What Christmann would have done had Déricourt actually placed Bodens on the next Lysander is unclear; most probably Déricourt would never have got that far. It is certain that Christmann was instructed to try and interest Déricourt in a supply of diamonds from Holland. (Christmann had already hinted this to Agazarian, who seemed very keen.) It seems certain that the lure of diamonds was meant as an extra incentive to Déricourt – to ensure that he and Christmann actually met. Since the war, Christmann has always been very vague about what his next move would have been, had he and Déricourt actually made contact. However, a veteran ADC to Colonel Reile has stated there was only one thing

Christmann would have done – lured Déricourt to some quiet spot and shot him.[10]

Unfortunately for the Abwehr, Déricourt was warned that the two agents were Abwehr men and that it would be unwise to go to the rendezvous. Who actually warned Déricourt is not known. It was no one from PROSPER's people, and certainly not Agazarian, who was completely convinced of the men's bona-fides. Nor did the warning come from Boemelburg, as might have been expected – on the contrary, it was Déricourt who informed the SD that he was being set up for a rendezvous with Abwehr agents. The Avenue Foch was not familiar with Christmann and Bodens and would never have linked them with the Abwehr, which was precisely why the Abwehr sent the lying Dutchmen in the first place. Boemelburg decided to deal with the matter by asking Kieffer to lay a trap.

But before we examine what happened next, the question still remains: who did tip off Déricourt? Could it have been Claude Dansey? Since 1941, British code-breakers had been reading Abwehr ENIGMA communications and were often able to track an Abwehr agent's progress across Europe, right to Southampton docks. But Christmann is unlikely to have needed to communicate by radio with his controllers, and all the Abwehr's top security communications between The Hague, Paris and Berlin would have been conducted by landline – which made them undetectable. Another possibility, and one that really does open a can of worms, is this: since MI6 had lost control of SOE's communications, Dansey had instructed Bletchley Park to monitor Baker Street's signals, and so might have been privy to the communications between Baker Street and the Abwehr-controlled sets in Holland. He would also have known that the Abwehr controlled all the SOE networks in Holland (something the SOE didn't know), and thus conclude that the Abwehr was trying to pass Arnaud and Anton on to GILBERT. It was possible, but it is an unproven hypothesis.

An ex-employee of the Government Code & Cipher School, who prefers to remain anonymous, has confirmed that they did occasionally monitor SOE's signals on behalf of MI6, but it was not a constant operation and there is no way of knowing whether in fact they caught the particular transmissions concerning 'Anton'. If Dansey knew about the Abwehr's ruse, and if he did forewarn Déricourt, it is impossible to prove now. Whatever the answer, on 9 June Déricourt made sure he was nowhere near the Restaurant Capucines.

Christmann and Bodens arrived early and chose a table inside. Most of the establishment had been roped off for cleaning and was relatively empty. Then, a gentleman in a grey hat and raincoat took a seat at a table on the terrace. A minute later Agazarian arrived and joined 'Amaud' and 'Anton'. After a few minutes Christmann noticed over his shoulder a pair of Feldgendarmerie moving amongst the clientele, asking for papers. The restaurant which had been empty a moment ago was now suddenly full; outside, the gentleman in the raincoat sat alone with nothing on the table before him. Bodens got up from the table and moved quickly towards the door. Once he was outside he was approached by a man who escorted him across the street. An incredulous Christmann exclaimed, 'They've arrested him!' Agazarian and Christmann remained at their table while the Feldgendarmerie examined their papers. Once they'd been returned, they left separately.

Agazarian, unmolested, got safely away to see Andrée Borrel and report what had happened. Christmann was not so lucky. As soon as he was out of the café, he was arrested and driven off towards Fresnes Prison, protesting wildly that he was a German agent. He persuaded them to take him to 84 Avenue Foch, where he saw Obersturmfuhrer Gutgesell.[11] Later he had an interview with Obersturmfuhrer Kieffer which, by all accounts, was a withering experience.

Meanwhile Boemelburg made a report of the affair to Kopkow in Berlin and paid a call on Colonel Riele at the Hotel Lutetia. A visit from the SD, though never a comfortable affair, nearly always introduced problems of rank – especially as the SS/SD saw themselves as superior to everyone. SS-Sturmbannfuhrer Boemelburg's rank was the army equivalent of Lieutenant Colonel, a rank below that of Riele who was a full Colonel. Reile used to infuriate Boemelburg by addressing him with his civilian police rank of Krimminalrat. Little was ever accomplished at these meetings.[12]

Four days after the incident at Capucines, Francis Suttill prepared for his return to France. He was expected to return to one of Déricourt's receptions, but instead chose to parachute to a reception in a field in the Sologne. His anxieties about security had multiplied during his stay in London and he became suspicious of various people in Paris, including Déricourt. In fact, he was on the verge of paranoia and the prospect of being in GILBERT'S care completely unnerved him. In October 1942, at the very start of his messianic operation, Francis Suttill, consumed with hope and ambition, had parachuted into France and been greeted by the diminutive figure of Pierre Culioli; more than eight months later he preferred to return to the same man. Culioli was puzzled by Suttill's decision. In the first place, when he made his first drop into France, Suttill came down very hard, damaged his ankle and had dragged his foot for some months after. Second, and more important, Culioli's area was crawling with Germans and he had just warned London of that fact.

Culioli and his 'soldiers' had been out virtually every night (as had other PROSPER sub-circuits) coping with the massive quantity of arms that were pouring in. Every night there were streams of 'personal messages' broadcast over the BBC, directing the various groups to a particular field where they would await the Halifaxes. On the night of 11/12 June, a typical drop was going smoothly until one container flared dramatically and then exploded on impact. This began a small chain-reaction, causing other containers to explode and sending debris and shrapnel in all directions. Two of Culioli's men were wounded. The operation had been a disaster and they all expected to be surrounded by Germans at any moment. In fact they were not discovered, but the following day the Germans poured men and armoured vehicles into the area, set up barrage balloons to entrap parachutes and patrolled the area looking for hidden arms dumps. Culioli sent a message to London, requesting they cancel all air operations in his area for the time being. The very next night, Culioli was informed that Suttill was arriving by parachute on the 14th and wanted a reception. For some reason, Culioli's message had not reached London.[13]

It seemed the sky was filled with danger that night as Culioli and his team stood in the field and watched for the grey floating shape of the parachute. Out of the sky

Suttill came, with a sound like the thrash of linen on a clothesline. Not a word was said until the three were safely at Culioli's brother-in-law's house. 'I asked you to receive me because I didn't want to be received by anyone else,' Suttill told Culioli. The latter asked, 'Was there any news of the invasion?' Suttill replied bitterly, 'It will have to wait until the autumn. During the next full moon, everything will double and then double again in July.'[14]

The following morning Suttill briefed them about another proposed drop in a day or so, when two young Canadians were due. He arranged for Culioli to bring them up to Paris around the 21st or 22nd, where they would be accommodated at Armel Guerne's place. Culioli, though loyal, was almost at the end of his tether. 'Does London know how dangerous it has become?'

'London expects us to be ready by September,' Suttill replied.

In Paris, Suttill moved quickly to prepare himself and his team for the long, hard wait. He believed that from the moment his feet touched French soil, every action, every conversation, every word almost, was a potential trap that might cause the invasion to founder, and for the first time he felt vulnerable and exposed. One of his first actions was to eliminate someone of whom he had come to despair: Agazarian. The young Mauritian radio operator, over the course of his current mission, had made contact with a large number of networks that had nothing to do with PROSPER. He was even known to some circuits in Holland. Suttill had warned him not to extend himself or to maintain his contacts with other circuits. In fact Agazarian had been transmitting messages for more than twenty separate individuals. The recent incident at

Capucines topped it off. Jack and his wife would return on the next Lysander.[15]

–

During the first weeks of June, Déricourt had decided to get out of Paris and take Jeannot away for a break. They were doing their best to overcome a big disappointment about the new flat at 58 Rue Pergolese. After they'd spent a great deal of money re-decorating and furnishing, the owner had changed his mind about selling. The Déricourts would have to rent. It was a great blow to Jeannot who had for so long dreamt of owning her own place. (In fact they were never able to buy the flat.) So, no sooner were they inside the apartment than they left again, took the train down to Tours and spent a week or so bicycling along the rivers Loire and Loir. Henri used the break to note down a few more fields, while for Jeannot it was one of the first opportunities she had to be alone with her husband since they had moved to Paris.

They avoided hotels or pensions and mostly camped out under the stars. When he went on these journeys, Déricourt used to wear an old suit of 'country clothes' that would make Jeannot despair. After a few days, Henri would look like a vagrant and sometimes when they called at a farmer's door to ask about a certain field, they'd be set upon by vicious dogs or packed-off like beggars. Even so it was a time of real happiness between them, and one she cherished long afterwards.

If given the opportunity Henri would talk with the locals about soil and rainfall and the quality of livestock – and never ceased to amaze his wife at how much he knew – or seemed to know. Sometimes they would pause on the brow of a hill to take in the scenery, and Henri would repeat a promise to her that 'one day they would own land down here in Loire'. She believed him absolutely.[16]

On the night of the 16th/17th, Déricourt handled another double Lysander operation. On the first aircraft was Charles Skepper, who was headed south towards Marseilles where he was to establish a new network which would last for nine months. With him was Diana Rowden, a courier who was to link up John Starr in the ACROBAT network, over in the Jura. Jack and Françoise Agazarian climbed into the plane and settled themselves into the rear cockpit. Déricourt waved them off back to Britain. On the next aircraft to arrive were another two women; Cecily Lefort, who was to join the JOCKEY circuit in the Basses Alpes, and the enigmatic Noor Inayat Khan, the famous MADELAINE. Noor Khan was to join up with Gilbert Norman, in Paris, as a supplementary wireless operator. The passengers returning to Britain were Paul Lejeune, who had arrived on Déricourt's first operation, and two escaping French politicians.

The SD had been informed well in advance and their Bony-LaFont agents were already waiting to follow the newcomers. They tailed Skepper, but lost him in Lyon. They had better luck with Diana Rowden and Cecily Lefort, but were discouraged from following Noor Khan, as she travelled up to Paris in the same compartment with Rémy Clément – someone they'd been ordered to avoid.

Boemelburg, like Déricourt, had expected PROSPER to return on that operation. When GILBERT told him that PROSPER had already parachuted back, it was Kieffer who sifted through all their intelligence and concluded that, if he was back, then he would probably have been received by the group down in the Sologne.

Kieffer wanted to make an arrest; Boemelburg resisted the idea. The situation sparked off a brief and extremely rare row between the two men.

Obersturmfuhrer Kieffer had carried the brunt of the work in dealing with BOE/48, organizing the surveillance operations and at the same time guaranteeing the FARRIER group's safety, the most frustrating aspect of which had been fending off the Abwehr's spoiling tactics and their brow-beating of German agents. Kieffer had never met (and never did meet) Déricourt and he frankly dismissed Boemelburg's unswerving faith in him. However, the real source of disharmony was the disagreement over how best to deal with PROSPER. Kieffer wanted to swoop as quickly as possible and decapitate the entire network, before PROSPER had time to distribute his orders. Boemelburg was more cautious. His stakes were far higher than Kieffer's. Boemelburg wanted the glory of having discovered the date of the invasion, something he did not believe PROSPER would divulge under interrogation. He believed that information would come from BOE/48. The other, and over-riding, motive was that he didn't want GILBERT linked with any of the arrests. If they bungled it, GILBERT'S credibility would be destroyed.

While Kieffer and the 60-year-old Nazi argued over PROSPER's fate, the man himself was moving from safe-house to safe-house, seeing as many people as he could. For reasons known only to himself, he misled Jean Worms about the date of the invasion saying, 'it was a matter of weeks away'. Gilbert Norman met up with the ebullient Jacques Bureau, the wireless expert, and told him PROSPER had actually seen Churchill during his trip to London.

A few days later, Bureau and Suttill met at the Hot Club in Montmartre, where the latter told the jazz fanatic, 'The invasion will come at the beginning of September, on the northern coast. I cannot tell you precisely where, or precisely when.'[17] Gradually Suttill made his way around the inner circle, but many who saw him remarked at how different he seemed. At the point when he ought to have felt at the peak of his power, he appeared 'grey and strained'.[18] He was exasperated that London was sending out to him two Canadians, whom he doubted would ever pass as Frenchmen and who would need cosseting until they'd settled down into obscurity. It was another of Buckmaster's brainstorms, but at the worst possible time. With so much activity going on, the Germans were on their toes – and everyone was under that much more pressure. Added to which every week news arrived of the arrest of some distant contact out in the field. Each scrap of bad news brought more anxiety and Suttill began to feel the edges of his empire were crumbling. And yet, all around him his colleagues seemed indifferent to the danger. He needed to make new contingency plans.

Suttill wanted to organize another tour to see all his lieutenants in the field, but he somehow lacked the will to motivate himself. He was passing through an interminable nightmare of doubt and depression, feeling that his great operation was about to slip from his fingers – or be snatched from his grasp.

Introverted and tormented by suspicion, he suspected Déricourt, he suspected Armel Guerne and even Gilbert Norman.[19] He had become obsessed with the idea that there was a traitor, either at the very heart of their group, or in London; and he began to lose sight of his goal. Jean Worms spent a day with him and remarked to a colleague how careless PROSPER seemed, as though gripped by some suicidal fatalism. 'One would almost think he felt something was going to happen to him. These English are queer people. I don't understand them.'[20] To another colleague Suttill remarked, 'When the blow comes, and it won't be long, it will come from London.'[21] To others he seemed irritable and impatient, barking orders about tightening security.

Francis Suttill had been sent into France to organize a secret network whose sole purpose was to produce coordinated guerilla warfare behind enemy lines, in support of the forthcoming invasion. To that end he had built a massive army of trained and well-supplied men which was waiting for the signal to rise up. Then, with everyone stretched beyond their resources, they were being told to hold out until September. Suttill felt forsaken by his colleagues in London whom he believed were leading him – or allowing him to be led – towards some terrible disaster. Over and over he repeated to his friends his anxiety that, 'unless the invasion comes now, during the summer, we are lost. We should otherwise all be arrested.'[22] Not only would there be no invasion that summer, there would be no invasion that autumn either.

Suttill slept very little. On some nights he preferred to stay on the streets, risking arrest for breaking the curfew and then turning up at a colleague's flat at dawn and collapsing with exhaustion. Ironically, as he was out pacing the streets, struggling with his fears about the network's security, Boemelburg and Kieffer were invariably awake too and the lights at Avenue Foch blazed deep into the night. On Saturday, 20 June, without informing anyone Suttill left his flat and moved to a small hotel in the Rue Mazagran, up in St Denis. It is indicative that he should have sought security close to his communist contacts in the working-class streets of the so called 'Red Belt', and forsaken the Parisian West End.

The final decision to move in on the PROSPER group was made as a consequence of a series of events that occurred ninety miles south of Paris. On the night of 15/16 June, two Canadians, Frank Pickersgill and John Macalister parachuted to a reception organized by Culioli, who then took them to the same house that had sheltered Suttill. Sturmbannfuhrer Bauer, the SD commandant in Blois, had a signal from Kieffer warning him to be on the look-out for PROSPER, whom he was certain would parachute into the Sologne any day now, 'or may already be there'.

The SD were already conducting a profitable *ratissage* in the area, attempting to stamp out the unprecedented resistance activity. Each night dozens and dozens of containers of equipment rained down from the sky and virtually everyone on the road after curfew was invariably engaged in resistance. Around midnight on the 20th, a small truck was halted at a road block near Dhuizon. Inside the cab was one of PROSPER's sub-organizers, Roger Couffrant, and the local garage mechanic, André Habert. In the back, the Germans discovered nine containers of arms and explosives hidden under a layer of straw. The men were dragged out of the truck and beaten unconscious on the spot. A little later the same night the local school teacher, another PROSPER soldier, was arrested on his way home, after having disposed of a load of material. He recalls his interrogator saying, 'We weren't looking for you or your stuff. We were looking for someone arriving from England.'

Operation COCKADE was driving loyal British and French men and women to run the most horrendous risks. Buckmaster and his colleagues in F Section were doing no more than they'd been ordered, 'to prepare for D-Day', while out in the field, the unidentifiable 'little people' were throwing themselves into what they believed would be their proudest moment.

Early the following morning, Culioli set off for Paris in his little Citroën, with Yvonne Rudellat and the two Canadians. As they approached Dhuizon they were confronted by the same road block that had caught Couffrant and Habert the night before. Miraculously, they had no trouble and passed through to the next checkpoint at the gates of Dhuizon. At this stage the two Canadians were ordered out of the back of the car, while two SD men got in and ordered Culioli to drive up to the Mairie. The Canadians followed on foot.

At the town hall the four from the car were taken to the Assembly Chamber where sixteen other prisoners, men who'd been arrested the night before, stood silently together. Culioli convinced the SD he was a local forestry official and he and Rudellat were allowed to go. They sat in the Citroën outside waiting for the Canadians, and worrying whether their hopeless French accents would convince the SD. Suddenly an officer stepped out of the Mairie and asked them both to come back inside. Culioli didn't wait, he put his foot down and raced the little machine as fast as it would go. The Germans took up pursuit in a couple of powerful French Fords, drew up within a few metres of the Citroën and opened fire.

The windscreen was shattered, the tyres exploded and Rudellat slumped forward against the dashboard with bullets through her head and shoulder. Culioli swerved the car towards a brick wall, but missed and skidded into a field where he was flung out of the vehicle. The SD arrived and pummelled him with rifle butts and the steel-capped toes of their jackboots. Back at the Town Hall the SD unwrapped a parcel that had been discovered in the car. It was addressed to a non-existent prisoner of war in Germany and inside it they discovered some radio crystals and four notes. One was inscribed '*Pour Prosper*', two others '*Pour Archambaud*' (Gilbert Norman) and a third '*Pour Marie Louise*'.[23] SS Sturmbannfuhrer Ludwig Bauer telephoned 84 Avenue Foch and asked for Kieffer. He read the contents of the messages and when Kieffer passed the information on to Boemelburg, he simply replied, 'Yes, bring them in.'

The day the arrests had begun down in the Sologne, Saturday, 20 June, Francis Suttill had moved to the little hotel in St Denis and then taken the train down to Grignon to see the Balachowskys at the Agricultural College. He claimed to be looking for fields for the gliders that would come with the invasion. In truth he just needed to talk with people whom he felt would understand his anxiety. He missed the society that had gathered in those grounds. Madame Balachowsky recalled that at lunch he revealed his anxieties about the rest of the group, saying that he had lost faith in GILBERT, and felt 'haunted' by the others, who seemed oblivious to the danger around them. He felt utterly lonely and abandoned.

After lunch, Suttill and Madame Balachowsky walked together under the fruit trees. The blossoms had all fallen and early apples were ripening at the uppermost reaches of the trees. Madame Balachowsky mentioned to him the name of a woman, Madame Monier-Vinard, who had organized an escape service from France, through Gibraltar to Britain, and was in regular radio contact with London. She would probably handle his communications if he felt he could not trust GILBERT, or anyone else for that matter. He thanked her for her generosity but said there was no point. The Germans, he felt certain, had an agent in Baker Street.[24]

They travelled back to Paris together and as they parted company outside the Gare Montparnasse, he repeated his certain fear: 'The Germans seem to have known all our movements for some time now.'

On Sunday the 21st Suttill went to the Gare d'Austerlitz to meet Culioli and the Canadians. He had also arranged a rendezvous with Déricourt and brought with him two passengers for Britain – Richard Heslop, organizer of a network in the Savoyard Alps, and an RAF pilot named Taylor who'd been shot down. Déricourt took the couple to one side and told them to return that evening to get the train to Amboise.

Meanwhile, Suttill waited at the entrance for Culioli and the Canadians. When they failed to turn up he was not alarmed and resolved to return at the same time the following day. When they failed to arrive on the Monday he presumed the worst.[25] At one o'clock he turned up at Armel Guerne's flat, alone but agitated. Andrée Borrel arrived a little later and during lunch watched her commander deteriorate into an ever more distressed and irrational state. The cracks were widening; the trusted ones were disappearing and yet they still had to hold out for another two and a half months. Finally Suttill crashed his fist on the table and declared, 'if there were not an Allied invasion soon, he and Norman would provoke one, by calling out the entire network, which would cause all the others to rise up in its wake'.[26] It was symptomatic of his deluded state that he believed this would force the Combined Chiefs to accelerate their invasion plans. Perhaps it is just as well he never knew just how cheaply PROSPER stock was being traded in London that summer.

The following day, Tuesday the 23rd, Suttill decided to get out of Paris and travelled down to Triechateau, near the ancient town of Gisors. He met with George Darling, an organizer who worked closely with Culioli. Suttill needed to know if there had been any precise news of Culioli and the Canadians. Darling confirmed his worst fears.

In Triechateau, they had a safe-house that belonged to Darling's fiancée, Madame Guepin. Rather than return to Paris, Suttill decided to stay the night there. He looked so tired and wretched that Madame Guepin wondered whether he wasn't very ill. 'I can't tell you what weighs on me,' he replied. 'But it's not my health.'[27]

As Suttill tried to get to sleep, listening to the trains that ran all night up to Dieppe, Kieffer's men in Paris finally moved in. At precisely midnight, several black Citroëns pulled up in the Avenue Henri-Martin. Some fifteen plain-clothes men emerged and began to surround number 77, on the corner with the Boulevard Lannes. When all were in place a young Rottenfuhrer knocked on the door of Nicholas and Maud Laurent, another couple on the fringe of the network, and asked for Gilbert Archambaud (ARCHAMBAUD being Gilbert Norman's codename). When Norman came to the door he found half a dozen Lugers trained on his head. Upstairs Kieffer's men found Andrée Borrel asleep in bed. The Laurents,

Norman and Borrel were bundled into the cars and driven to the Avenue Foch and were taken upstairs to the cells.

Down in Blois, Pierre Culioli and the two Canadians had been interrogated constantly since their arrest. Having been shot in the knee after he attacked one of his guards, Culioli was later stripped and chained to a bed where he was beaten around the groin and face with a large buckled belt. On the Tuesday he'd been driven up to the Avenue Foch and was lying, almost comatose, in a neighbouring cell when Borrel and Norman were brought in.

About one thirty on the Wednesday morning, another squad arrived at PROSPER's hotel in the rue Mazagran and awoke the terrified patronne, Madame Fevre. They demanded her register and found the name François Desprée, Suttill's pseudonym, recorded against room 15. Madame Fevre told them that Monsieur Desprée had been away for a few days. They took the spare key and decided to wait.

That same morning, the 24th, Suttill rose early to catch the 7.00 am train to Paris, where he had a number of meetings to attend. After breakfast, Madame Guepin accompanied him to the station at Gisors to see him off. Suttill knew he would not see her again and after saying their farewells, he twice returned to embrace her. At about ten thirty, he approached the Hotel Mazagran, cautiously looking for any signs that would suggest it was being watched. He entered quietly, not disturbing the patronne, and climbed the stairs to his room. As his key rattled in the lock, three SD men drew their pistols. Suttill swung the door open and then stood there, framed in the doorway, slowly raising his hands above his head. It had come at last.[28]

XIII

Consequences

The news of PROSPER's arrest was signalled to Berlin by midday and passed on to Adolf Hitler before he sat down to dinner. Kopkow immediately sent congratulations to Boemelburg with a request that he be kept informed of the interrogations.

–

How had the SD known where Suttill was staying? Neither Gilbert Norman nor Andrée Borrel spoke a word to their interrogators for more than two days. No one else knew. Except, perhaps, for Déricourt. The last time Déricourt and Suttill had met was on the morning of 21 June, at the Gare d'Austerlitz when Heslop and Taylor, the two homeward-bound passengers, were introduced and told by Déricourt to return to the station that evening. They did, but Déricourt did not. Heslop and Taylor went to ground again and awaited an explanation. That night, over the field at Pocé-sur-Cisse, Squadron Leader Verity circled in vain, looking for the reception lights.

Déricourt never gave a reason for his absence, but he did have to contact Suttill again (the only man who knew where the passengers were hiding), to re-schedule the operation and ensure the passengers would come to the same rendezvous the following day. Which they did. Then it was Verity's turn to miss the party, having suffered a generator failure over the Channel.

The following night, that of the 23rd/24th, the night Norman and Borrel were arrested, Déricourt's operation was finally completed under the silent gaze of the SD's agents. Out of Verity's Lizzie had come Robert Lyon, on his second mission to the ACOLYTE network, and a Free French agent called Colonel Bonoteau. Both men were followed to their destinations. The SD eventually lost track of Lyon, but Bonoteau was arrested that same morning.

Meanwhile Suttill and Norman were undergoing their calvary. It was not uncommon for prisoners to have to withstand some tough punishment during their interrogation at the Avenue Foch. Though it was not, in the strictest sense, a torture chamber, there were a number of instruments for enthusiasts to use to extract information: rubber or wooden truncheons, thin leather whips – rather like riding crops, knuckle-dusters and, of course, the standard issue jackboot. Suttill's interrogation began in the presence of SS Feldwebel Josef Placke, who was relieved by SS Hauptsturmfuhrer Karl Langer and he by one Dr Josef Götz. These men were not responsible for any beatings, but maintained a presence while others did the heavy work. It lasted for three days, during which time Suttill was not allowed to eat, drink, sleep or even sit. Sometimes Kieffer conducted the interrogations and on one occasion SS Standartenfuhrer Knochen himself engaged in the breaking of PROSPER. In a separate room, Gilbert Norman underwent the same treatment in the presence of SS Hauptsturmfuhrers Scherer, von Kapri, Ruhl and Vogt. Boemelburg remained aloof from the entire procedure.

What Baker Street expected of its captured agents was that they would hold out for at least 48 hours, giving enough time for contacts to disappear. They were not expected to keep *absolutely* silent, a principle proceeding from the view that no intelligence that any SOE agent held would ever be worth a human life. Suttill and Norman had already agreed their scale of values, and it was understood that information about *materiel* would come low on the list. To all their colleagues they had given the same instructions, 'Don't try to hold out. Give them something. A little at a time, but don't give them everything.'[1] For three days Norman, Suttill and Borrel spoke not a word. In fact Borrel never talked at all.

On the fourth day Kieffer removed from his safe a file marked BOE/48 and presented for Suttill's gaze the photographic copies of his letters, reports, instructions – everything that he had sent as mail to London, or that had been sent from London to him. Probably the most devastating sight was a list of his 'personal messages', broadcast by the BBC since January.

> Mes genets sont fleuris dans le jardin,
> Après les fraises, les framboises,
> Il faut compter les marches de la Tour Eiffel,
> Quand les lilas refleuriront,
> Archibald aura 10 ministres,
> La morue est salée,
> Halte-là qu'on vous rattrappe,
> Ils seront toujours verts,
> Prenez garde au lion perdu,

Congestion à la gare de Lyon,
On plombe la dent du midi.[2]

Out of the thousands of messages the BBC had broadcast
to the agents in France, the SD knew precisely which were
his – and more importantly, what they signified. It was a
blow of devastating effectiveness, for all his worst nightmares had come true – there *had* been a traitor in Baker
Street. Most of the material that was presented to Suttill,
Norman, Culioli and others bore the stamp '*von BOE/48*',
which Suttill and a few others took to be this phantom
German agent in Baker Street. No one presumed it was
someone who lived just round the corner. The SD had
other mail, also from BOE/48, that revealed a great deal
of information about the forthcoming invasion, including
other BBC messages that were to 'alert' the network that
the invasion was imminent. Then there was a piece of
correspondence brought by the Canadians from London,
in clear, which was a schedule of 'arms drops' leading up
to D-Day. Suttill could see no point in prolonging his
agony. He could neither stand nor speak, but he could
just about hold a pen.

Kieffer had received an instruction from Kopkow in
Berlin to offer Suttill a promise of clemency in return
for information about the hidden arms dumps. It was
Hitler's personal wish that the entire network be eliminated as swiftly as possible, while Boemelburg insisted
on pursuing the date for the invasion. Suttill considered
Kieffer's proposal carefully and then asked for a guarantee from the Reichssicherheitshauptamt in Berlin –
from Kopkow[3] or even Himmler himself, that in return
for information about arms and equipment all captured
agents would be treated as prisoners of war.

On the fifth day a document arrived bearing Himmler's signature and the marque of the RSHA. After going over the document innumerable times and talking it over between them, Suttill and Norman agreed to accept the guarantees. Later that same day Josef Placke and some French agents of the SD called on George Darling out at Triechateau, and presented him with a letter in Suttill's hand. The letter requested that Darling hand over all the arms in his care to the bearers of the letter. Darling mounted his motorcycle and led them, unsuspecting, to the Bois de l'Etoile where the arms were hidden. Once the arms were loaded onto the back of a truck, Darling climbed onto his bike again and kicked the motor into life. One of the Frenchmen, sensing that he might be trying to escape, took out his pistol and ordered him to stop. Darling swerved into the forest, a volley of shots cut through the clear air and Darling was found – a mangled heap beneath some thorny undergrowth. He died in hospital within the day.

On 1 July Gilbert Norman was led into Culioli's cell to acquaint him with the details of the pact. 'They have known everything about us for so long. No one will be shot so long as they recover the material.'[4] Culioli eventually agreed to help the Germans uncover nearly a hundred containers: Roger Couffrant at Ramorantin, 30 Containers; André Gatignon at Noyers-sur-Cher, 20 Containers; August Cordelet at Chaumont-sur-Loire, 25 Containers; and Albert le Meur at Chambord, 14 Containers. Culioli was driven around to each location where he did his best to reassure the local Resistance of Suttill's pact with the SD. Norman did the same. The scene was repeated in the Paris suburbs, in dozens of départements, in hundreds of villages and towns.[5]

By the second week of July, both Suttill and Norman had divulged the date of the invasion. It seemed to be supported by the scraps of information in the mail, but Boemelburg wanted corroboration from other sources. On 14 July, Jacques Bureau, the radio specialist, was arrested, taken to Fresnes Prison and placed in a death cell. The previous occupant had been shot the day before. Bureau was there hardly any time before the door swung open again. He presumed he was about to be shot. Instead he was driven to the Avenue Foch, where he was confronted by Gilbert Norman. Despite the treatment to which he'd been subjected over the past fortnight, Norman seemed very relaxed. Bureau was impressed. Norman wasn't cowed or beaten, indeed he projected a sense of pride – of rescued honour. 'Don't let them depress you,' he said, 'retain your dignity. We have made an arrangement with these gentlemen,' he continued, 'and Jacques, I want you to shed some light. Understand?'

Bureau believed there to have been a hidden message in Norman's statement. He had employed an obvious grammatical error in his French which signalled that his meaning was to be interpreted as, 'give them something, but not everything'. Bureau had understood. As Norman moved to the door he repeated, 'A little light, monsieur, and in return no one will be shot.' Then, for the guard's benefit as well as Bureau's, 'And you know it won't be long now.'[6]

Assigned to an interrogator, Bureau was escorted down a long corridor of small 'torture' rooms that were used for the less significant detainees. At each room his interrogator knocked, but found it occupied. They were all occupied. With a macabre shrug, the German told him, 'We will have to wait.'

Bureau's thoughts raced through all the information in his head regarding PROSPER, grading it from the insignificant to the critical. For a number of days he was able to satisfy them with information about the location of hidden radio sets and crystals. But he knew that couldn't last. He knew the invasion was due in September and it was to that question the SD returned time and again. 'Other people have told us the date, why don't you?' Finally he relented and decided to tell his little lie: 'November.'[7]

From all the interrogations and written material that had been gathered, Boemelburg was sufficiently confident to send a report during the third week of July to Kopkow in Berlin that stated the invasion would fall at the Pas-de-Calais during the first week of September. From this point Kopkow's priorities would switch to the next stage of the SD's operation against an invasion – the radio game.

Each morning Dr Josef Götz would step out of a small hotel in the Avenue Grand Armée and walk to the Avenue Foch, where he had an office on the second floor. On rare occasions he would wear his uniform but mostly he preferred civilian clothes, being as he felt more of a civilian, and though he always carried a concealed weapon, he was grateful he had never had cause to use it.[8]

Josef Götz was born in Michelbach in 1910. He studied French and English to university level, graduated with a doctorate in philosophy and became an inspector of schools in Karlsruhe before the war. He was transferred to Paris in June 1941 to work with the Abwehr but was commandeered by the SD on 21 November 1942. He initially baulked at the idea of working with the Nazis, but was quickly won over by the threat that if he refused to bring his linguistic talents to the Avenue Foch, he would be transferred to a punishment squad.[9]

After the final arrests of the Red Orchestra, Götz had been briefly involved with playing back to Moscow a few of the captured Soviet radio sets. Since then he had been engaged on translations, interpreting documents and a bit of code-breaking. Most of his attention was focused on the product that had been coming out of the sophisticated radio listening station at Boulevard Suchet. There, the German technicians would listen in to all the transmissions to and from SOE's agents in the field. It was Boulevard Suchet that had first given Boemelburg a clue, back in November, that a new network seemed to be developing in northern France. During all the months since, they had put together thick files on each of the radio operators they had monitored, with information on their call signals, wavelengths, strength of transmission and most significantly, the operator's 'signature' – that is, the pattern of an operator's individual 'touch' on the Morse key. Now all this scrupulously gathered information was going to be put to the test.

At the beginning of June Götz had returned to Germany on leave, but this was abruptly cancelled by a call from Kieffer. On 29 June he sat in Kieffer's office and was told in the broadest terms about the recent arrests. His next engagement would be to begin playing the game with PROSPER's radios. Boemelburg presumed that London would send in reinforcements to try and salvage something from the disaster before the invasion. He wanted to know who and where those agents would be, before they left London. He also wanted to ensure that any change in the Allies' plans was not missed.

Götz began with Gilbert Norman's transmitter, which had been captured with all the codes. He transmitted to London, as if from Norman, 'There have been arrests. Am safe and gone to ground. Await instructions.' London responded and Götz was ecstatic. He composed another message and awaited another reply. This time London signalled, 'Where is PROSPER?' Götz hesitated, then chose to ignore the question. The exchange continued.[10]

While Dr Götz concentrated on his radio game, Kieffer concentrated on what he was best at. His priority was simple police work and the eventual eradication of every last vestige of PROSPER's army from the field. The arrests continued throughout July. Armed with information from Suttill or Norman – and sometimes with Norman accompanying them, the SD swept through the countryside like a scythe through ripening wheat. At first scores and then hundreds of French men and women were delivered to the prisons around northern France. At Fresnes, people were crowded sometimes five or six to a cell.

Following the initial arrests, most of Suttill's contacts went to ground or left the city. Many did not. Jean Worms and Armel Guerne were arrested on 1 July at the little black-market restaurant not twenty yards from Déricourt's flat; the rest of Captain Darling's staff at Grignon on 1 July; Dr Balachowsky on 2 July; Jacques Bureau on 14 July; Rowland Dowlen by radio direction finders on 31 July; Charles Grover Williams on 2 August; Robert Benoist on 5 August (but he escaped). Then there was Pierre Culioli, Yvonne Rudellat, Frank Pickersgill, John Macalister, Gilbert Norman, Andrée Borrel and Suttill himself. But these are only the names that have been recorded. The full account simply can't be given. Francis Suttill had 144 full agents (classified P1) within his network, but when you count everyone officially connected to PROSPER – all the P2s and P3s, the number rises to 1015.[11]

All over Paris and the surrounds, wireless sets signalled the news to Baker Street. Noor Khan, Rowland Dowlen, Dubois, Cohen, Johnny Barrett, Ben Cowburn and others all sent the black tidings. The news crept around the corridors and began to sink into people's hearts. Buckmaster found it very hard to believe at first. Suttill had been the best, the very best that they had sent in – or so he believed. Vera Atkins recalls her first concern was for all the people that had been associated with Suttill and what had become of them. Atkins was right. The loss of PROSPER was nothing compared with the devastation that rained down on the SOE's networks in northern France as a consequence of those initial arrests. By August the SD would be in almost total control.

Across London, at Broadway Buildings, the young Patrick Reilly, Sir Stewart Menzies' personal assistant, was at work in his office across the corridor from 'C's' when Claude Dansey marched in, clapped his hands and declared, 'Great news, Reilly. Great news.' Reilly naturally presumed Dansey was about to tell him of some major intelligence coup against the Germans. 'One of the big SOE networks in France has just blown up!'[12]

Dansey's isolation within the service could not have been more acute. Reilly thought him 'a wicked man, undoubtedly'. Indeed, one of Reilly's contemporaries actually claimed 'Dansey was the only truly evil man I ever met.' Many of Dansey's colleagues, however, never saw any evil. General Sir James Marshall-Cornwall, who admired Dansey and served under him for nearly two and a half years, never learnt the full details of any of his operations. And as for his agents, 'Only Dansey knew anything about *his* agents, who remained very much his own.' He would come and go from his office unannounced, 'making for secret meetings elsewhere, conspiratorially wrapped in his long dark overcoat'. He was unashamedly 'the most unpopular snake in the business', as the author Charles Whiting described him. But like him or not, he was there for the duration.[13]

One evening during the first week in July, around 9 p.m., Karl Braun cruised one of his master's Citroëns along the Boulevard de Beausejour, watching for GILBERT'S familiar shape loitering by the kerb. Braun was another who resented the special treatment this man seemed to receive. Their trips to the Château in Neuilly were always conducted in mutually contemptuous silence.

Boemelburg greeted Déricourt by the large circular table in the hall and led him across into the salon. Though Déricourt would be the very last to admit it, that visit – in substance no different from any other – rocked the great survivor to his very foundations.

Boemelburg's tactful, one might say even sympathetic, approach was to catalogue the extraordinary bravery and resilience PROSPER's people had shown under interrogation. 'The Jew Worms has not uttered a syllable! And DENISE (Andrée Borrel), she has impressed everyone.' This conversation took place before the SD had really begun to reap their rewards out in the field, and before news of it had drifted into Paris.[14] Nevertheless, Déricourt had felt the first cracks of an arctic wind clawing its way through. Again, he received the same reassurances that he would be well taken care of. How attractive these reassurances felt that night in Neuilly, is anyone's guess.

The Déricourts' move to Rue Pergolese had its uncomfortable side. Emerging from the metro at Porte Dauphine, he would have to walk past the blazing lights at 84 Avenue Foch on his way home. How did he cope with the knowledge that each day more and more of his colleagues were being driven through the steel gates and down into the basement garages?

On 17 July, Déricourt was scheduled to run an operation down near Tours, on a field Clément had discovered. Joseph Antelme, the organizer of BRICKLAYER, and Jean Savy, a lawyer colleague of his, were on their way to London and away from the chaos. Following his meeting with Boemelburg, Déricourt also decided to get out. He sent an urgent message to London saying he was taking advantage of the next mission to catch a lift back. This message wasn't sent to SOE but to MI6. SOE were never informed he was leaving his post.

Then, as with the previous operation, Déricourt failed to make the rendezvous. Flying Officer McCairns circled the area for no less than 25 minutes before giving up. The operation was set up again for the 19th/20th. Déricourt rarely had trouble with unwanted German patrols interfering with his operations, quite the reverse. So why did he miss the rendezvous?

The night for which the operation was originally scheduled happened to coincide with a critical MI6 Lysander operation on the other side of Paris. From a field near Brez-Brouillancy, Marie-Madelaine Foucarde, the leader of the famous MI6 intelligence network 'Alliance', set off on her long-overdue trip to London to meet with her controller, 'Uncle Claude'. It would have been very careless if Dansey had allowed two agents, from two vastly different operations, to get anywhere near each other as they passed through RAF Tangmere.

So, two days late, on the night of the 19th/20th, Antelme, Savy and Déricourt climbed into the back of McCairns' Lysander. As the aircraft began to roll across the meadow grass, Savy and Déricourt watched the lonely figure of Rémy, giving the thumbs-up to them as they passed.[15] Déricourt knew it was incredibly callous of him to have left Clément at that particular time, the latter's safety being subject to an arrangement with the enemy, but he knew he wouldn't be gone for long. The SOE had hastily put together a Hudson operation three nights hence, the 22nd/23rd, for what they expected would be a veritable exodus of PROSPER people still at large. As the Lysander lifted up and out over the Loire valley, Rémy was already organizing bicycles and the luggage. The SD were not on station that night – Déricourt had told them nothing about the operation.

Dansey arranged for an MI6 reception officer to actually meet the aircraft on the hardstanding and whisk Déricourt away from his SOE colleagues.[16] He was taken to MI6's own little safe-house, Tangmere, where two nights before Foucarde had enjoyed her first English breakfast. From Tangmere he was taken up to André Simon's flat in Harley Street, where he slept until late in the morning.[17] After lunch he was driven to a meeting at one of Dansey's 'service flats'. No one at Baker Street headquarters (except André Simon and Bodington) knew that Déricourt was in London. Nor did they ever know.

Déricourt's de-briefing served a variety of purposes. He was extremely keen for everyone to appreciate the delicate state of the situation in Paris. He needed to hear the same sort of reassurances from Dansey as he'd recently heard from Boemelburg. No doubt he was given all the encouragement and expressions of confidence he needed. But if Déricourt had harboured any hopes of being withdrawn from the field, he was disappointed. 'I went secretly to London. There I received the order to carry on my mission as Air Movements Officer [for SOE] and other orders too. These related to the intelligence side.'[18] Naturally Dansey couldn't pull Déricourt out without revealing his hand? On the contrary, it would seem that Uncle Claude was of the opinion that the greater part of Déricourt's work was still to be done.

He was told to return to France and maintain his contacts with Boemelburg. Déricourt was concerned, however, that his integrity in the field was beginning to be questioned. That would be dealt with, he was told, by an old friend who was flying out to join him. Nicholas Bodington had convinced his superiors at SOE that before anyone else went in, he should fly to France to report on the situation and make any necessary decisions 'on the ground'. News of this decision had already reached Dansey.

Bodington would go on the next available SOE flight, with the radio operator Jack Agazarian. F Section must have lost their concentration for a moment to have allowed the Deputy Head to fly to occupied Paris; but on the other hand, Bodington knew he'd be in safe hands. After the war, Déricourt claimed Bodington had known all about his operation from the beginning – '...he had been present in the room at the War Office when I was briefed to approach the Germans on my return to France'.[19] Whatever argument he used with

SOE, Bodington's real purpose in going was to seal-up any cracks that had appeared in Déricourt's reputation, something he'd become very adept at ever since Baker Street had heard the name Déricourt.

Bodington had already come to Déricourt's rescue just a few weeks earlier, following yet another of those worrying reports from MI5. Back in April, during his Easter trip to London, there had been the report, gleaned from French intelligence sources, about Déricourt's contacts with the Germans in Paris during 1940 and 1941; now the same sources had reported that '...the Gestapo are aware that Déricourt had been to the UK [the Easter trip] and that they would try and get in touch with him in order to use him rather than arrest him'.[20]

The provenance of such a report must be seriously questioned. Certainly there would never have been any leak from 84 Avenue Foch regarding Déricourt, he was one of the SD's best-kept secrets. On the other hand, the report does date from the same time the Abwehr began their campaign to 'discredit GILBERT' – it may even have come straight from Hugo Bleicher.

At any rate, it was a serious piece of news and should have laid seeds of doubt for the safety of Déricourt's entire operation. F Section chose to deal with it by asking Déricourt himself for an explanation – the perfect opportunity for him to exploit his greatest talent. As every basic manual of deception will tell you, you start from the truth, and proceed sideways.

Déricourt had written: 'One day two Lufthansa pilots called at my home. I had met the two officers before the war, when they were civillian pilots. I think I remember the name of one of them, Mittelhauser, who use to fly Paris–Cologne in 1939.' Déricourt claimed they invited him to work for the German air-transport organization, Luftflotte, which he described as 'an organization of the Lufthansa ... which consists solely of French pilots ... but is controlled by Colonel Kingsburg of the Luftwaffe'. (Luftflotte was also concerned with aerial reconnaisance.) Déricourt claimed he had extricated himself from 'any further involvement' by getting declared medically unfit for flying. He also claimed, 'this little adventure had for a time made me fear for my security'.[21]

He sent the letter by the Lysander that had taken the Agazarians out of France in June. It was a neat piece of work. Déricourt had dove-tailed the SD's very real visit to his wife, with an offer he had received back in 1941 to work for Luftflotte. It was an important step, for he was able to refer to this fictional visitation, with suitable elaboration, whenever his activities were called into question.

Referring to Déricourt's letter, on 21 June Bodington pencilled a most cryptic memo which, once again, put paid to any suggestions that Déricourt might be engaged in anything untoward with the enemy. 'D. is now in France and doing well. I don't feel there is much we can do about this. [The report that the Gestapo might try to contact Déricourt.] We know he is in touch with the Germans and also how and why.'[22] The last sentence employs what civil servants call an economy of truth.

Having played 'back-stop' for Déricourt at Baker Street, Bodington would now do the same out in the field, for Dansey must have had Déricourt down as a long-term operation.

From SOE's point of view, Bodington's mission would provide a much needed picture of the 'situation on the ground'. Apart from establishing precisely who was secure and who was not, Bodington was also required to solve some confusion over Gilbert Norman's radio. There had been many reports announcing Norman's arrest; and yet, his radio was still on the air. SOE's signals branch had been suspicious of the transmissions from the outset. The very first transmission under Götz's control had been too halting and with an uncertain 'signature'. They reported, 'unusual, hesitant – quite easily the work of a flustered man doing his work under duress', implying that the SD were forcing him to transmit. But Buckmaster was of the opinion that Norman was not the type who would co-operate with the Germans. Unfortunately, Buckmaster wasn't aware that the SD required very little assistance from Norman – and what they did need, they got from London.

Every operator had a secret code that he had to transmit, known as a security code, a meaningless series of numbers or letters that confirmed to the receivers in Britain that they were listening to the man himself. Often there were 'double security checks', one transmitted at the beginning and another sent sometime during the course of the message. While transmitting as 'Norman', Götz was surprised to receive from London a criticism for neglecting to use his 'double security check'. Norman was pretty amazed too when Götz showed him the message from London and demanded to know his 'double security check'.[23] So Buckmaster wanted to believe Norman was still at large but Signals had their doubts. Bodington would clarify the situation.

Déricourt spent the night of the 20th at Simon's flat in Harley Street and the afternoon of the next day in Bodington's company. That evening, 21 July, an MI6 conducting officer drove Déricourt out to RAF Tempsford. MI6 already had two officers going into

France that night on Operation FLORIDE; Dansey secured a place for Déricourt as the third passenger. They were put down to an MI6 reception at Chateauroux.[24] Déricourt leapt from the craft and began a lightning dash across country to Angers where he was scheduled to receive his first Hudson operation for SOE.

He caught the first train up to Vierzon, where he changed to another heading west to Nantes in the Loire Atlantique. He got off at Angers, long before Rémy arrived for their rendezvous. The army of SOE fugitives that both Déricourt and London presumed would try to get on that flight didn't materialize. While Rémy and Henri sat in a café waiting for nightfall, Déricourt told Rémy he should go to London soon and be properly trained. Rémy shrugged. 'By the way,' Déricourt said, 'my chief is coming on this flight.'

The virtue of the twin-engined Hudson was that it could carry about a dozen passengers and yet had similar landing and take-off characteristics to the Lysander. Running up towards one of those craft really was an awe-inspiring experience, especially when it had just dropped out of the night sky towards a series of simple torches stretched out across a meadow. Once again, it was an operation the SD knew nothing about, though that isn't to say they didn't know Bodington was coming.

Agazarian looked after himself, while Déricourt put Bodington up at Charles Besnard's flat in the Avenue Malakoff, which Besnard now shared with Julienne. He was completely devoted to Julienne and it was really for her sake he allowed his place to be used as a safe-house. He was reconciled to the fact of Julienne's involvement with Déricourt and the Resistance, though it would always be a source of deep apprehension. Lately, however, Besnard had grown a little more anxious for Julienne's security. No one, not even he, could have been unaware of the new season of terror that had broken out since the PROSPER arrests. Déricourt sensed Besnard's anxiety and so moved Bodington across to his own place in Rue Pergolese, where in fact he stayed for most of his time in Paris. For Déricourt it was the very pinnacle of success to emerge from the Metro at Porte Dauphine with the Deputy Head of F Section and walk past 84 Avenue Foch. It was the first time Bodington had met Jeannot. They spoke very little to each other, except that Nick told her that 'London thought Henri was doing a good job'.[25]

The secret that Bodington was at large in Paris was not kept so for long. Kieffer telephoned Colonel Reile at Abwehr headquarters to find out – in a roundabout way – whether they had yet heard the news – but before Kieffer had a chance to begin probing, Reile popped the question: 'By the way, did you know the Deputy Head of F Section is in Paris?'[26]

Kieffer had no sense of humour. He telephoned Boemelburg and asked whether GILBERT had already informed him? Boemelburg confessed that he had not been informed. The only thing concerning Kieffer was who got to Bodington first, the Abwehr or himself. He also suspected that if Bodington was in Paris, GILBERT would certainly have known about it and was holding out on them. Kieffer also began to have his doubts about Boemelburg.

One of the first items Bodington dealt with, was the confusion that was often created over Déricourt's codename. GILBERT had often been mistaken for Gilbert Norman and vice-versa, so Déricourt had to be re-christened. Someone with a secret sense of humour plumped for CLAUDE.

The most pressing problem to deal with, however, was the question of Gilbert Norman's radio transmissions. During the course of Baker Street's conversations with Dr Götz, they had asked *Norman* for 'a contact address where friends could reach him'. Götz duly supplied one. Baker Street then signalled to Bodington, through Agazarian, the details for a rendezvous with Norman at 'Madam Ferdi-Filipowsky in the Rue de Rome'.[27] The SD were amazed at how audacious, not to say foolhardy, London could be in sending Bodington into the field. Both Kopkow and Kieffer wanted him; Boemelburg was oddly indifferent. But Kieffer must have sensed he was onto a hiding to nothing, that Déricourt would surely protect Bodington. Nevertheless, Kieffer had his orders from Berlin, and he had to persist.

Naturally Déricourt protected Bodington. They both knew Norman was under arrest. They knew the transmissions were coming from the SD. They knew the address in the Rue de Rome would be a trap, but Baker Street was clinging to the possibility that Norman was still at large. Why? Why should Baker Street have any doubts about whether Norman was arrested? Why had London requested a contact address and then passed it to Bodington, if they hadn't wanted the address tested? A rendezvous was made for 30 July. Bodington hadn't actually been ordered to turn up, but it was clear Baker Street expected someone to go. There were many more subtle ways of testing the authenticity of Norman's transmissions but Baker Street hadn't thought of any and Bodington was damned if he was going to test the bloody address, so – they sent Agazarian. His arrest was as swift as it was predictable.

Another piece of business that had to be dealt with was the purchase of a small bar in the Rue St André des Arts, near the Place St Michel. Déricourt wanted a proper establishment that could be used as a mail-drop and contact point for escaping personnel. Bodington had brought a sizeable contingency fund and a substantial part of it was used to buy the bar. Charles Besnard, being a lawyer, would look after the purchase, and he and Julienne would run the place. One evening, while Bodington was at Besnard's place to finalize the details, Charles took the opportunity to air his anxieties about Déricourt. Bodington listened intently.

Besnard claimed he did his best to ignore the work Julienne was involved with, but he was naturally protective and couldn't help but wonder sometimes precisely what was the nature of Henri's operation. He had noticed that Déricourt appeared to have regular contacts with the Germans, which naturally seemed an odd thing to do, given that he was supposed to be working with the Resistance. Bodington asked Besnard what Julienne knew.

'She knows he has contacts with the Germans. She says he's seeing old friends from before the war and that he's doing a black market in oranges. She doesn't suspect anything else, she believes in him completely.'

Bodington asked Besnard straight out, what he believed. He replied, 'Déricourt is, in my opinion, a double agent acquainted with both parties.'

Bodington didn't see any point in fudging an answer, Besnard was an intelligent lawyer. 'I know that Déricourt is working with the Germans. I encouraged him to do so.' Besnard was naturally a little taken aback, but Bodington told him 'not to worry about it, London has recommended it'.[28]

Besnard shrugged and shook his head, but if that was what London wanted Henri to do, who was he to question? It was agreed that it would be the wisest thing not to disturb Julienne's ignorance.

Bodington actually got around quite a bit during his visit and saw a number of people. One person he had to meet with was Henri Frager, the DONKEYMAN organizer. It was a conference he'd put off for as long as possible, having been warned by Déricourt from the outset that Hugo Bleicher had an agent within the DONKEYMAN group. A meeting with Frager was a potentially lethal operation, further complicated because Frager himself had no idea his network was compromised. Frager was an honest and devoted officer, but highly excitable and often given to fits of temper. He would not have been easily convinced that his lover Roger Bardet was also a German agent. And besides, Bodington wouldn't have been able to tell him without giving away his source.

Before Bodington and Frager finally met, Frager had been primed with highly damaging information about Déricourt. On 12 August, an extraordinary meeting took place between Frager, Roger Bardet and Hugo Bleicher. The German was introduced as 'Colonel Heinrich', a dissident Abwehr officer keen to be rid of the Nazis. This Colonel Heinrich confided in Frager that the SD had a most valuable agent within SOE's Paris circuits. '*Gilbert, L'homme qui fait le pick-up.*' This fuelled Frager's already smouldering suspicions and seemed to explain much that had occurred that summer. Colonel Heinrich was quite frank with Frager, and admitted his motive was the Abwehr's fight with 'those people at Avenue Foch'.

When arranging the meeting between Bodington and Frager, Déricourt went to considerable lengths to evade Bardet and Bleicher, by employing Vera Leigh, a courier in the INVENTOR circuit, as a 'cut-out', a go-between who could not compromise anyone. Just as Bodington expected, he was subjected to a fierce tirade against Déricourt. 'GILBERT,' Frager pronounced, 'is an agent of the Sicherheitsdienst.' It wasn't what Frager said that concerned Bodington, but the vehemence with which he said it. Frager threatened that unless Déricourt was taken out of the field, he would send a report to Baker Street himself. Bodington said that he would include Frager's remarks in his report.[29]

Bodington immediately warned Déricourt that Frager knew about his contacts with the SD and that he would doubtless repeat the accusation to Baker Street. Déricourt was never in any doubt where Frager had received the information but all he could do about it was to ask Boemelburg to intervene. This Boemelburg did in no uncertain terms. Bleicher was ordered to present himself before Boemelburg at the earliest possible moment. The elderly Nazi didn't mince his words, repeating himself again and again to emphasize that GILBERT must remain inviolate and that, if necessary, he would demand further orders from Berlin to protect BOE/48. Whatever placatory noises Bleicher might have made at the time were quickly swept away by his actions, for within days he ran into Bardet and Frager again, and 'Colonel Heinrich' gave Frager even more intelligence on Déricourt.

'You spoke to Bodington about GILBERT?' Bleicher enquired.

'Of course.'

'Then Bodington warned GILBERT about you.' Frager could not understand why Bodington had revealed what Frager considered to have been a strictly confidential conversation.

'How do you know this?'

'From the SD, where else? Oh, by the way, you should know that he is no longer GILBERT, but CLAUDE. That is also from the SD.'[30]

Bodington's own position had begun to look a trifle exposed by now and Besnard recalled noticing just before Bodington's departure, that he looked a man consumed by some internal struggle, 'like two people within the same skin'. It must be said that, throughout the course of Déricourt's operation, great pains were taken by Bodington and others to protect Déricourt's integrity, while Bodington's probity seems to have been neglected.

There is a (probably apocryphal) story that before Bodington returned to London, he and Déricourt dined secretly with the one they referred to as 'notre ami' at his château in Neuilly. Unfortunately, it is now too late to confirm this story though there is evidence that Boemelburg boasted of it to some of his colleagues.[31] Within a few weeks half the SD interrogators at Avenue Foch were making the same boast to their victims.

In 1982, Colonel Reile explained that just before Bodington's departure, during a rare consultation with the SD, the Nazis proudly revealed that they knew the date of the '1943 invasion' and argued against the pursuit of Bodington. 'Bodington was in France a few days [weeks] before the invasion and it was decided not to arrest him because they [the SD] felt the English would conclude we were aware of the date of the invasion.'[32]

On the night of 16/17 August, Bodington was shepherded down to the field near Pont-de-Braye, to a rendezvous with Claude and Lise de Baissac. The great SCIENTIST network, so closely associated with PROSPER, was also disintegrating. Their story was remarkably similar to PROSPER's.

A network claiming to have some 11,000 fighting men and women, strategically placed in the west and embracing the Biscay coast, it had been an obvious choice for exploitation. Since June, de Baissac's group had received nearly 121 aircraft loads of equipment; that is nearly two thousand containers of arms and explosives – three times as many as had been sent to PROSPER. During the first weeks of August, SCIENTIST received BBC messages indicating that the invasion was on for September.[33] But in July, just at the time the PROSPER network was being swept from the field, the Germans began to move in on SCIENTIST. By the time the de Baissacs were clambering aboard the Lysander, the Germans were making hundreds of arrests throughout their region.

All three passengers snuggled together in the cramped fuselage, each preoccupied. Bodington spent most of the journey running through his head the outline for one of the least 'enlightening' reports in the SOE canon.

In that report he dealt with the arrest of Agazarian by claiming that both of them had had their doubts about the address at Rue de Rome, but it had been agreed they would 'toss for which of them would go', and Agazarian lost. (The question of Agazarian's arrest and subsequent death was one that dogged Bodington for some time. Long after the SOE had passed into history he was interviewed about his trip to France. This time he was able to volunteer the information that following his arrest, Agazarian had withstood the most punishing treatment and not said a word. Where he had obtained that information was not revealed.)

As to Frager's accusation that Déricourt was an agent of the SD, Bodington concluded (rather disingenuously) that it was highly unlikely, as he himself had not been arrested while he was there, and so Déricourt must have been sound. He went on, 'I can say here and now that GILBERT's (Déricourt) organization, which consists of three people, has not the slightest possibility of being infiltrated and that the Germans obviously do not know the real identity of GILBERT.'[34] [I cannot explain why Bodington persisted in referring to GILBERT when it was he who had informed Déricourt that he was henceforth CLAUDE.] Bodington's report bolstered Déricourt's reputation and went a long way towards fending off future slings and arrows. But unfortunately Déricourt was soon to lose his friend at court. Only a matter of weeks after his return from France, and somewhat mysteriously, Bodington moved to the Political Warfare Executive (PWE). The official record states that Bodington took up the post to 'lecture soldiers on conditions in France'.[35]

While Bodington had been away, Dansey and 'C' were making use of the material Déricourt had given them during his secret trip in July. He had provided details of the SD's sweeping arrests throughout the Loire, Normandy and Pas-de-Calais regions, just as they'd been described to him by Boemelburg. It provided Menzies with invaluable ammunition for a campaign they were about to unleash on the SOE. This goal – which was also Dansey's – was to have the organization finally abolished. On 26 July, Menzies sent a note to Sir Charles Portal to be read to a meeting of the Chiefs of Staff Committee of the War Cabinet.[36] The purpose of Memo CX 108, 'based on reports from most secret sources, on the situation of certain of the Resistance groups in France', was to direct opinion towards MI6's view that the SOE had no proper control over its affairs in France and ought to be restructured as a sub-section of MI6. A copy of Memo CX 108 was sent to a highly embarrassed Gubbins, by then the Head of SOE, who recovered quickly enough to challenge Menzies' view 'that at the present moment Resistance groups are at their lowest ebb and cannot be counted on as a serious factor unless and until they are rebuilt on a smaller and sounder basis'. Gubbins countered by claiming that the 'groups under [our] own direct control have not been penetrated by the enemy to any serious extent'.[37]

Gubbins had fallen into a trap. On 1 August, a Joint Intelligence Sub-Committee pronounced that on the basis of Memo CX 108 and despite Gubbins' protestations, they were forced to the view that SOE had been less than frank in their reports about their situation in France. Moreover, because the JIC had been obliged to learn the truth from MI6, they felt doubly disappointed with SOE, who had a responsibility to keep them and the Chiefs of Staff informed. After reiterating the tenet that wherever the two organizations' interests coincided, MI6's should always prevail, they concluded that if SOE and MI6, 'formed part of the same hierarchy ... under the Ministry of Defence, we cannot believe that the information regarding the situation in France would have failed to have reached the Chiefs of Staff before now, nor that when it did reach them they would have had only half the story'.[38]

They went on to recommend the Chiefs of Staff to consider just such a reorganization. The SOE were not only fighting for survival in France, but in Whitehall too.

XIV

Cockade

One of the first rumours that circulated soon after news of the PROSPER disaster had spread was that Francis Suttill had been very lax in his security measures; that virtually the whole PROSPER network had been terribly amateur and had more or less invited German attention. That view has been sustained in a great many accounts and histories. I can find no evidence to support it. Of course there were lapses and small indiscretions, as there were in the very best networks, but it seems to me there are a great many apocryphal stories of carelessness and indiscretion that have been incorporated as fact in the SOE canon.

The premature collapse of the PROSPER network came as a surprise to John Bevan at the London Controlling Section. He had hoped it would survive right up to D-Day and beyond. No one, except perhaps Dansey, had any idea how badly compromised it was. Consequently, PROSPER's departure from the scene created a gap in that part of Bevan's scheme to promote COCKADE – with still two months to go. Most people who knew how PROSPER was being used to promote COCKADE naturally presumed that the increase in the network's activity to cope with all the arms drops was the only reason for its collapse. Déricourt's involvement was still a watertight secret. In a particularly insensitive approach, senior officers in SOE were asked if they thought they could contribute something to fill the gap left by PROSPER.

A directive was sent from COSSAC inviting the Political Warfare Executive (PWE, the black propaganda organization) to collaborate with the SOE in a scheme it was hoped would, on the one hand, support COCKADE, and on the other cope with the sort of disasters that had befallen PROSPER. It seems odd in retrospect, but SOE were very enthusiastic about contributing to COCKADE.

On 13 July, three weeks after PROSPER's arrest and a week after the news had been circulated, a top secret meeting was called at the War Office to discuss and draw up new security instructions for STARKEY.[1] Bevan was present and hinted that a joint plan was being created by PWE and SOE that would hopefully prevent the occurrence of similar disasters. By 18 July, five days before Bodington's departure to France, the joint PWE/SOE plan was presented to Morgan's HQ. It described their objectives:

(i) To counter the repercussions of STARKEY upon the patriotic armies (Resistance) of Europe.
(ii) To counteract the effects of the enemy's counter-propaganda which will doubtless present the outcome of STARKEY as a failure to invade.

They suggested that by producing a steady flow of false messages and BBC broadcasts they would present the Germans with a picture of the Resistance 'subject to the strictest discipline derived from the Allied High Command' as being fully prepared to 'rise-up' when commanded – or, likewise, 'stay their hand'.

One of the most alarming aspects of the plan was to deliberately mislead the BBC into reporting false stories. 'The BBC should be treated as an unconscious agent of deception, i.e. that it should react to the news and inspired leakages created by the forthcoming operations in a normal and uninformed way.' This could be very dangerous.

The BBC held a very important responsibility during the war for broadcasting informed and impartial reports of the war to an audience both at home and abroad desperate for the truth. It was also the agency through which SOE delivered its 'personal messages' to the agents in the field. It seemed as though no one had properly considered the harm this new proposal might cause in the long term, when genuine BBC messages would be crucial.

But this was only the beginning. The PWE and SOE also felt they had a positive contribution to make to the prosecution of COCKADE, 'by producing the symptoms of underground activity, prior to D-Day, which the enemy would naturally look for as a prelude to a real invasion'. 'SOE would produce a number of subversive operations on a scale sufficient to disturb and confuse the enemy, but be so devised as not to provoke premature uprisings.'

This would be achieved, they said, by repeatedly warning the Resistance by means of broadcasts to 'stay their hand until given the order to rise'.[2] This was incredibly confusing. First, the SOE would be carrying out operations of 'considerable scale to disturb the enemy', then at the same time their agents would be told to 'stay their hand'. The safety clause was this: seven days before the fictitious D–Day, leaflets and broadcasts would alert the Resistance that the operation had just been an exercise. It was precisely what had been attempted with PROSPER, but with the added features of a guarantee of discipline.

PWE and SOE were so confident about their scheme, that in conclusion they added a piece of hard sell, suggesting that unless they were allowed to make their contribution,'…COCKADE might lack the full colour of authenticity'.[3]

General Morgan was utterly confused by the plan and its stated objectives. He sent copies of it to the Chiefs of Staff, with a typically amusing memo:

> …Now where are we?
> You will see that PWE suggests leading the BBC up the garden path and refers to the press going the same way.
> Now for pity's sake, tell me who tells who what and when, and what he expects them to believe anyway. I refuse to see anybody in the information world about any of this until I am absolutely clear as to what it is all about, which looks to me like being never.[4]

The Chiefs of Staff perceptively noted, 'Our disciplinary control over the Resistance groups in occupied territories might fail and the groups might take premature action … and be subjected to severe reprisals.'[5] For those who cared to notice, their comments echoed a similar warning set out by the Army Intelligence officers in May.

By August the stories had begun to trickle into the press. United Press International proudly revealed, 'An official source states that the Allies will move against Germany by the autumn and the race for Berlin is on ... Signs multiply that the Allies may land in Italy and France within the next month.'[6]

Suddenly newspapers all over the world joined in the chorus. The *New York Times* ran a banner headline, 'ARMIES READY TO GO' SAYS EISENHOWER.[7]

And again, the United Press' source in London told them, 'French underground leaders were revealed today to be confidently expecting an early invasion of France ... there was widespread speculation in Great Britain that zero hour for the assault on Western Europe was approaching.'[8]

On 17 August, the day Claude de Baissac and Bodington returned from France with the SCIENTIST network destroyed, the BBC broadcast the following:

> ...the liberation of the occupied countries has begun. We are obviously not going to reveal where the blow will fall. All those elements that are to contribute in any way whatsoever to the success of operations on French metropolitan territory must be fully equipped to carry out their task. You must prepare yourself, day by day and week by week, for the role you will have to play at a future date, which may be near, in the liberation of your country.[9]

The BBC had also broadcast a series of 'personal messages' that alerted the Resistance to expect the invasion within a fortnight. Drops of arms and equipment had not abated. In July 2200 Sten guns were dropped, in August 7378. The number of pistols went up from 445 to 1740, grenades from 2780 to 9527 and incendiaries from 6533 to 13,288.[10]

The USAF conducted over 200 heavy bomber sorties over the Cap Gris-Nez/Boulogne area while vast numbers of troops were deployed in peculiar mobilization exercises. The 59th Staffordshire Infantry Division recorded in its *War Story*, 'Tented camps sprang up all over Kent and the roads became littered with direction and location signs. All contact with civilian population and the outside world was forbidden.'[11]

At Avenue Foch, every signal was being monitored and digested. Boemelburg and Kieffer marked off the calendar day by day. They were working round the clock, processing all the interrogations of the enormous numbers of people pouring into the prisons. Kieffer's view had prevailed, and arrests had become a priority. 'The more men we brought in before September, the fewer would support the Allies on D-Day.' Boemelburg's major preoccupation was convincing Von Runstedt, Commander of the German Forces in the West, that the intelligence he had received in July was accurate and that all the subsequent signs confirmed it. On this one point, the withering figure of the Abwehr was in complete agreement with the SD.[12]

Von Runstedt was not anxious, but cautious. He had initially found the reports of a planned invasion in 1943 unconvincing. He was confident that the Allies had so many resources already committed in the Mediterranean that another major operation in the same year was unlikely. He was not prepared to start calling up reserves. But Boemelburg would not give up and Von Runstedt was peppered with reports from the SD that the Allies were more than able to launch a cross-Channel operation of ominous size. The next few weeks would test his nerves.

However, in London, the earliest intelligence reports were already claiming that COCKADE had failed. On 14 August, an Army Intelligence review headed: *Enemy Order of Battle in the West* revealed,

> ...at no time before have [German] troops in Brittany been so thin on the ground.
>
> The Germans have ... dispatched one division (113) to Russia. It would appear, therefore, that whilst STARKEY had caused minor reactions in the increase of photographic reconnaisance over this country, the operation at present cannot be considered to have constituted a sufficiently serious threat to contain even the normal number of German divisions in the west.[13]

Added to which, a concerned and influential number of Army Intelligence officers, devastated by reports of the chaos in France, renewed their attacks and were lobbying for the whole thing to be called off. Already nearly a thousand members of the Resistance were languishing in prison.

With the reports from France getting worse, General Morgan was furious at the way the press reporting had got completely out of hand. PWE had actually overdone it. There was too much news about an invasion, whereas in reality one would expect there to be none at all. On 20 August, Colonel Bevan called an emergency meeting to deal with the disquiet over the press and the BBC broadcasts. COSSAC, PWE and SOE were represented, the latter being particularly concerned about morale and keen to transmit to their people that 'it was just an exercise'. But Bevan wasn't keen to stop the carnival yet. A compromise was reached whereby the 'Be ready' broadcasts were replaced with a series of 'Be calm, today is not the day' broadcasts.[14]

Confidential advice was sent to all newspaper editors explaining why a clampdown on all press speculation should occur. The most embarrassing element of this back-tracking was the way in which the BBC was rescued from ignominy. It was decided to blame the enemy. It broadcast:

> Be careful of German provocations. We have learnt that the Germans are circulating inspired rumours that we are concentrating armies on our coast with the intention of invading the continent. Take no notice, as these provocations are intended to create among you a situation where you may be caught. Lay low! Be careful! Do only what you are told to do by the BBC.[15]

Then, less than three weeks before 'D-Day', MI6 reported a change in German attitudes. A few cracks had begun to show. On 13 August, Hitler had redeployed the 25th Panzer from Norway to France. Photo-reconnaisance was stepped up, and Von Runstedt had revised his contingency plans for the deployment of reserves. On 23 August, he wrote in his weekly report that arms drops to the Resistance in August were already twice those for July; and for the very first time that year, he used the term '*Zweiten Front*'. It was possible COCKADE might work after all.[16]

It was touch and go. In London, opinion still seemed to be swinging strongly towards calling it off. General Morgan suggested as much on 2 September, 'Up to date enemy reactions to our operations have not been sufficient to justify the laying on of the final phase of STARKEY.'[17]

If Morgan was serious about cancelling COCKADE-STARKEY, then no one had informed SOE about it. They still had networks in northern France that were expecting a fleet of landing craft off the Calais coast in a week's time. An essential part of their contribution towards COCKADE was being able to broadcast to their groups nine to seven days before 'D-Day' that it had all been an exercise. With less than four days to go they were getting very jumpy.

On 3 September, the operational section of COSSAC received a handwritten memo from their intelligence section, reminding them of the understanding with SOE. An anxious Colonel Rowlandson from SOE had been in touch to inform COSSAC that they had recently been ordered *not* to inform their networks that it had been an exercise.

> Col Rowlandson states that there are at present no signs of an upheaval, but if the Boche get into a panic, it will probably communicate itself to the patriots.
>
> Although all is quiet at present, Col Rowlandson could give no guarantees and he would like to be able to give his boys a line as soon as possible.[18]

In the meantime, MI6 reported '*The German Secret Service considers cross-Channel operation imminent.*'[19]

On 7 September, Dr Josef Götz intercepted a BBC 'personal message' that contained the secret codeword for a large-scale uprising meant to coincide with the invasion. Pandemonium broke out at Avenue Foch. Telephone calls were made to Kopkow in Berlin. Boemelburg was triumphant – the codeword had originally been passed to him by Déricourt. But would Von Runstedt believe them? Boemelburg called him personally. Kieffer sent a report by car to St Germain-des-Pres, Von Runstedt's headquarters.[20]

On 'D-Day' itself, a fleet of 95 landing craft, escorted by two naval vessels, left port at 06.30 hours filled with troops and equipment. The armada set sail for the Pas de Calais. The sun shone brightly, there was a slight swell. A cine-cameraman had recorded in loving detail the process of loading the artillery and other equipment. Then during the lull before the storm, he busied himself taking shots of rugged-looking Tommies glaring out to sea, or the anti-aircraft batteries scanning the sky for German aircraft.[21]

In the Kent countryside, the 59th Staffordshire Infantry suddenly got the order to move out.

> When units began to move, they found themselves passing with unusual smoothness right through the system of staging camps. The anti-climax came when we reached the sea, we marched down to the shore – and about turned. That must have confused the Jerries.[22]

In the English Channel, the armada waited. Not one German aircraft flew overhead. Not one shore battery opened fire. Nothing happened at all. There was just the sound of the engines and the sea-wash. Then at around 10.00 am, a German radar station near Calais that had been out of action all morning, began to pick up faint traces of the invasion fleet. Later, a spotter plane confirmed... that it was sailing back to England.

The bare facts were that COCKADE had been devised, in lieu of a real invasion, with the purpose of pinning German forces in the west, whereas precisely the opposite had occurred. From April through to December 1943, there was an unstaunched flow of trained front-line troops from France to Italy, the Balkans and Russia – 27 divisions in all. A post-mortem reported that the Germans had clearly perceived STARKEY for what it was, a deception. But the truth was the Germans didn't perceive it at all – and certainly not as a deception until they heard the BBC announce, 'a major invasion rehearsal in the English Channel today'. Apart from the SD, German attention was elsewhere – in fact, at the precise spot from which COCKADE had been designed to draw it: the Russian Front. The only consolation that could be retrieved from the ashes was the fact that the Sicherheitsdienst had been utterly convinced of an imminent invasion.

–

COCKADE failed to convince the Germans for a number of reasons, but perhaps the single most significant factor was the premature collapse of PROSPER. Following the arrests in France in July, Hitler was utterly convinced there would be no invasion in 1943.

Kopkow had received almost daily reports from Kieffer and Boemelburg, cataloguing their remarkable successes in the field. Berlin was at first incredulous and then ecstatic at the vast numbers of men and women Kieffer was hauling into prison. Then there was the massive amount of arms and munitions that had been uncovered and were being shipped east to the Russian Front. No one in Berlin had ever imagined a secret army could be that large.

Hitler made the perfectly intelligible observation that PROSPER must have been meant to play a vital role in the Allied invasion. In one of the cruellest ironies of the war, the Fuhrer concluded that once the network had been eliminated, the Allies' invasion prospects were shattered.[23]

XV

Denunciation

The events of that June and July became a spectre that haunted Déricourt for years. He once wrote, 'Why is it that I am neither mad nor dead?'[1] Frager had spread rumours about him among the other resisters and he had taken to carrying a pistol whenever he left the apartment. Nevertheless, he still expected to be around for at least another year and somehow managed to maintain the absolute confidence of his chief in London. 'If they lose me, they'd never find anyone else to do this work.' His life settled into a regular routine again, though with one small alteration.

Dr Josef Götz had been drawn into the PROSPER campaign, first as an administrator who organized the surveillance groups of Déricourt's operations, then later, he was drawn in deeper because of his talent for conjuring with captured radio sets. In July, he was introduced to GILBERT himself. Kieffer and his staff were so stretched coping with all the arrests, there was no one else to oversee the regular meetings. Götz was extremely flattered to be included in something which everyone in Avenue Foch knew was Top Secret. But by the same token, he was a little frightened by the prospect of meeting such a famous double agent.[2]

Götz's instructions were very precise. He had to establish a link with GILBERT – a telephone number, through which they could arrange their meetings at one of the apartments. At each meeting he had to take the details of incoming flights, the date, the place, the number of aircraft etc. Then he had to telephone the Luftwaffe and anti-aircraft units, give them the details of each flight and ensure they didn't attack it. Then he had to write a report for Kieffer.

Once he had explained everything, Kieffer leant forward, crossed his two index fingers and held them in front of Götz. 'Boemelburg and GILBERT are like that. Boemelburg thinks GILBERT will make our fortune for us in Berlin. Kopkow speaks of him with Himmler and everyone. Who knows, perhaps he will make us famous?' Kieffer admitted he had never actually met GILBERT, 'but even so, I don't like him and I don't trust him'.[3]

Götz understood immediately that he was just another face to GILBERT, someone to whom he passed the small stuff, the trifles; while Boemelburg received the important material at his meetings with GILBERT in Neuilly.[4] Götz also appreciated that the meetings between GILBERT and Boemelburg were very regular and in private, so he would have to watch his step.

The routine began with a phone call from Boemelburg, 'GILBERT, tomorrow.' Götz would walk to the flat, let himself in and wait. GILBERT would arrive a little later; there would be a few words of conversation and then immediately down to business.

Götz soon developed a genuine admiration for Déricourt:

> …A real agent, a true professional. He spoke carefully, infrequently and not before he had considered the whole question.
>
> [Metaphorically] … he was a man who always seemed to look around himself before moving and when you spoke with him, you had his complete attention.

He found him very personable, 'but without offering anything of himself'. Götz's admiration quickly turned to fascination.

To Déricourt, Götz was always simply 'the Doctor'. Though when in an expansive mood he once uttered, 'no enemy of the middle class'.

One long hot summer's day in August, Götz arrived at the flat and had removed his jacket and placed it over the back of a chair. He was not permitted to open the windows or shutters and as a result the place was like an oven. GILBERT arrived and followed Götz down the corridor into the living room, but before they could get down to business the telephone rang. Götz excused himself and went to answer it. While he was out of the room, Déricourt reached into Götz's jacket pocket and took out his wallet. He carefully removed every single item, examined and returned it, slipping the wallet back into the jacket.

When Götz returned they concluded their business and GILBERT left. He always left first. A few minutes later Götz was stepping out of the flat and wondering about buying a beer before returning to Avenue Foch. When he opened his wallet he noticed that all the contents had been disturbed. He tried to think of how to explain it to Keiffer. 'It was all there, just in the wrong order.'

'Of course,' said Kieffer. 'What do you expect? I told you not to trust him.'[5]

Just three days after he had dispatched Bodington and the de Baissacs to London, Déricourt organized another Hudson operation at a new field down at Soucelles near Angers. It was a massive operation – altogether ten people were expected to converge on that little patch of meadow. In Paris, some were lodged in JuJu's pied-à-terre while others, like Tony Brooks, found their own accommodation. Brooks was the organizer of a remarkably effective and secure little network called PIMENTO. He met up with Déricourt to get the details of the operation and was immediately subjected to an irritating barrage of questions.

'Aren't you the organizer of PIMENTO?'

Brooks claimed he was just a courier returning to London for some dental work.

'Where are you staying? When did you arrive? When do you expect to return from London?' Brooks was incredulous but said nothing. He took the details of their rendezvous and departed.[6]

On the night of the operation, with just half an hour to spare, Brooks, Déricourt and Clément turned up and began to lay out all the torches. Unknown to Brooks, in the bushes lay hidden the entire SPRUCE group – Marchand, Boiteaux, Regnier; G. Gerson, VIC; Octave Simon, SATIRIST – one of the sub-circuits connected to PROSPER; Robert Benoist, co-organizer of the CHESTNUT group, south-west of Paris, caught up in the PROSPER *rafle* (Benoist had just escaped from the SD); Madame Le Chêne, courier to the PLANE network down in Clermont Ferrand.

Once the Hudson was down, just one passenger emerged while the others made their way towards the shuddering mass of machine. Halfway across to the aircraft, they became aware of a herd of bullocks that had been grazing at one end of the field and had now begun slowly moving towards them. The noise of the engines and all the movement finally started a stampede. Everyone was rooted to the spot with fear. Déricourt's major concern was the aircraft, which could have been torn to shreds by one of the crazed beasts. Miraculously, no harm was done to man or machine and the outgoing passengers climbed aboard. At the last minute, however, the operation was held up by Madame Le Chêne, who found it difficult, in her fashionable dress, to get her leg up high enough to reach the bottom of the ladder.

Brooks surveyed the scene for a moment or two but could see only one solution. He planted his shoulder beneath the woman's buttocks, straightened up – and Madame Le Chêne shot into the Hudson to a chorus of 'Bravo!'[7] It was an incident the Bony-LaFont men neglected to mention in their report. They also lost sight of the single incoming agent, who had not waited for Déricourt's assistance – and when the Hudson had gone, so had he.

Soon after that operation Clément paid a visit to Madame Menon in Tours, to deliver a message. She was the headmistress of the little school where, back in April, Frager and his party were disturbed by the SD. Curiously, they were disturbed again. Without warning, a squad of SD men turned up, charged into the schoolhouse and arrested everyone.[8] When the news reached Déricourt that Rémy had been arrested, he telephoned Boemelburg, demanding he be released immediately. Boemelburg told him to be calm, Clément would be free soon. The local SD commander was contacted and the entire party was released within two days. Clément was seriously shaken by the ordeal and described in graphic detail for Henri every moment as it had happened. Déricourt took the whole thing seriously too and planted Clément on the next flight to London.

There had been no SOE operations anywhere near the COCKADE-STARKEY 'D-Day'. Déricourt's next operation was exactly a month after the last. Outgoing with Clément were Colonel Zeller, Ben Cowburn, Goldsmith and a couple of Polish couriers. Incoming were Yolande Beckman, wireless operator to the MUSICIAN group near St Quentin; Harry Peuleve, new organizer of the AUTHOR group; H. Despaigne, courier for the DETECTIVE group; and a Gaullist agent called H. d'Evaigner. All were discreetly tailed by the SD's agents. Déricourt's arrangement was operating just as smoothly as ever. You would think PROSPER had never happened.

Clément returned on a Lysander on 16/17 October and brought with him six small diamonds from SOE, which Déricourt sold on the black market. He also brought with him the dapper little figure of André Watt, who had been assigned to FARRIER as Déricourt's official radio operator. Watt and Clément standing side by side were a comic sight; Rémy stood a full head and shoulders above the diminutive radio operator. He quickly settled into the FARRIER team and flourished under numerous nicknames, from 'Tich' to the imaginative 'demi-Watt'. André became another for whom Déricourt arranged protection. He took Watt to the Bar Lorraine at the Place des Ternes, where he 'displayed' him for the benefit of Boemelburg's men. In fact Déricourt took a lot of trouble to protect his team. Radio operators were particularly vulnerable. SOE's radio sets had by Watt's time evolved down to the size of a small valise though they were still pretty weighty objects. Carrying the device was always a tense operation, for although it looked completely innocent, anyone could be subjected to a spot check by the Feldgendarmerie and being discovered with one was the end of the line. How could one explain it? Déricourt never allowed Watt to carry the set. Though Watt always assumed it as part of his responsibilities, Déricourt wouldn't argue and simply took the thing and strode off.[9]

Unfortunately, just when Déricourt had begun to think the whole thing was becoming too easy, Henri Frager raised his head again. Hugo Bleicher, still masquerading as Colonel Heinrich, continued to meet with Bardet and Frager. At one of these meetings he told Frager that he'd seen copies of some of his July mail which had passed across from Avenue Foch. It was mail that Frager had given to GILBERT to send to London. Frager exploded. He resolved to go to London and blow the whistle on Déricourt.

By October the bar in Rue St André des Arts was now functioning as planned. Three homeward-bound agents had approached Besnard and asked if GILBERT could get them back to London. Besnard gave each of them a password that would identify them to Déricourt. At one of these rendezvous, Déricourt was surprised to discover that one of the passengers was none other than Roger Bardet. He was delighted with the prospect of shovelling this one onto an aircraft to London. He told Bardet to catch the evening train down to Angers where he would be met at the station at about nine.

Having inspected the field first, Déricourt and Clément cycled back to Angers and their rendezvous. Bardet and four others stood waiting inside the Angers station doors: Francis Nearne, brother to the more famous Jacqueline Nearne; Alexander Levy who was a chief engineer with the French Public Works; N. LePrince, a Gaullist agent; and Bardet.

Déricourt liked to kill time before operations at a little café in the town square. As the party walked across the square, Déricourt noticed that Bardet seemed to be lagging behind. He stopped to wait for him to catch up and then noticed that behind Bardet, lurking in the shadows, was Henri Frager. There was nothing Frager could do, but shuffle forward and be confronted. As the two Henris glared at each other, Déricourt accused Frager of stalking one of his operations. Frager denied it, but then admitted that in fact he was the one meant to be flying to London, not Bardet.

Déricourt put it all together in a flash. Because Frager didn't trust him, he'd sent Bardet to make all the arrangements and then had hoped at the last moment to slip himself onto the aircraft in Bardet's place.

Déricourt was furious. 'How dare you tell someone else the password!'

By this stage Clément had stopped to see what the disturbance was about. He ushered the other passengers into the restaurant and then approached the belligerents. He had never seen Déricourt lose his temper before and it must have been a sight to behold. Through clenched teeth, Déricourt explained the situation to Clément who was equally infuriated but had the presence of mind to realize that the middle of the town square was not the place to discuss it. Levy now joined the scene, intervening just at the point when fists were about to be thrown and the police called.

The group of hotheads moved inside the restaurant and sat silently through their meal, during which time Déricourt had gathered his thoughts and tried to rescue something from the fiasco. He suggested that as both men knew the password, both should be transported to London. Bardet nearly spilt his soup. The argument flared up again and the patron despaired lest the police should arrive. The other passengers too had become distressed at the apparently unremitting dispute. Bardet had no intention of setting foot on British soil.

As far as the other passengers were concerned, this was a battle between Déricourt and Frager over protocol and passwords. They were completely unaware of the delicately balanced game of bluff that hinged on what each knew – or did not know about the other. There was a great deal more at stake than simply the success of the operation.

Having reached a stalemate again, Déricourt changed the subject and instructed everyone where to assemble, close to the field. Three hours later, six figures stood together at the break in a hedge that bordered the field. Clément dashed off across the open space to organize the torches when from behind him he could hear drifting voices. The row had errupted once more.

It was interrupted by the drone of the Hudson, banking away to the west. After the great machine had thumped and thudded its way to a halt, Déricourt helped first Levy, then LePrince and Nearne into the aircraft. Then finally Frager helped himself aboard. Suddenly Déricourt took hold of Bardet and heaved him bodily towards the doorway. It was hopeless; the door was some two or three feet above the ground and it would have taken two men to hoist him up.

Déricourt and Bardet struggled bitterly, their voices drowned by the roaring engine, while the pilot waited for the thumbs-up. Bardet kicked and screamed, flailing his arms in all directions until finally he managed to get away from Déricourt. Clément didn't know what to do. Déricourt turned back to the aircraft and looked up at Frager, now standing in the doorway – hand outstretched; not to help someone aboard, but to shake Déricourt's hand. He had won. Déricourt turned away. Clément rushed forward, clasped Frager's hand and, having checked everyone inside was secure, closed the door.[10]

Meanwhile Déricourt's attention had switched to Bardet, now a receding figure in the gloom. His hand closed round his pistol; he would never have a better opportunity to be rid of him. But he paused – Déricourt had realized in time that Bardet's death would mean his own end. There was nothing he could do about Frager now and so long as he remained in London, Bardet was insured. After all, there were the three incoming agents to be looked after and the sight of someone being shot would hardly have been an advertisement for Déricourt's services.

Frager's debriefing by security officers at Baker Street began the day after his return to London and lasted four days. He began at the beginning, describing the very first operation where his party were disturbed at Madame Menon's schoolhouse, then expanding he described how over the summer a number of operations to recover dropped arms and equipment were foiled by the presence of Germans, apparently alerted to the location of the drop-zones. Then, closing in on the meat of his subject, he introduced and described the enigmatic figure of Colonel Heinrich and the information that Déricourt was an agent of the SD and was giving them the mail that SOE's agents had entrusted to him. The clincher for Frager was that Heinrich had learnt that Bodington had warned GILBERT immediately after his meeting with Frager and that somehow the SD were aware that Déricourt's codename had been changed to CLAUDE. Following Frager's lengthy de-brief, SOE's security section decided to instigate a proper investigation into Déricourt. The security section was headed by an MI5 officer called John Sentor, seconded to the SOE to provide a little professional expertise in that department.

Before him was Déricourt's entire SOE file, beginning with MI5's initial report received 23 November 1942 stating they would not recommend him for employment. That of course had been countered by Bodington's own personal recommendation. Subsequently there was the report from MI5 in April, which stated that Déricourt was known to have had contacts with the Germans in Paris after the French Armistice and to which MI5 had commented, 'This seems very dangerous.' Bodington had dealt with that one by dismissing it as 'typical French back-biting'. Then another report dated 11 June, from a Belgian source, stating that when Déricourt was in London he talked freely of his work in France. Then on 18 June MI5 sent yet another report, which again came from the French and which claimed that the Gestapo knew about Déricourt and were going to try and use him. This was quashed by Déricourt and Bodington between them. Finally there was Bodington's stirring testimonial delivered in the report of his trip to Paris. If Sentor appreciated that any pattern had developed between the MI5 reports and Bodington's comments, he chose not to express it on paper. (There now began a long struggle between SOE's security section, which was simply trying to do its job and protect SOE operations, and various forces ranged against them. Some of these were innocent, others were not.)

Sentor's principal difficulty with the case was that Buckmaster considered *both* Frager and Déricourt completely reliable. In fact Déricourt's record had been particularly good, given all the chaos of the PROSPER collapse. To Buckmaster especially, Déricourt had shone like a beacon of light while all around was dark and destroyed. In his final analysis, Sentor was forced to conclude, in the absence of any evidence to substantiate Frager's statement, that it was just 'one agent's word against another's'. It was formally noted that the matter of Frager's statement would constitute not an accusation, but a denunciation. However, Sentor perceptively concluded, 'If he is a traitor, he won't cause any substantial casualty. The enemy won't want to lose him so won't compromise him.'[11] Sentor passed the report to Archie Boyle, the man who had sponsored Déricourt into the SOE. Boyle annotated it, 'Most disturbing.'

When the report reached Buckmaster there clearly developed a private struggle between what was implied in the report and what Buckmaster felt 'in his guts' – that Déricourt was completely reliable. All agents passing through Déricourt's hands were advised to consider him a security risk and avoid all unnecessary contact. So long as he remained 'a vital link in the transport system' he would remain in place. If however any of his operations should result in the arrest of agents in the field then, '…he should be liquidated on the spot'.[12]

But at precisely the same time as the security section were looking into Déricourt's record, moves were afoot to quash any doubts there might have been about '*l'homme qui fait les pick-ups*'. Since the beginning of October there had been a sniff of a rumour that Déricourt was being recommended for a DSO. Later it was confirmed that, indeed, he was to be cited for the Distinguished Service Order. This was news of very great moment. The DSO was an award of extremely high merit and more to the point, it would be SOE's very first DSO. Naturally the news generated a great deal of interest, enhanced Déricourt's image somewhat and perhaps even cloaked his work in a kind of mantle of distinction. Now he really was a star. The question was, though, who had recommended him?

Colonel Buckmaster was not behind the recommendation, nor was Bodington. Indeed no one in F Section had anything to do with it. The actual recommendation was written up by Brigadier E. Mockler-Ferryman who was the officer responsible for all operations in north-western Europe. Mockler-Ferryman, or 'The Moke' as he was known, was also not the instigator – he simply wrote it up 'as instructed'. No doubt. But instructed by whom? Just what The Moke wrote is almost as intriguing as the question of its provenance. The citation recognized Déricourt's excellent work in the field and that his technical competence had earned the complete confidence of the RAF's Special Duties Squadron. In addition, it drew particular attention to the fact of his relations with the Germans. It referred to the 'particular difficult and highly dangerous' circumstances in which he operated.

This involves keeping up many very dangerous acquaintances, particularly [though not exclusively] with pilots of the Luftwaffe and Lufthansa. He has been successful in achieving this and in preserving the security of the other members of our organization.[13]

Given the sacrifice of people like Francis Suttill (who received the DSO posthumously), Jack Agazarian, Andrée Borrel and dozens of others, this particular recommendation seems rather to oversell Déricourt's significance within SOE's operations, especially in the light of it being their *first* DSO. It seems perverse, to say the least, that it should have been drawn up at the same time that Frager was accusing Déricourt of working with the Germans. SOE's files do not reveal 'the precise origins of that recommendation'. According to Harry Sporborg, who later became intimately familiar with Déricourt's case, the DSO recommendation did not come from within SOE. If nothing else, one has to commend Claude Dansey's timing.

Despite news of the DSO the security section's concern about Déricourt continued into November and involved Frager's accusation that Déricourt might be passing SOE mail to the Germans. They memoed Buckmaster:

The constant tapping of courier [mail] yields the Gestapo in the long run a far higher dividend than the arrest of a few agents engaged in sabotage, or even the break-up of a whole organization which we can restart

with entirely different personnel, unknown
to the Gestapo.

Buckmaster, perhaps under the influence of the news
that his star man in northern France was in line for
the Section's first DSO, dismissed Sentor's argument, 'I
cannot agree … The courier that might have been seen
by the enemy is of very little practical value.'[14] When flight
after flight, month after month everything Déricourt
touched ran so smoothly, it would have been almost
impossible for Buckmaster to exercise a rigorous examination of other people's doubts. Emerging from the ruins
of PROSPER, the like of which no one in F Section ever
wanted to see again, all the section officers were united in
their admiration for Déricourt. But the doubts continued.

In mid-November, a Gaullist agent named Yeo-
Thomas returned from France and delivered another
report on 'the one who does the pick-ups'. In substance
it seemed to be the same as Frager's. When the security
section interviewed Yeo-Thomas he told them, 'Through
his treachery two men and one woman were arrested in
August.' Security could find no evidence of who these
might have been, and dismissed Yeo-Thomas' report as
'inter-service rivalry'. F Section were determined not to
remove Déricourt from the field.[15]

However the situation in Paris was changing dramatically. Given all the odds against him, it was remarkable that
Déricourt had held out as long as he did, but by October
the writing was on the wall. Significantly, it had nothing
to do with Frager or any other denunciation. Déricourt's
mission began to draw to an end because of a decision
made in Berlin.

Boemelburg had assumed that after the summer's
success, he would be fêted as a hero. Instead, he saw his

stocks fall. There had always existed a degree of tension between himself and Kieffer, whose far more straight-forward approach to his work, obsession with making arrests and filling the prisons had finally won him greater recognition than had Boemelburg's insistence on restraint and pursuing 'the date of the invasion'. One evening in October, Boemelburg entertained Déricourt at Neuilly to explain to him that he was being sent to Vichy, where he was to be given command of the local SD detachment. It was a post that had been enchanced by the added respons-ibility of liaison with Maréchal Pétain. Boemelburg would return to Paris only infrequently, but no longer in charge of counter-sabotage for France. He said candidly, 'I have not been tough enough.'[16]

The atmosphere under Kieffer's reign was very different. There would be no more drives through the Bois de Boulogne, no more quiet little tête-à-têtes, no more confidences. Kieffer wanted the details of the flights and the mail, for which he was prepared to maintain the protection over Déricourt's group. The latter's meet-ings continued with Dr Götz, to whom he gave the details of the next operation: a Hudson down near Angers for the night of 15/16 November. Déricourt had been instructed to expect five incoming passengers. In and around various addresses, Déricourt had secreted nearly a dozen personnel on the run. Amongst them were Francis Cammaearts and Chartrand from the JOCKEY group, four colleagues of Ben Cowburn – Mulsant, Johnny Barrett, Rechenmann, Madame Fontaine; and the current President of France, François Mitterrand.

In one other aspect the relationship was different. Kieffer now insisted that in future he and his men must be allowed actually on to the field to watch the operation. He didn't trust Déricourt an inch. On the night in question, a group of SD men huddled under their camouflage bushes peering into the dark with their night-binoculars. They watched Wing Commander Hodges bring his Hudson down to the row of lights, and taxi to a halt. Out of the aircraft stepped Gerson to start another mission, Captain Jean Menesson, André Maugenet, Paul Pardi, Lieutenant Eugène Levene and Captain Fille-Lambie. As Fille-Lambie stepped out he recognized his colleague Mitterrand stepping in and there was a brief embrace. The outgoing group boarded the aircraft and it was off the ground within eight minutes.

Déricourt took three of the newcomers who bicycled with him to the little station of Tiercé. There they caught the train from Angers to Le Mans, calling at Ettriche on the way. Clément with the other three boarded the train at this point. At Le Mans they all changed trains and Fille-Lambie left the party to make his way down to Rennes.

As they waited for the Paris express, Déricourt recognized a group of men who had been on the train since Angers. The heavy raincoats, hands thrust deep into their pockets – they were Kieffer's men. Déricourt had warned his group to avoid displaying any signs of mutual recognition and to spread themselves out along the carriages. The SD did precisely the same. It was all very heavy handed and had all the hallmarks of a disaster. Déricourt warned Clément and together they warned each of their passengers that the SD's agents were on the train. That was all they could do.

At the Gare Montparnasse Déricourt and Clément took their time getting off, watching the carriages slowly empty. Then down on the platform they noticed a scuffle taking place in the crowd ahead. They watched as Menesson, Maugenet and Pardi were arrested. Levene and Gerson got away.[17]

Déricourt could not survive any more operations like that. His mission was coming to an end. Meanwhile, Jeannot had heard from her relatives of a plot of land that was up for sale down in the Midi — its price was two million francs.[18]

XVI

Arrangements

From Broadway Buildings, Claude Dansey could look out across a view of Green Park strewn with copper-coloured leaves. He had just been in conference with Menzies about two recently received decrypts, one from ULTRA and the other from American sources. Both decrypts were of Adolf Hitler's most recent military command for the defence of the West. Dated 2 November, Directive 51 outlined plans to strengthen the Atlantic Wall, re-fortify aircraft and submarine resources and build up well-equipped and seasoned units that could be mobilized to 'throw the enemy back into the sea'. The September invasion threat long gone, the Germans were now preparing themselves for the most obvious, '...an offensive against the Western Front of Europe no later than spring, and perhaps earlier'.[1]

It could hardly have escaped Dansey's notice how dramatically his war had altered since 1939 when he stood at the helm of the Z Organization. Now, Stewart Menzies had in his hand two copies of Hitler's most recent directive, 18 days after it had been promulgated. The major headache with this new form of intelligence was not one of acquisition, but of digestion for quantity had arrived with quality. The success of ULTRA — of signals intelligence in general, of photo-reconnaissance and all the other scientific developments, had slowly eroded the value of the 'network' of agents.

As 1944 and the invasion crept closer, Dansey was beginning to appreciate what others had realized long before – that the 'man in the field' was not a war winner anymore. He might in future play a much more specialist role, like advanced tactical intelligence, but his heyday was over. Dansey's immense influence within the 'community' had begun to wane and the young intellectuals seemed a lot less deferential. While Menzies had got his 'K' in the New Year's honours and was riding high on ULTRA, Dansey had begun to be seen for what he was, an anachronism – a man out of his time whose methods no longer had a place in the modern service. Frankly, he was becoming something of a liability.

During September and October there had been a series of particularly vitriolic rows with SOE that had still not been resolved. All year long Major-General Gubbins had kept up a campaign of attacks against Dansey, having somehow got it into his head that Dansey was interfering with SOE's networks. Gubbins' meetings with Menzies were invariably fruitless – especially as Menzies could always swear with his hand on his heart that he knew nothing about any of Dansey's alleged improprieties. Menzies had neither the will nor the inclination to ease Dansey from his job and remained loyal to his deputy throughout the war. In the meantime, with the help of Déricourt's intelligence, Menzies and Dansey were waging a successful campaign to have SOE in Europe shut down.

Following the meetings with the Combined Chiefs in August and September concerning Menzies' Memo CX

108, the Joint Intelligence Committee recommended that SOE's activities should cease immediately and that the organization be liquidated, or absorbed into MI6. (The JIC came to that conclusion in December, encouraged by strong representations from the RAF that aircraft and resources currently supplying SOE networks in France would be more usefully deployed in support of the bombing of Germany. But the JIC were unable to proceed any further with their recommendation because Winston Churchill was abroad and it was felt only he could make the final decision. In the event, Churchill reprieved SOE.)[2] While all this was still in the balance, Gubbins made a concerted effort to have the Dansey thorn finally removed from their side. He was aware of the stakes and appreciated the limit of his influence on the Chiefs of Staff, but nevertheless if he could stick a crow-bar under Dansey and force him out, then he would. SOE shared with MI6 a liaison officer in the United States, in the person of Sir William Stephenson. 'Little Bill' Stephenson flew to London each month for consultations with both organizations and was regularly obliged to listen to Gubbins' long harangues about Dansey. Unlike Menzies, Stephenson was a sympathetic audience. He had known Dansey since 1930, had long been sickened by his machiavellian methods and was now one of a growing number of people within the service who wanted to see the old man go. Gubbins wrote to Stephenson a cry for help:

> Since I told you about the Dansey menace
> in May and you talked with Stewart about it,
> Dansey has somehow accelerated his jabbing
> interference to the point that I am losing

> good men. I would be grateful if you would
> help me put a stop to his actions.[3]

Stephenson flew to London on 1 October to meet Gubbins. Afterwards he organized a series of meetings with other prominent people within the intelligence community: Sir Robert Bruce Lockhart, Director General of the Political Warfare Executive (PWE); Guy Liddell, MI5; and Desmond Morton, Churchill's special adviser on intelligence matters. Finally he called on Stewart Menzies to lay what facts he had before him. Menzies was an honest man, but he found it hard to stomach one of his own officers running an errand for the SOE. The meeting became heated and when Stephenson sensed he might not succeed, he threatened to pay a call on SOE's own Godfather – Winston Churchill.

Menzies angrily agreed that Dansey's interference would cease from that moment, adding that he would take 'whatever action was required to assure compliance'. According to Stephenson, it was as a result of his meeting that Menzies finally asserted his proper authority over Dansey.[4] That may be so, but then it may also have been ill health that caused the 67-year-old Uncle Claude to loosen his grip – but he loosened it only very slightly. He was fully occupied in organizing a new series of networks in preparation for D-Day, while in the meantime he and Menzies still had SOE on the ropes.

With all that in hand, there was the tiresome little problem of Henri Déricourt, who had lost his target Boemelburg and was now fruitlessly giving away information to Kieffer – someone who showed no sign of falling under Déricourt's influence. The Frenchman had to be brought out, but how without revealing Dansey's hand?

After Stephenson's confrontation with Menzies, Dansey could hardly afford to further inflame SOE's sensitivities. Despite what they all said, he was a loyal controller and would not abandon his people. Déricourt would not suffer any recrimination for the consequences of his work. But removing him from the field did pose a problem. The only practical solution would be to force SOE's hand – and make them recall him.

Although in theory very simple, in practice getting F Section to pull Déricourt out would be almost like drawing teeth. SOE's security section had been racked with doubts about the man for months – and they hadn't succeeded in shifting Buckmaster at all. The only way Dansey could force Buckmaster's hand was to pass to the SOE incontrovertible evidence that Déricourt was working with the Germans – and then cope with the consequences afterwards. On 6 December, SOE received a report, passed on from one of Claude Dansey's agents returning from the field. It was similar to a report they had already received in June: 'The Gestapo are trying to get in touch with GILBERT.'[5] Unfortunately, all it did was to confuse SOE's security section. First it wasn't news-worthy and second it employed the old name GILBERT. SOE weren't at all sure it didn't refer to Gilbert Norman. However, the fact that it had come from MI6 gave it a significance the other reports had lacked.

The security section invited MI5 to take a look at Déricourt's case, to which they reluctantly agreed, providing they were not required to take an active role. It would seem that SOE's security people were completely at a loss over the case, but they received no comfort from the inscrutable MI5, whose officers pored over Déricourt's file but declined to comment. If they formed suspicions, they did not share them with SOE.

A month passed and SOE received a communication from Section V, the counter-espionage section of MI6. At the outbreak of war, Section V had been given the task of penetrating the enemy's intelligence groups, the Abwehr and the SD, and revealing their order of battle. Later it formed an effective bridge with MI5 and was responsible (with MI5) for running all the great 'double' agents abroad. Having discussed Déricourt with MI5, Section V requested a meeting with John Sentor at SOE's security section.

At that meeting, on 4 January, the Déricourt file was examined in detail again, but this time the visitors did express an opinion. They made it very clear.

> Déricourt does not have a case to answer. If
> Déricourt comes back he will not return as
> a suspect character but as a victim of denun-
> ciation and must be allowed to answer. The
> original allegation [Frager's] is really a subject
> of denunciation.[6]

Still no decision to bring him out. Then on 13 January, SOE received a message that one of Dansey's agents had recently returned from France and had made an accusation about Déricourt. SOE asked for details and received a report that sounded oddly similar to the one Yeo-Thomas had delivered in November, 'A French Captain in the RAF has been working for the Germans. Through his treachery two men and one woman picked up in August.'[7] It contained a little more circumstantial evidence than the November report and it mentioned a number of

BBC messages that had been used in connection with Déricourt. But the security section were not convinced. They requested a copy of the agent's actual report and for permission to meet with the agent himself. (Perhaps they sensed there was something slightly bogus about these reports.)

It took a week for a copy of the report to arrive and nearly two weeks for permission to debrief one of Dansey's agents. Finally on 26 January, Flight Lieutenant Miller from SOE's security section was granted an audience with the MI6 agent, and returned satisfied with his bona-fides. Miller wrote up his report the following day, in which he stated that although Déricourt still had no case to answer, the MI6 agent's report did recommend Déricourt be brought back.[8] John Sentor concurred and passed the recommendation on to Buckmaster who minuted, 'Déricourt is coming back and security are relieved.' Dansey's plan had worked, so far.

Wing Commander Hugh Verity, who had been posted to SOE as Air Operations Manager, was informed by Buckmaster of these reports from MI6 and the decision to bring Déricourt out. Verity just couldn't believe it, 'I thought of Henri as my friend.'[9] F Section's operations officer Gerry Morel was brought into the conversation and was equally incredulous, but offered to go to France himself to bring Déricourt back.

A proposal for Operation KNACKER was submitted to the Air Ministry as an attempt '…to remove Déricourt from one of his own fields, at the point of a gun if necessary'. The Air Ministry told them to forget it. They would never countenance sending one of their aircraft on a mission where there was the distinct possibility of a shoot-out – and to kidnap someone who had an honorary commission in the RAF and had been recommended for the DSO! It took a good deal of reasoning from Air Intelligence before the operation was accepted and KNACKER was finally scheduled for the night of 4/5 February.

Déricourt already knew that he was coming out, he just didn't know when. Jeannot was down in the Midi with a deposit to put on the plot of land. He daily waited for a signal that would tell him when to move. When it came, it took him completely by surprise. Baker Street had told Déricourt KNACKER would be a Hudson operation, with ten incoming passengers. On the evening of 4 February, Déricourt had nine outgoing passengers making their way down to the field at Angers.

When the Hudson came to a halt by the leading light, the door was flung open and out jumped Gerry Morel, dressed in full RAF uniform and a brand new peaked cap. Déricourt and Clément could barely believe their eyes; there he stood insignia and pips gleaming in the moonlight. This was to be a formal affair. Morel braced himself, but before he could utter a word, the Hudson's slipstream tore his new cap off and sent it cartwheeling across the field. That was the end of the ceremonial aspects of the operation. Clément dashed off after the cap, which couldn't be left in a French field, while Morel explained to Déricourt that he'd been ordered to return to London tonight.

'Why tonight?'

'Buckmaster wants to give you a medal.'

It couldn't have become more ridiculous. Déricourt, doing his very best to keep a straight face, informed Morel that immediate departure was completely out of the question. Now Morel was unbelieving.

'Why ever not?'

Déricourt simply repeated that it wasn't possible. Morel insisted. By this time Clément had returned with the cap and had caught the gist of the conversation. He began dancing around the two of them, waving his arms about and yelling at the top of his voice, 'Don't go. Don't take him away and leave me here on my own!' It had become farce. Morel, though armed with a pistol, was not really used to this sort of business and dreaded having to actually use the weapon. Déricourt, on the other hand, was all calm and good reason. He explained that Baker Street had told him to expect ten incoming passengers for which there were now ten redundant bicycles hidden in some bushes about 200 metres away that had to be disposed of. 'Clément couldn't do that on his own.' Rémy had ceased his dance and was now nodding his head vigorously.

Déricourt told Morel that if they came for him in five days' time, he would be waiting to be collected. To Morel, this seemed a solution preferable to the pistol and so, a little disappointed with himself, he climbed into the aircraft with the homeward-bound passengers. As if to mollify him, Déricourt climbed on board too, just to re-confirm the details. With Déricourt in the aircraft, Morel seriously considered taking out his pistol and ending the argument right there, but Déricourt was fully in command of the situation. 'Five days!' he said then leapt out, closed the door and left Morel to ponder on how he would write up his report.[10]

On the train back to Paris, empty but for some rather under-occupied SD men, Déricourt mentioned the bit about the medal. Clément nodded. He had heard about it in October, 'A DSO.'

'A DSO? Is that very good?'

'Oh yes. In London they think very well of you. You are the best.'

First things first. He telephoned and organized an emergency meeting with Boemelburg who was fortunately up on a visit from Vichy. Next he telephoned Jeannot and told her to return to Paris as quickly as possible.

At about eight o'clock on 5 February, Karl Braun pulled up by the kerb and Déricourt got into the black Citroën. Twenty minutes later the car crunched its way up the drive of the château in Neuilly and round to the side door. Boemelburg stood there to welcome him.

Dr Götz arrived a little later, was met at the front door and ushered into the hall. It was his first visit to the château. Off to the left was a large living room and a fire in the grate. In one of the armchairs sat GILBERT with a drink in his hand and an expression of calm familiarity. When everyone was comfortable Déricourt explained again for Götz's benefit that he'd been recalled. Boemelburg was very distressed. He was absolutely certain Déricourt would be arrested. Frager had betrayed him, London was suspicious. 'This was all Bleicher's work.'

Déricourt disagreed. He was not suspected, it was just a new assignment and he offered to continue to work for Boemelburg from London. The idea had some appeal and Déricourt played on it, reassuring Boemelburg as he went. What Déricourt was searching for was a guarantee that Clément, JuJu and André Watt would not be harassed while he was away. When they said goodnight at the side door, Déricourt shaking Boemelburg's hand for the second last time, he had his guarantees. Dr Götz arranged to meet with him again as soon as he knew the details of his departure.[11]

Two days later, Dr Götz received a telephone call asking him to meet Déricourt at the apartment. Götz, a little nervous about facing this last rendezvous on his own, asked Ernst Vogt, one of Kieffer's interpreters, to come with him. They let themselves in first and then waited for GILBERT'S knock. When Déricourt arrived he confirmed that he was leaving for London in a day or two – he kept it vague. To satisfy everyone he offered to arrange a BBC message, a code which would signal that he was in London and safe. They agreed on 'The Green lantern is still lit' – and then Déricourt left.[12] On 8 February, he was collected again by Karl Braun and taken for a drive in the Bois de Boulogne. Sitting in the back of the car with Déricourt was Boemelburg, who handed him an envelope full of cash.[13]

Déricourt left the cash, two million francs, with Charles Besnard along with instructions to complete the purchase of the property down in the Midi. He hugged JuJu, shook hands with Charles and said his farewells to demi-Watt. Then he and Jeannot, clutching what they could carry in two suitcases, boarded the train for Tours. Jeannot was very unhappy about going to London, 'there is bombing in London, it's not safe'.[14] Dressed in her best fur, she and Déricourt tried to stay calm as they sat and drank coffee with Clément in a little café near the field.

Suddenly Déricourt's nerve went, he was bathed in sweat and clearly tortured with anxiety. Clément had never seen him like that before; he found it quite infectious. Although Déricourt trusted his controller, he could not be completely certain what to expect in London. Clément didn't ask, but had assumed that because Jeannot was going, there was trouble. The parting was particularly painful.[15] All depended on Boemelburg's word.

At Tangmere, the escorting officers were a little surprised to see a woman with Déricourt. He introduced his wife to them and explained that 'She is here to do some shopping and then later, we will parachute back together!' Thankfully Jeannot had not understood a word of the conversation.[16]

Jeannot was dropped at The Savoy, while Déricourt was driven to Orchard Court, a block of flats where SOE had an apartment used for briefing and de-briefing their agents. Colonel Buckmaster, Wing Commander Verity and Déricourt sat in a little semi-circle in comfortable armchairs. It was a setting not dissimilar from the one he had just left in Neuilly. They chatted about nothing for a few minutes and then Buckmaster finally confronted Déricourt with the accusation that he'd been working with the Germans. Déricourt didn't bat an eye. With an absolutely dead-pan expression he explained, 'In order to do my work for you efficiently, I have to be on good terms with the German authorities in Paris. As a matter of fact, I sell them black-market oranges.'[17]

It was a stunning performance and went some way towards easing the tension. However, Buckmaster made it clear that the security people were very suspicious and were conducting a special enquiry. Verity left Orchard Court utterly convinced 'he was no double agent'. In fact he was so saddened by the way Henri had been treated that he arranged to treat Déricourt and his wife to a dinner dance that evening at The Savoy.

Déricourt and Buckmaster were driven directly to the Northumberland Hotel where the enquiry was being held, away from the corridors of Baker Street. It had been decided not to treat this as an ordinary security case but to entrust it to officers of the highest rank. A suspicion had crept into the minds of those familiar with the case, a suspicion that they might not be dealing with just an ordinary 'double'. Air Commodore Archie Boyle, the head of SOE's security and intelligence section, was accredited with being in charge of the enquiry, but in fact he was not involved with it at all. The proceedings were handled entirely by Gubbins' deputy, Harry Sporborg.

As it had been a series of MI6 reports that had actually provoked the decision to recall Déricourt, Sporborg had sent a message to Dansey alerting him to the fact that they were about to interrogate Déricourt and might require MI6's assistance. Sporborg was advised before the enquiry began to restrict himself just to Frager's report and that the MI6 material was, for security purposes, completely inadmissible. Surprised and somewhat hamstrung, Sporborg went through all the reports they had ever received, starting from the very beginning and ending with Frager's. Déricourt dealt with each one convincingly but left Sporborg certain they were not going to get anywhere near the truth through him.

> Déricourt made a good impression during his interviews – but insisted on restricting his replies to the narrowest possible interpretation of the question. He gave nothing more than was asked of him.[18]

Buckmaster sat in on the first day, presenting his opinion of Déricourt's remarkable record (thanks to the SD): 17 successful operations involving 21 aircraft, which had brought in 43 people and taken out 67. Buckmaster stressed again and again that throughout Déricourt's mission, no casualties had occurred. Sporborg noted:

The fact that casualties do not appear to have occurred does not necessarily disprove his treachery, as the Germans might be waiting till nearer D–Day before they pounced.

Sporborg concluded:

> ...but if, in fact, he has been working for the enemy (as has been alleged), then he is a high grade and extremely skilful agent and no amount of interrogation will shake him.[19]

That night at The Savoy, Hugh Verity and his wife tried to raise Déricourt's spirits. Jeannot looked 'rather brassy' in her fur coat while Henri paraded in an RAF officer's uniform, with the yet un-gazetted DSO ribbon on his breast. Despite the music and the good company, there was nothing that would cheer him up; Déricourt was feeling badly cornered. Then suddenly Jeannot piped up, having been peering at a woman in the crowd, 'I have seen a dress just like that in Paris.' You could have heard a velvet curtain drop. Paris, in February 1944, was on the other side of the moon.[20] That night, the BBC broadcast Déricourt's secret message to Dr Götz.[21] SOE knew nothing about it but the message ensured Watt's, Clément's, and Juju's continuing safety.

The following day, the 10th, Sporborg spent in closed session with John Sentor. They were far more hamstrung by the MI6 restrictions than they had originally presumed. Section V had advised them that if they chose to use Frager's accusations as a basis for their enquiry, then they should not refer to any of the material that had come from the 'Colonel Heinrich' character. Section explanation, which didn't explain anything at all, was that this 'Colonel Heinrich' may in fact be a real German security officer genuinely seeking to collaborate with the Allies.[22] 'All the more reason,' argued Sporborg, 'to use his material, for it would more likely be genuine.'[23] No reply from Section V.

Suddenly all the internal dissent about Dansey had been submerged. MI6 was responding to a problem with a single voice. Even Section V, a department that despised Dansey, was co-operating to frustrate SOE's enquiry. Each way Sporborg turned, someone from MI6 had an answer. Sporborg had managed to get hold of some very sensitive 'intercepts', decrypted German signals which were clear evidence that:

> The Germans were making use of their connection with Déricourt in a way that went far beyond anything Déricourt had indicated to us in his story about being approached by pilots.

The signals also indicated that Déricourt '…had kept up these contacts for some time'.[24]

By that stage Sporborg was in no doubt that Déricourt had been working with the SD. Again he enquired with MI6 about the status of the 'intercepts' and was informed they were completely classified and consequently inadmissible. Sporborg asked to see Dansey personally, but received no reply. 'Dansey knew about the Déricourt investigation but was singularly unhelpful and curiously uninterested in the proceedings.'[25] Sporborg felt the organization was being humiliated by the way they were being forced to conduct the proceedings. James

Langley, Dansey's man in MI9, once said, 'What Dansey wanted done was done, and what he wanted undone was undone.'[26]

On the 11th, Déricourt was driven to the Northumberland again. On this occasion, MI5 were represented. Sporborg was advised that his questioning should 'in no way press Déricourt in case he is *soured*'.[27] Patiently, he proceeded in the only way left, by putting certain points to Déricourt and asking him to comment. It was no longer an interrogation.

A day or two later, Henri and Jeannot decided to take a walk along the river to find some form of distraction. Just as they left the Savoy, Henri decided it looked like rain and went back upstairs to fetch their umbrella. When he opened his door he found two gentlemen with a large box of tools making 'repairs' to their telephone. Déricourt apologized for disturbing them and left them to get on with their work.[28]

Meanwhile Sporborg and John Sentor pored over all the evidence they had on Déricourt and tried to find a path through what was admissible and inadmissible. It seemed to Sporborg absolutely ridiculous that if MI6 knew of Déricourt's connections with the Germans, they should prevent SOE coming to the proper conclusion and having the man interned. Sporborg asked for MI5's opinion, which they gave in very uncertain terms. 'Although it is only fair to say that GILBERT makes a good impression under interrogation, and that his antecedents seem to be remarkably unexceptional...' (Unexceptional antecedents? In the past six months, MI5 had sent four separate reports to SOE about Déricourt's contacts with the Germans. What made them change their mind?)

> ...we should if the decision was entirely
> [ours] regard the case against him as serious
> enough to prevent him from undertaking any
> further *intelligence work* outside this country[29]
> [author's italics].

One would presume that MI5 were aware that 'intelligence work' was not what SOE had employed Déricourt to do. Either the officer who wrote that up had lost his concentration or MI5 knew more than they were telling. At any rate, MI5 had effectively recommended precisely what Claude Dansey had wanted. SOE were forced to admit that Déricourt had 'no case to answer' but at the same time, on the advice of MI5, Sporborg decreed that he would not be sent back. Buckmaster was furious. So was everyone else in F Section, but there was nothing they could do. Normally, SOE agents who had finished their service were sent up to a country house at Inverlair in the Scottish highlands, where they were provided with suitable cover stories before they re-entered the outside world. Nothing of the sort occurred with Déricourt; instead he and Jeannot settled down to life at The Savoy.

Whenever Boemelburg was up to Paris on business he would call in to see Dr Götz at Avenue Foch, to hear of any news from Déricourt. There never was any. As the weeks became months, Boemelburg became resigned to the fact that he was unlikely to hear from Déricourt again. Sitting with Götz one day, Boemelburg sighed, 'Ah well. That's the last we'll see of the two millions.' Götz thought for a moment and then ventured, 'That's exactly the price of a property he wanted to buy down in the Midi.'[30]

At the café in the Rue André des Arts, business was a bit slow since Déricourt had left. In fact they did no more operations at all. In April a confusion over code-words led JuJu to believe the Germans had rumbled the place. (Kieffer had known about it from the start.) She radioed through Watt that they wanted to be brought out and it was agreed. Rémy preferred to stay in Paris and was ordered to lie low.

On 5/6 April, Charles, JuJu and André Watt climbed into a Lysander and were brought out safely. While the latter was in London, he and Déricourt met for dinner and chatted harmlessly about business. Déricourt never explained why he had not returned to France.

To discourage similar contacts, the Déricourts were moved to the Swan Hotel at Stratford upon Avon, then to a place in Birmingham and finally to a flat in Barons Court, in London's western suburbs, SOE were finished with Déricourt and had re-directed their attention to the preparations for what promised to be the real invasion. Déricourt took no part in that operation, but he did have one more brief role to play in the war. He had been put in touch with de Gaulle's intelligence service, the BCRA, where he'd been recommended as a skilled pilot. He made a number of useful contacts there, and with the Free French preparing for the liberation they were keen to have him. Unfortunately, MI5 would not clear him until well after the invasion had taken place. At the end of August, he resigned his RAF commission and was assigned as a Free French officer to a top secret Allied communications squadron. He was given a very high security classification and attached to the staff of the French Military Commander, General Koenig. In October and September, Koenig's mission was to make contact with all the Resistance groups; Déricourt, flying an Auster light aircraft, was responsible for flying Koenig or his staff to their rendezvous.[31] On 9 September 1944, Déricourt's war came to an end. While on a low-flying reconnaissance mission he crashed near Chateauroux and was nearly killed. He was rescued by some farmers who eventually got him to the hospital at Issoudun where he was examined and found to have a ruptured lung, eight fractured ribs, a fractured skull and lacerated liver. He was transferred to Orléans and then finally up to a liberated Paris where he spent some months recuperating.[32] Déricourt always maintained that he was shot down by a column of Germans, but there was a rumour at the time that it had been some of the Resistance taking their revenge. The official report stated that he had flown into some power cables.

–

Towards the end of May 1944, Dr Götz was handed a list of BBC messages. Götz recognized immediately they were the 'alert' messages for the invasion. He informed Kieffer and was told to send a written report to the German High Command in the west. Each night they listened for the 'B message' that would signal the invasion was scheduled for the following day. Götz had by that time compiled a list of fifteen messages that were meant for fifteen separate circuits. These had come from a number of sources, some from captured agents. Many came from Déricourt, who had handed them over to Boemelburg in the back of his Citroën. On 5 June, the messages were all there – action!

'That's it. It's the invasion!' Götz cried. He telephoned headquarters, then sat down at the typewriter and tried hard to compose his report. He felt he was part of history. The report was sent to Kopkow and to military headquarters. By the time Götz went to bed, he felt confident they had won the war. Many of the messages Götz had received were real; some were designed to distract attention; *none* of them were heeded. Götz's report was not opened until the morning of the 6th, and by then it was too late. The military had been warned by the SD too many times about invasions in the past.

One other legacy of 1943 became evident during the weeks and months of fighting after D-Day. Almost daily, Götz had to plant bright red pins into a map of France to represent acts of sabotage. The centre and south of France was awash with the red markers, while the north – the great belt that had been covered by PROSPER – was almost clear.[33] SOE never succeeded in re-establishing a presence in the north on the scale or significance enjoyed by Suttill. The SD had it under control.[34]

-

In the summer of 1945, when the war in Europe was over and people once again had time to stop and reflect, Harry Sporborg began wondering about that GILBERT thing back in 1943. Why, he wondered, had MI6 shown such intense interest in Déricourt while he was still in France, but then 'lost interest and were notably unhelpful in the investigation into Déricourt's activities after his recall in February'? Sporborg finally managed to see Claude Dansey before he retired and he asked him about 'that man Déricourt'. Sporborg didn't record what Dansey told him, but he did recall this:

> Claude Dansey. You knew full well he never told you the whole of any story. I rather liked the old boy, though deception came second nature to him. There was no doubt

whatsoever in my mind that Déricourt was being employed by MI6 for functions which were outside SOE's sphere of operations and knowledge. Make no mistake about it, MI6 would never have hesitated to use us or our agencies to advance their own schemes, even if that meant the sacrifice of some of our people.[35]

But that's not what it said in the official record. In October 1945, the British Government under Clement Attlee announced that the SOE would be wound up and closed down by the end of the year. All the files and records were handed across to MI6. The cover-up had begun.

XVII

Trials

Not everyone was keen to rush out into civvy street the moment they closed the doors at SOE. Vera Atkins, who became Head of F Section in June 1944, felt particularly badly about the decision to liquidate. Atkins felt very strongly that before the books and files were closed for good, there was much that still had to be accounted for. Her major preoccupation was the fate of the Section's women agents who had not returned. There were twelve in all. Atkins spent many frustrating months lobbying various authorities to get permission to go to Europe and track down the threads of these lives cut down in the service of F Section. Through a great deal of persuasion and a tiny degree of threat, Atkins got herself attached to the United Nation's War Crimes Commission which allowed her access to the files on hundreds of German prisoners and the opportunity to interview most of them.

In Berlin Atkins did the rounds of the various agencies, from Military Intelligence to the Red Cross, gathering information; then she finally drove down to see the War Crimes Investigator at the Rhine Army HQ at Baden-hauser. Through him she was put in touch with the camp commandants of Ravensbrück, Sachsenhausen, Buchenwald, Auschwitz and so on. Gradually she was able to cross each name off her list.

The final account of PROSPER people is very incomplete since most of the SS's and SD's records have not survived. However, the fate of the key figures in the network has been well catalogued. Andrée Borrel was given a fatal injection and then incinerated at Natzweiler in July 1944. Yvonne Rudellat recovered from her wounds only to succumb to typhus at Belsen soon after it was liberated; Noor Inayat Khan was kept in chains at Pforshiem and then sent to Dachau where she was shot; Gilbert Norman, John Macalister, Frank Pickersgill, Johnny Barrett and Dubois were hanged at Gross Rosen in September 1944 – as was Robert Benoist, though he was arrested in a different operation; Francis Suttill was hanged at Sachsenhausen in March 1944 as were Cohen and Jean Worms. Of the hundreds more arrested in the country, there is no account.[1]

In the course of her investigation, Atkins found herself in the pretty little German town of Gagenau. There, she had the opportunity to interview one Josef Kieffer who was being held for the murder of a unit of SAS men. They sat opposite each other at a simple table and proceeded through the details of how each woman was arrested and when she was deported to the concentration camps. Suddenly, in the course of their conversation, Kieffer mentioned the word Déricourt. Atkins looked up from her notes.

She quickly recalled the French pilot they had employed during 1943 to arrange Lysander pick-ups and who had been so unfairly accused by Frager and others of having dealt with the Germans. She asked Kieffer about Déricourt. He explained that he, GILBERT/Déricourt, had given them a great deal of information about PROSPER and other networks, which they had been able to use most successfully. When the full import of what Kieffer had said sank in, Atkins asked if Déricourt had actually been working for Kieffer. 'No. He was not my agent, he was Boemelburg's agent. He was BOE/48.'

After all this time, months of interviewing some of the worst criminals of the war, the last thing Atkins expected to feel was shock. But this was still business. She took a separate statement in which Kieffer explained the relationship with Déricourt in detail and she had him sign it. It was then sent to the War Crimes Commission in London.[2] It was standard procedure for these reports to be handed on to the relevant government authority involved in the pursuit of war criminals. Déricourt had been employed by a British service, so the report was passed to MI6.[3]

At the time Vera Atkins was engaged in her investigations, Déricourt was putting together a new career as a pilot with Air France, for whom he regularly flew the Paris to London route. Having recovered from his crash, Déricourt had taken his unauthorized and fabricated Flight Logs to Air France, and been accepted straight away. Rémy Clément, Léon Doulet and Robert Marotin were all there too. But whereas most Frenchmen were trying to re-create order in a world that had too long been turned upside down, Déricourt was of course doing his best to exploit the chaos.

France during the first half of 1946 was a country on the brink of civil war. The national uprising that had so long been heralded as the prelude to the invasion, now threatened – long after the liberation – to tear the country apart. Until October 1945, de Gaulle had effectively governed France under the constitution of the Third Republic. At that stage a referendum produced an overwhelming vote to abolish the old constitution and start again.

The National Assembly was dominated by left-wing parties, the most influential being the Communists, a party which had displayed a singular unity throughout the occupation. De Gaulle had been determined to create within the new constitution a Presidency with wide executive powers. The Communists in particular were opposed to any formula that created a President that was anything other than a mere ceremonial head. An extraordinary constitutional situation existed however, for although the politicians were set for a long process of conciliation, out in the country the Communists still had at large secret armies that had been armed and trained during the war by the SOE – and by PROSPER in particular. So long as the threat remained of what they saw as a de Gaulle dictatorship, the Communists refused to disarm. Five years of clandestine warfare had forged a national conscience bent on intrigue and distrust. From the moment of liberation de Gaulle had determined to crush the Communists. Conciliation had failed so he resorted to methods with which he was more familiar. He resigned over the constitutional impasse and while the Assembly debated, he plotted. Many of his old cronies from the wartime intelligence services were now in key positions of the re-formed Deuxième Bureau, though regrettably bereft of funds.

Into this milieu stepped a young captain who had been a desk-bound officer in SOE's Belgian Section. His name was Peter Belgeonne. In March 1946 he was involved in the liquidation of SOE matters in Brussels, in the course of which he was obliged to travel to Paris to liaise with certain French authorities. While in

Paris he was put in touch with a Colonel in the Deuxième Bureau who engaged him in conversation about the armed communist groups. The Colonel suddenly leant forward and solemnly asked Belgeonne 'to convey a message to the British authorities'. He then proceeded to lecture Belgeonne about the great threat to national security from the Communists and then pronounced, 'Were the British prepared to give [us] the means to do so, right wing resistance "reseaux" are ready to make every endeavour to crush the communist organizations.'

Belgeonne was a little taken aback by the Colonel's directness but said that he would convey the request to the relevant authority, though he cautioned the Colonel that he did not think the British Government would want to get involved in French domestic affairs. Belgeonne went down to the British Embassy and asked to see one of the officers of the MI6 station. He then repeated the French Colonel's request to the sound of the MI6 officer's ribald laughter.[4]

Within a week Henri Déricourt was contacted by someone by the name of Gaillot. Henri Gaillot had been a member of de Gaulle's BCRA in London where he had met Déricourt and they had become friends. Since the liberation Gaillot had joined a somewhat sinister secret rightwing 'reseaux' largely made up of ex-BCRA men, which enjoyed a loose association with certain officers in the Deuxième Bureau. He asked Déricourt if he would be prepared to collect some money from London; there would be £100 in it for him. Déricourt was prepared. On 10 April he was scheduled to make two flights to London's Croydon Airport. After the morning flight, he telephoned The Savoy Grill and asked for a Mr Robert Marshall (no relation to the author), but failed to make contact. He flew back to Paris, then returned to Croydon in the late evening and telephoned again. This time Marshall was there. A meeting was arranged for the following day, 11 April, at The Savoy.

Déricourt stayed overnight at Croydon, flew back to Paris first thing in the morning and made contact again with Gaillot. He was given a child's handkerchief by which he would be identified, then he flew the midday flight to Croydon, took the train up to Victoria and a taxi to The Savoy. He made contact with his 'Mr Marshall', showed him the child's handkerchief and a few minutes later stepped out into The Strand carrying nearly £6000 worth of gold and platinum.

At Croydon, he showed HM Customs a canvas bag, which he said contained cigarettes and coffee. As he walked down the corridor towards his aircraft, he was observed by another customs officer to pick up a briefcase that no one had seen before. He was approached and asked what it contained. Déricourt said a box of cigars. Inside, underneath a pair of pyjamas, were found 14 pieces of platinum and a gold nugget. In the canvas bag were 139 pieces of gold bullion and 1320 one-pound notes. In Déricourt's jacket pocket they found another £100. Detective Sergeant James removed Déricourt to the local station where he was charged.

Déricourt admitted the entire story in every detail and naturally the police didn't believe a word of it. He was remanded before the local magistrate the following day where 'another authority' managed to convince them that the case should be adjourned until Déricourt could have the benefit of proper representation.[5]

Many years after the event, when Déricourt was questioned about the Croydon affair, he explained somewhat coyly, 'I had simply let them know I was in an embarrassing situation and asked if they could do something to help me out and they did.'

On 23 April, Déricourt appeared again at the Croydon Magistrates' Court, in the company of a formidable array of 'silks'. He was represented by no less a figure than Mr Derek Curtis Bennett, a King's Counsel, and two junior counsels. Déricourt repeated his story precisely as he had told it to the police and customs people, after which Mr Curtis Bennett rose to his feet and pronounced, 'His story is true! The French resistance movement still existed to protect democracy should it again become necessary and the defendant, who was still a member of it, was doing a job for them.' Then he described in lavish detail how Déricourt had been involved in espionage during the war, '…working for the British secret service in France…' How he had been awarded the Croix de Guerre and recommended for the DSO. Mr Curtis Bennett then continued, 'I suppose that for his work in France he would think nothing of carrying about two dozen fictional passports. He has spent most of his life doing unorthodox things for which he has had credit.'[6]

The message was perfectly clear. Déricourt had not been engaged in criminal activity, but *unorthodox activity* and had apparently done this sort of work before with complete impunity. The sheer presence of Déricourt's eminent counsel convinced the suburban magistrates that they were dealing with the secret workings of national governments. The prosecuting counsel acting for HM Customs pointed out that the standard fine for the offence was in the order of £18,000 plus imprisonment. The senior magistrate, Mr D. A. Lawrence, clearly impressed by Mr Curtis Bennett's argument, fined Déricourt £500.

The fine and Mr Curtis Bennett's services were paid for by 'another party'. In due course HM Customs returned the gold and platinum to Déricourt, though not the currency, and he departed under a deportation order on 2 May.

The loot had been part of de Gaulle's secret service fund, an unorthodox stash that had been gleaned from every imaginable source and squirrelled away under various names over the course of the war. Much of it was inadvertently left under the benevolent eye of MI6, until long after the liberation. It was not MI6's gold, but it was MI6 who had come to Déricourt's aid when he fell foul of HM Customs. Contrary to requirements, there is no record of Mr Curtis Bennett's instructing solicitors and HM Customs have no record of ever having prosecuted the case.

This was not the long arm of Claude Dansey at work, he had retired. But his legacy lingered on. The most disturbing element of the case was the fact that MI6 were in possession of a statement signed by Josef Kieffer which detailed Déricourt's involvement with the SD. There was never any question of taking any action on it. (A copy of the statement now lies in Déricourt's SOE personal file.) Despite the iniquities Dansey had perpetrated during the war the service still had its obligations to those he had employed. Menzies was still in charge and although it seems unlikely he knew about Déricourt from the beginning – and sanctioned the operation, he clearly felt Déricourt's work deserved some reward and Curtis Bennett's services were a down payment.

–

Three months after Déricourt finally delivered the gold to his contact in France, he was rewarded by a grateful

President with the Chevalier de la Legion d'Honneur.[7] Unfortunately, just as he received his French honour, his British award was withdrawn. Peter Belgeonne's future wife returned from a trip to Paris in April 1946 with the news that the French DST were conducting a massive investigation into one Henri Déricourt. Belgeonne was outraged to learn that this same fellow was still in line for a DSO. (It had been frozen since April 1945.) He spoke to Phillip Rea (Lord Rea) who took it up with the Foreign Office. Any risk of embarrassment was neatly avoided because the DSO cannot be awarded to anyone with a criminal record, and the Croydon case had just been concluded.

The French were not governed by such sensibilities. It is typical of Gallic bureaucracy that they would present a man with a highly significant award – and then arrest him for treason. On 22 November 1946, just as he and Jeannot were having their evening meal, three men from the DST arrived at 58 Rue Pergolese. The search for traitors and collaborators had begun even before a government was in place. DST interrogations from as early as August and September 1944 were liberally sprinkled with references to a GILBERT who had worked with the Germans. A dossier on Henri Déricourt was opened even before de Gaulle made his triumphant march down the Champs-Élysées. Throughout 1945 and 1946, Commissaire Rene Gouillaud conducted a slow and thorough investigation, under the supervision of the Director of the DST and great Anglophobe, Roger Wybot.

The DST had already interrogated Hugo Bleicher, Roger Bardet, an aide to Colonel Reile named Commandant Shaefer, and one of Kieffer's staff officers, Josef Placke. At the DST headquarters in Rue Saussaies,

Gouillaud confronted Déricourt with a series of accusations. That he had passed information to the SD about when and where F Section agents would arrive at night; that he passed the SD secret documents and notes; and that the Abwehr envied the SD's relations with him, for through him they had 'one of the most brilliant coups'.[8]

The French investigation had taken him completely by surprise, especially after the work he had done for them. Initially he denied everything, then as his thoughts gathered and imagination went back into gear, he drew upon the story of the 'two German pilots'. This time he elaborated it by adding that these genial flyers introduced him to a Dr Götz. 'In the course of their drive through the Bois de Boulogne, Götz had shown him that he knew all about his work for the British.' Then Déricourt claimed Götz blackmailed him and forced him to give details of his operations. Déricourt claimed that he agreed to do this with the hope of exploiting the situation to his own ends; that is, he claimed he sent the Germans to the wrong fields while his flights came in safely elsewhere.[9] Gouillaud continued:

> It appears from his first interrogation that he
> was unable to deny the evidence and so tried
> to minimize the importance of his contacts
> and their value, particularly with reference to
> the number of arrests that could follow.[10]

On the basis of what he admitted in his initial interrogation, Déricourt was charged on 26 November with having had 'Intelligence With the Enemy' and the DST were instructed on 29 November to pursue their enquiries further, 'to establish the consequence of Déricourt's treason'.

The DST had also interviewed SS Standartenfuhrer Dr Helmut Knochen, the man who had overall command over Boemelburg and Kieffer; Ernest Vogt, who had been Kieffer's secretary/interpreter; Richard Christmann and Dr Josef Götz. The quality of their testimony was excellent.

KNOCHEN:
Regarding the man in charge of the landing sites in France, and who Kieffer prided himself in controlling, Kieffer told me that he supplied the details of all his sites and the means necessary to decode BBC messages.[11]

PLACKE:
One day, Götz told me that Boemelburg had an agent named Gilbert Déricourt under his control and he gave me an address near the Place Malesherbes and a telephone number to contact him. I had a meeting with him in the company of Boemelburg at the abandoned apartment in Place Malesherbes. Déricourt told Boemelburg that there was an emergency landing that he had to deal with quickly at one of his fields down near Amboise. During a briefing with Dr Götz, before he went on holiday, he warned me of his suspicions of Déricourt, not to talk too much. Keep my mouth shut. One day, I heard Dr Götz say to some German functionaries that when it came to dealing with the 'landings' they had to take great care not to arrest Déricourt and not to arrest anyone in his presence. Great care must be taken

in choosing the right people from the ranks of the Bony-LaFont gang to do the work. Those who were involved had to be shown Déricourt, so they would make sure he was not arrested.[12]

DR GÖTZ:
Since 29 June 1943, I had deduced that the massive arrests which had occurred in the Buckmaster network were due in part to information already previously supplied to Boemelburg by GILBERT or Déricourt. I took part in five or six meetings with Déricourt. We knew that he was in charge of the air operations and the point of these meetings was to find out exactly when he was planning the Lysander, Hudson or Double Lysander operation. During these meetings, everything that concerned the operation was discussed. He told us the date, the moon, as well as indicating the number of agents. Sometimes even mentioning their names.

He also handed over agents' mail en route to London. Technical reports, political reports. If they seemed interesting they were photographed, otherwise they were simply copied or read.

He had three colleagues whose activity was known to our service. They were MARC (Rémy Clément), his right-hand man who assisted him in his operations. I did not know him, but GILBERT told us about him. CLAIRE (JuJu) who was for a time the contact address for Déricourt and

GEOFFROI (André Watt), his W/T who only worked for him for two months before his departure to London. To avoid his arrest, GILBERT had informed us of his existence and the areas in which he transmitted.

By his information on his air operations, GILBERT enabled us to carry out arrests. It was agreed that these arrests would take place with utmost care, not to burn GILBERT.

Finally, I believe this was Boemelburg's grand dream – GILBERT was of great importance to him for the future. Boemelburg saw in him the possibility of knowing the exact date and definite place of the landing, which would have been vital to the German defences.[13]

VOGT (Translator used in many of the interrogations of Suttill and Norman):
For this interrogation Kieffer had given me a series of photographic documents containing copies of the reports and letters sent to the London French Section by Suttill, Norman and other British agents of French Section. These photographic copies were all marked 'from BOE/48'.

They contained precise information about their activity in France, indicating their parachute drop fields, BBC messages for these drops, the names of direct colleagues and Frenchmen in charge of receiving these drops. Later I learnt that BOE/48 was none other than the above mentioned GILBERT or CLAUDE.[14]

For months Déricourt languished in Fresnes Prison without knowing what sort of strategy to pursue. The major problem was his admission to having had some kind of contact with the Germans. By doing that he had already signed his death warrant. Then about late February, he was contacted by someone from MI6. The contact's name was simply 'Robert'. He called on Déricourt at Fresnes and between them they began to reconstruct some kind of defence. 'Robert' told Déricourt to get Jeannot to enlist the services of the lawyer Maître Giafferi Di Moro, who had been de Gaulle's Minister of Justice in 1944 and 1945. Di Moro was not cheap and Déricourt distrusted him, even accusing him of seducing Jeannot.[15] But somehow, from this very unpromising start, they began to construct a defence.

Meanwhile Jeannot took the whole affair very hard. She had no idea what was going on and Henri would explain nothing. In her solitude she had begun to drink heavily and at that stage Henri was ready to throw in the towel. Just before he was about to appear before the Juge d'Instruction in April, Nicholas Bodington turned up on the scene. He made a habit of calling on Jeannot to see that she was coping and on every occasion asked if she needed any money. He usually produced an envelope containing bundles of notes, which Jeannot claimed she always refused.[16] Anyone familiar with Bodington would appreciate that the money was definitely not Bodington's own.

Appearing before the Juge d'Instruction on 24 April 1947, Déricourt's defence was built on the figure of Dr Götz. He elaborated on the story of being tricked by two German pilots to take a drive with their friend 'The Doctor', during which Götz said they knew all about his mission and that he would have to co-operate or suffer. Déricourt claimed that he gave Götz the details of eight out of his fourteen landing fields, which allowed him to continue his operations unobserved at the other six. It was a ploy that should have backfired, for Götz was also in French custody and had read Déricourt's statement in some press reports. Three days later, in the waiting room of an examining magistrate, Déricourt and Götz ran into each other. Götz asked him why he had invented just a ridiculous story.

Déricourt replied 'I was told you were in Spain.'[17]

Déricourt's spirits began to flag. He felt the whole affair was outside of his control and that great wheels were being turned that he knew nothing about. He was right. He wrote to Jeannot:

> The day before yesterday I had a visit from 'Robert' – neither good nor bad. He told me his colleagues were coming to see me and that's all. He sounded me out, listened to what I said to him and left. Impossible to know what's in his head. I don't count very much on them before the New Year because time is so short.[18]

In his spare time he busied himself with the design of an advanced form of automatic transmission, based on the British classic 'Hayes Selfselector'. He produced reams of highly detailed drawings and notes for what he called the VEGA 439. Jeannot spent almost as much time going back and forth from the Patents Office as she did visiting Di

Moro's. In the end, the idea cost too much to patent and the scheme was dropped.[19]

The year 1947 dragged on. There were hundreds, if not thousands, of cases waiting to come to trial and the French were doing their best to put them in the correct order. So many testimonies depended on another's corroboration. Two important developments occurred during the wait. The Government, sensitive to accusations that some of the trials had been conducted like kangaroo courts, passed a law requiring that in future mere contact with the enemy would not serve as sufficient grounds for guilt; a specific crime had to be proven. For example, that as a result of the passing of information an arrest had actually taken place.

The second development was the DST's inability to get hold of a number of key witnesses who would have made their case rock solid: namely Boemelburg and Kieffer. They had learnt that Boemelburg was living somewhere in the American zone of occupied Germany, but could not get him out. This was not because of any American intransigence – Boemelburg really had disappeared. Two American officers tracked down Frau Boemelburg but she denied having had any contact with her husband since the end of the war.[20] A story was spread that he'd been killed in Holland during a bombing raid.

Kieffer was a different story. Initially, he was a prisoner of the French but had been taken from Strasbourg Prison in 1946 to Gagenau where he was interrogated by the British. The French made persistent requests for his return so that they could interview him, but were denied access. While at Gagenau, Kieffer was seen by Vera Atkins and by MI6 but not by the French. He was tried and hanged in March 1947 for the murder of some ten or eleven members of the SAS – an act he had carried out on orders from Berlin.

There was also a problem in getting hold of Ernst Vogt, Kieffer's secretary cum translator. The DST had taken a very detailed statement from him (see extract above) on 3 March 1947, while he was a prisoner at Dachau. Since then he'd been passed back and forth between the British and the Americans and then finally to the British. By July, having failed to get hold of Kieffer, the French requested access to his translator, but were told there was no knowledge of his whereabouts.[21]

On 28 May 1946, the British handed over Feldwebel Josef Placke, another of Kieffer's staff officers, to the DST for an agreed period of fifteen days and on 10 April they took a statement from him specific to Déricourt (see extract above). A few months later, when the DST requested access to him again, the British simply refused. The DST demands, and there were a series of them, went all the way up to the Foreign Ministers and still the French got no satisfaction. As of 26 March 1948, two years after his initial statement to the DST, Placke was still in British custody.[22]

By the end of 1947, the DST could see their case beginning to fall apart at the seams. Commissaire Gouillaud was completely frustrated while the Director of the DST, Roger Wybot, could see the hand of Albion everywhere. Even Déricourt sensed the DST's case was crumbling. He wrote to Jeannot on 29 January 1948:

> ...they will have to release me for I have done nothing to be reproached for. The witnesses for the prosecution vanish one after the other and the accusations no longer have

substance. Besides the judge doesn't even know what to question me about because he says everyone lies in my dossier and everyone on whom one would wish to base an accusation declares themselves incompetent and tells the same facts in three different ways. I am the only reliable person who doesn't change the grounds of defence. Still I can't shake off the pestering bastards…

Di Moro recommended Déricourt ask for a general hearing, but 'Robert' advised against it. He told Déricourt to insist on a Military Tribunal. If he was found guilty, he would face the death penalty; if on the other hand he was found innocent, then the case was closed for good. There could be no further appeal and no one in France could call him a traitor with impunity. Déricourt elected for MI6's advice.

Eventually the Déricourt affair had begun to collect a little notoriety, as the press began to take note of cases that seemed to be going stale inside Fresnes. The DST were equally aware of the delay, caused by their vain attempts to collect the witnesses they needed for the prosecution. Finally, the trial was set for 8 May and the DST were forced to present their case without Boemelburg, Kieffer, Placke or Vogt. They did have Bleicher, Bardet, Götz and Knochen. The press reports state that a mysterious British Colonel Bodington suddenly appeared, to take the stand. In fact Bodington had been around almost constantly, organizing Déricourt's defence witnesses.[23]

Some few days before the date of the trial, Bodington heard that Vera Atkins was in Paris and went to look her up at her hotel. He feigned surprise when they ran into each other and proceeded to plead with her to have lunch with him. Atkins wasn't at all pleased to see him and the prospect of lunch was not at all appealing, especially as he would probably leave her with the bill. His pleas became more persistent; Atkins took a deep breath and agreed. During their meal, Bodington brought up the subject of Déricourt's trial. Atkins admitted she hadn't noticed it was on.

'I take it you'll be a witness?' she asked.

'Yes,' said Nick.

'I take it you'll be a witness for Déricourt?'

'Yes.'

Atkins thought for a moment. She had, after all, taken a very specific statement from Kieffer and was in no doubt what the outcome should be. She presumed Bodington's testimony would be in the form of character material with perhaps some reference to the trip he made out to Paris during August and September 1943.

Atkins spoke very quietly, making sure he understood the full measure of her feelings.

> Now Nick. So long as you limit your evid-
> ence to the fact that you got back safely, and
> explain the reasons why you got back safely,
> because you know why. Had you not got
> back safely it would have been the end of
> Déricourt's line. And you know that. You
> must in fairness to other people who did not
> return, give your evidence, I fear, only in that
> sense.[24]

She had put it in a nutshell. If Bodington had not got back to London in September 1943, SOE would have thought the worst of Déricourt – and Boemelburg knew that too. Bodington took the measure of her words.

At 10 am on 8 May 1948, Henri Alfred Eugene Déricourt entered the courtroom at Ruilley Barracks on the eastern side of Paris. From the moment the courtroom was brought to order, it was evident there was a singular lack of enthusiasm on the part of the prosecution to pursue its argument. Most significant was the testimony of people like Götz and Knocken which bore virtually no resemblance to that which they had each given twelve months ago. This can be partly explained by the fact that the prosecution for some reason failed to ask the right questions. But even so:

> Q: What exactly were the revelations made by Boemelburg concerning the agent Gilbert/Déricourt? And can you tell us the exact role that Déricourt played in Prosper's and Archambaud's (Gilbert Norman) arrest.

> Götz: The expression 'revelation' doesn't correspond with my memory of these things. At the time Boemelburg spoke to me of an agent, but at the time I didn't know who he meant – Prosper, Archambaud, Valentin (Macalister), Bertrand (Pickersgill), Culioli or Déricourt? It's impossible to say who provided the basis for the arrests.[25]

Later the good doctor claimed not to have known whether BOE/48 was Déricourt, that he never actually saw any documents marked BOE/48, that he didn't actually know about Déricourt until July, long after the PROSPER arrests (he knew of him in May), and that he was only concerned with his radio game. But the problem still remained, that Déricourt did have contacts with the Germans and unless it could be explained why, he still wasn't off the hook. Then, straight after lunch, up stepped Nicholas Bodington. It was to be his last great scene in the story and he would make it a memorable one. The press described him as laconic, mysterious, even enigmatic.

> I had to return to France in July '43 to check on several points in the PROSPER network. I saw Déricourt constantly, I was in permanent contact with him. I know the Germans had learnt of my arrival in Paris but I was never bothered. I had total trust in Déricourt and recommended he maintain his contacts with the Germans.[26]

As the reporter from *Le Parisien* put it, 'From then on, the other testimonies lost all significance.' The unanimous verdict of the French Press was that Déricourt's connections with the Germans was not something undertaken as a contingency measure, but an authorized operation conducted for definite objectives.

Bodington left everyone in no doubt that he spoke for 'British Intelligence'. A classic double bluff? The Foreign Office immediately disavowed any knowledge of his actions. Bodington took the job knowing how exposed he would be and how much disapprobation it would attract. Those are the rules for 'unattributable acts'.

At 58 Rue Pergolese Jeannot and Henri toasted each other with champagne as they fought their way through the crowds of well-wishers in their tiny two-roomed apartment. '*L'affaire Déricourt*' had been embraced by the press as something almost akin to a cause célèbre. It was a very popular acquittal. After all, French honour had been reprieved, he had acted under orders. And who could say they were wrong? Friends and old acquaintances whom he had long forgotten were suddenly there to embrace him. For Jeannot, it was all over, all the emptiness and loneliness and doubt. Henri was home again and would never ever leave her. Rémy was drunk and so relieved that all his doubts had been dispelled. Charles and Julienne Besnard hugged Henri and Jeannot and talked of buying a chicken farm. Everyone was so blissfully happy. It was all over.[27]

And Bodington? The would-be MI6 man, the spy-*manqué*, the hero of the hour, Dansey's éminence grise – well, he was drunk too. Many months later, Bodington ran into Vera Atkins again and very Nick-like greeted her warmly. Atkins stared at him coldly and simply said, 'I'm sorry, Nick. But I don't know you anymore.'[28]

XVIII

Afterwards

Vera Atkins recalls that soon after she had carefully sorted
out SOE's files and handed them over to MI6, she was
told that most of the records of agents' messages and
debriefings had been accidentally destroyed. Atkins and a
team of FANYs (First Aid Nursing Yeomanry) had spent
some time organizing the archives into box-files, grading
everything in order of importance A, B and C. Only
category C, she was told, seemed to have survived. Atkins
had no way of checking this, took her colleague at his
word and it became yet another incident to arouse suspicion amongst SOE veterans that MI6 had something to
hide about those five years of war. It has been speculated,
however, that the files were never destroyed at all. After
all, once they were in MI6 custody, why bother to burn
them? No one would ever be allowed to see them.

The accidental fire, the lack of space, the over-zealous
secretary – stories proliferated for years. Despite those
stories, research by various parties has elicited a great deal
of information from Century House (MI6 Headquarters),
material that was originally in those category A and B
files, but without raising any hope that the full extent of
the archives would ever be made public. Atkins was told
the files were destroyed after she had made a request for

some papers to assist her enquiries with the War Crimes Commission. After all, how could they refuse SOE papers to someone who had just sorted them out and handed them over?

Locking the files away rarely proves to be the end of a story. People and their recollections live on and, inevitably, an account of these events relies a great deal upon those recollections. It has been my experience that in amongst the memories of those who were there at the time, lies an overwhelming determination to discover the truth. All that remains now is to give an account of those people who played a part in these events, and lived on.

Maurice Buckmaster returns each year to France for a reunion of agents connected with F Section. It is an annual event steeped in good champagne and vintage anecdotes. Memories of 1943, however, have a bitter taste and the name 'Déricourt' is almost too painful to utter, especially as he had meant so much to F Section. In December 1945, Buckmaster wrote a memo denouncing those who doubted Déricourt.

> It is indelicate to say what I think about this officer, as long as his case is *sub judice*. But when – if ever – the clouds are blown away, I am prepared to bet a large sum that we shall find him entirely innocent of any voluntary dealing with the enemy. His efficiency in Hudson and Lysander work was staggering and it was his very success that raised the ugly idea that he was controlled. People who did not know him and judged him on the results of his work said 'It's too good to be true – he MUST be a bad hat.' That kind of reasoning

would be scoffed at by any country section officer who has to judge his man far more closely than an outsider.

Suffice it to say that he never once let any of our boys down and that he has by far the finest record of operations completed of any member of SOE.[1]

That memo was written before the trial in Paris and all the revelations that followed. Buckmaster is a man still haunted by the knowledge that he has been betrayed.

Rémy Clément still lives in the same little artist's apartment in the Rue Fontaine, up in Montmartre. His wife, now dead, was a remarkable painter in the style of the Belgian surrealist René Magritte. Rémy's home is a shrine to her work, embellished here and there with photographs of old friends now departed. Clément and André Watt meet regularly and chat about everything that has been. Watt still has an old wireless set which works as well today as it did in 1943 and he still feels a tinge of fear whenever he carries it down the street.

Julienne and Charles Besnard are both dead as is Roger Bardet, who died as this book was being written. Nicholas Bodington moved to Strasbourg to work for UNESCO, then returned to Britain and took up journalism again. He died in Plymouth in July 1974 somewhat bereft of friends from the SOE. He and Déricourt did not meet again after the party at the Rue Pergolese.

Déricourt's two controllers died within months of each other, though in greatly differing circumstances. Sir Claude Dansey retired from MI6 at the end of 1945. He had finally collected his 'K' and added to it Chevalier of the Order Leopold from Belgium, Commander of the Legion d'Honneur from France, and Officer of the Legion of Merit from the United States of America. He married for the second time and moved to the village of Bathampton, near Bath. He and his wife lived together happily, though briefly, until his death on 11 June 1947.

Karl Boemelburg had been head of the SD in Vichy as the war was drawing to its conclusion. As the Allies advanced, he was ordered to escort Maréchal Phillipe Pétain to the Austrian castle of Sigmaringen. In April 1944, Pétain was granted permission to enter Swiss territory. But in the chaos of defeat, Boemelburg could not even find enough petrol to get the party to the border and had to sell his watch and ring to scrape together the money for the fuel. With Pétain safely handed over, it was time to disappear. Boemelburg managed to contact his wife and get her to come to Austria, bringing as much cash as she could find. With that he was able to purchase a new identity, that of a recently deceased 'Sergeant Bergman'. (There was a thriving black market in dead men's papers for those who might wish to avoid retribution.) As Sergeant Bergman, Boemelburg finally settled in a small village near Munich and his family moved nearby. They would meet secretly, at night or at weekends. Boemelburg obtained work as a gardener with a wealthy family in the village. Eventually he convinced them he had some education and offered to sort out the extensive family library. Boemelburg settled down to this quiet rural existence, content with the way fate had treated him. Then on New Year's Eve in 1947, he was out with his family celebrating when he slipped on the ice, cracked his skull – and died. He was buried in the little village cemetery under the name Bergman. Recently his son altered the headstone to read Karl Boemelburg.

Dr Götz returned to being an inspector of schools and is currently writing his memoirs about the 'radio game'. Dr Helmut Knochen spent twenty years in prison for his part in the SAS murders and other crimes and now lives near Munich. SS Obersturmbannfuhrer Horst Kopkow is also still with us. His original field of intelligence was communist espionage and consequently he was of great assistance to the Gaelen Organization, the post-war German Intelligence service that was sponsored by MI6 and the CIA. He lives today under the name of Codes, in the little village of Gelschen-Kirchen, near Essen. He still regrets the fact that no one would listen to their intelligence about D-Day. When pressed on the matter of PROSPER and the 'pact' that was made with Suttill and Norman, this is what Mr Kopkow-Codes had to say:

> It was well known the British just emptied all their prisons of murderers and criminal types, and offered them clemency if they would parachute into France. We only did what the British would have done to them.[2]

Immediately after his trial Henri Déricourt found employment a little hard to come by. He got some part-time work in 1949 with a flying club, and then in 1950 with a company that manufactured beds. He returned to flying again in January 1951 for a company called Aigle Azur which operated cargo routes to the Lebanon and Algeria. Later that year he began to fly a route to Hanoi and Saigon. It was while he was flying for Aigle Azur Indochine, that he won yet another award, the *Croix de Guerre – Etoile Argent*. It was the time of the colonial wars in French Indochina.

From 1953 to 1954 he lived in Beirut working for the Lebanese airline Air Liban. He returned to France in 1954 and joined a new airline, *Société Auxiliare de Gerance et de Transports Aeriens* (SAGETA) which had been created to fly cargo and troops out to French Indochina. On 29 January 1957, Déricourt was trying to land a large four-engined passenger aircraft, an 'Armagnac', in thick fog at Orly Airport when the plane crashed, flipped upside down and spilt 2000 gallons of fuel on the runway. There were a number of injuries but Déricourt escaped with just a pair of badly burnt hands.[3]

Following the accident he was dogged for the next few years by an interminable official enquiry that pursued him from Paris to Vientiane, in Laos. He managed to get official Laotian papers that claimed he worked for the government airline Air Laos, though in fact he worked for private enterprise.[4] Also in Laos at the time was Rémy Clément, now retired from Air France. Unlike Déricourt, Clément really did work for Air Laos. Déricourt had returned to the sort of work he knew made the best return. The Marseilles-based heroin trade, the so-called 'French connection', received its supplies from Thailand, Laos and Cambodia where the trade was controlled by the ubiquitous Corsican Mafia. The man at the centre of that trade was Bonavanture 'Rock' Francisci who operated an infamous charter airline he called 'Air Opium'. Francisci's airline, officially known as Air Laos Commerciale, consisted of a fleet of three twin-engined Beechcrafts.[5] One was flown by Rend 'Babal' Enjabal, who had run his own opium airline a few years before; the others by Roger Zoile and Déricourt.[6] Henri preferred the title 'Air Confiture' to 'Air Opium', explaining that raw opium looked just like jam.

His route was a triangular course from Wattay Airport in Vientiane up to any one of the little dirt strips in the highlands, Sam Neua, Phong Saly, Muong Sing Nam Tha or Sayaboury, his cargo – gold bars. There he would collect anything from three to six hundred kilos of raw opium and fly it to drop points in Vietnam or Cambodia. 'Rock' Francisci had good relations with all the government authorities, especially Ngo Dinh Nhu, the brother and chief adviser to the President of South Vietnam, who allowed Francisci's aircraft in and out of Saigon unmolested. Nhu then used these aircraft to fly his own intelligence agents secretly into Laos and Cambodia on the return trip.

Déricourt earned a great deal of money doing this work, money which he claimed was for a special day. An arrangement had been made with Air Laos, the government airline, to pay Déricourt a standard salary which went into his Credit Lyonnaise account as though he were an ordinary employee. Each month he would virtually empty that account, telegraphing the money to Jeannot in Paris.[7] His earnings from 'Air Opium' he took separately – and in cash – to Hong Kong, where it was transferred into sterling and sent to a bank account in London. Jeannot never knew about the London account, nor about the Vietnamese 'wife' and child Henri lived with at the Hotel Constellation.[8]

In August 1962, he wrote to a colleague in Paris, '…everything must come to an end and everything has its way. It's time for me to go.'

On 21 November 1962, he took off from Vientiane for Sayaboury with a quantity of gold and four passengers. Given the load he was carrying, he had only just enough fuel to reach the little mountain strip by changing-over to his emergency tank, an operation normally conducted with the help of the engineer. Déricourt neglected to take an engineer that day and had to make the change-over himself.

The engine stalled a few kilometres from the village strip. On this occasion the aircraft failed to glide the rest of the way in and came down amongst the tree stumps at the edge of the strip where it burst into flames. There were no survivors. The following day Rémy Clément flew over the wreckage to view the spot where they said his old friend had perished. All the remains were charred beyond recognition, even the gold bars had melted. On 23 November the press agencies Agence France and Reuters dispatched this report:

Funeral of French pilot Henri Déricourt

Vientienne, 23. This morning at the Christian cemetery at Vientienne the funeral took place of Henri Déricourt, French pilot distinguished for his heroism during World War Two. Representatives of the French Embassy and the British Embassy, as well as military representatives of the air and land forces of those countries attended the funeral of Henri Déricourt.

Pilot with the Free French Forces, Henri Déricourt had flown in Royal Air Force operations during the war and had been promoted to the rank of Lieutenant Colonel. He was awarded the Distinguished Service Order (DSO) and the Distinguished Flying Cross (DFC).

He died when his plane crashed on landing at Sayaboury, in Laos. According to a spokesman of the company, the causes of the accident are unknown.[9]

It seems a fitting tribute to Déricourt, that the last item of news he generated was a testimony riddled with lies. Alongside the British and French Embassy officials who attended the ceremony was the CIA station chief for Laos.

In February 1963, Clément arranged to ship Déricourt's 'remains' back to France, where they were buried at the little village of Vitry-aux-Loges, in the Loiret. Jeannot lived for another twenty-two years at 58 Rue Pergolese, slipping steadily into an alcoholic decline. She died alone, in October 1985, surrounded by mounting debts and the memorabilia of her life with Henri. She was buried in the grave containing her husband's remains. There wasn't even enough money to add her name to the headstone.[10]

Not long before he died, Harry Sporborg described what he had learnt as Deputy Head of SOE about Déricourt's involvement with MI6. When he was asked why these facts did not appear in the official record, he explained the rules of the game.

In this world you must understand one thing: if you're going to become involved in these things, you must never, never admit anything afterwards. Anything. You have to go into it determined that, no matter what happens, you will never reveal what you have done.

You must resolve to go to your grave still
resolutely denying that it ever happened.[11]

Bibliography

Christopher Andrew, *Secret Service*, Heinemann, 1985.

J. G. Beevor, *SOE, Recollections and Reflections*, 1940-45, Bodley Head, 1981.

Hugo Bleicher, *Colonel Henri's Story*, Kimber, 1954.

Anthony Cave Brown, *Bodyguard of Lies*, W. H. Allen, 1976.

Maurice Buckmaster, *They Fought Alone*, Odhams, 1958.

Mathilde-Lily Carré, *I Was The Cat*, Souvenir, 1960.

Winston Churchill, *The Second World War*, Cassell, 1954.

Alfred Cobban, *A History of Modern France*, Vol. 3, Pelican, 1965.

Prepared for British Information Services, *Vietnam, Laos and Cambodia: Chronology of Events 1945-68*, COI, 1968.

E. H. Cookridge, *Inside The SOE*, Arthur Barker, 1966.

Brian Crozier, *South East Asia in Turmoil*, Pelican, 1966.

Roman Garby Czerniawski, *The Big Network*, Ronald, 1961.

François Fonvielle-Alquier, *The French and the Phoney War*, Tom Stacey, 1973.

M. R. D. Foot, *SOE 1940-1946*, BBC, 1984.

M. R. D. Foot, *SOE in France*, HMSO, 1966.

M. R. D. Foot and J. M. Langley, *MI9, Escape and Evasion 1939-1945*, Bodley Head, 1979.

Marie-Madeleine Foucarde, *Noah's Ark: The Story of the Alliance Intelligence Network in Occupied France*, George Allen & Unwin, 1973.

H. J. Giskes, *London Calling North Pole*, Kimber, 1953.

Paul Guillaume, *La Sologne au temps de l'heroisme et de la trahison*, Orléans, Imprimierie Nouvelle, 1950.

Gordon Harrison, *A Cross-Channel Attack*, Dept of The Army, 1951.

Trumbell Higgins, *Winston Churchill and the Second Front 1940–1943*, New York, 1957.

F. H. Hinsley, E. E. Thomas, C. F. G. Ransom and R. C. Knight, *British Intelligence During the Second World War, Volumes 1, 2 & 3*, HMSO, 1979, 1981, 1984.

The Trial of German Major War Criminals: proceedings of the international military tribunal sitting at Nuremberg, 20 November 1945–1 October 1946, HMSO, 1947-49.

Heinz Höhne, *Canaris*, Secker & Warburg, 1979.

Heinz Höhne, *Codeword: Direktor. The Story of the Red Orchestra*, Secker & Warburg, 1971.

Heinz Höhne, *The Order of the Death's Head*, Secker & Warburg, 1969.

Patrick Howarth, *Intelligence Chief Extraordinary, The Life of the Ninth Duke of Portland*, The Bodley Head, 1986.

Paul Johnson, *A History of The Modern World from 1917 to the 1980s*, Weidenfeld & Nicolson, 1983.

Fleet Admiral William D. Leahy, *I Was There*, Victor Gollancz, 1950.

Herbert R. Lottman, *Pétain: Hero or Traitor?*, Viking, 1985.

Compton MacKenzie, *Greek Memories*, Chatto & Windus, 1932.

J. C. Masterman, *The Double Cross System*, Yale University Press, 1966.

Alfred McCoy, Cathleen Read and Leonard Adams, *The Politics of Heroin in Southeast Asia*, Harper & Row, 1972.

Malcolm Muggeridge, *1972 Chronicles of Wasted Time*, Collins, 1973.

Noguères, *Histoire de la Résistance en France*, Robert Laffront, 1979.

Jean Overton Fuller, *Double Webs*, Putnam, 1958.

Jean Overton Fuller, *German Penetration of the SOE*, Kimber, 1975.

Jean Overton Fuller, *Horoscope for a Double Agent*, Fowler, 1961.

Robert Paxton, *Vichy France*, Barrie & Jenkins, 1972.

Anthony Read and David Fisher, *Colonel Z*, Hodder & Stoughton, 1984.

P. J. Stead, *The Second Bureau*, Evans, 1950.

Hugh Verity, *We Landed by Moonlight*, Ian Allan, 1978.

Charles Weighton, *The Pin-Stripe Saboteur*, Odhams, 1959.

Nigel West, *MI5: British Security Service Operations 1909-1945*, The Bodley Head, 1981.

Nigel West, *MI6: British Secret Intelligence Service Operations 1909-45*, Weidenfeld & Nicolson, 1983.

Kenneth Young (Editor), *The Diaries of Sir Robert Bruce Lockhart II: 1939-1965*, Macmillan, 1980.

References in the Text

Chapter I

1. Letter from Henri to Jeannot, 9 December 1946.
2. Mme Déricourt, 9 May 1982. Mme Déricourt's recollection of that evening was so precise she could even recall what they had been eating: tripe.
3. Letter from Déricourt to his wife, 9 December 1946.
4. Complaint from unnamed DST officer noted in Déricourt trial papers.
5. *Inside the SOE*, E. H. Cookridge, p. 215.
6. A number of people have heard the 'trapeze artist' story. This particular version was taken from an interview with Rémy Clément. It is one of the more fantastic tales he had heard from Déricourt.
7. A story Déricourt had told two Belgian intelligence officers in London in October 1942.
8. Déricourt writes a great deal about the 'little people' in a series of letters to Miss Overton Fuller during 1959-1962.
9. Déricourt papers.
10. Farman Air School log book.
11. Robert Marotin, 14 March 1982.
12. ibid.
13. Air Bleu correspondence in Déricourt papers.

14. Déricourt flight log – confirmed by Ministère de L'Air, Contrôle.
15. Léon Doulet and Rémy Clément, 13 March 1983.
16. Robert Marotin, 14 March 1982.
17. ibid.
18. Bodington personal file, Reuters.
19. Contemporaries of Bodington recall his trip to Spain and his writing about Punter. Punter had links with Claude Dansey's Z Organization. *Colonel Z*, Read and Fisher, p. 253.
20. Boemelburg papers, Berlin Document Centre.
21. Rolfe Boemelburg, 23 January 1986. The only son of Carl Boemelburg, Rolfe was a student in Paris during his father's assignment in 1938. He is absolutely certain he never met either Déricourt or Bodington.
22. Private information.
23. Rolfe Boemelburg, 23 January 1986. His father enjoyed re-telling this story whenever he was home on leave.

Chapter II

1. *Secret Service*, Christopher Andrew, pp. 414–18.
2. *Greek Memories*, Compton Mackenzie, p. 324.
3. *Secret Service*, Christopher Andrew, Chapter 4.
4. Letter from Dansey to Major R. H. Van Deman quoted in *Colonel Z*, Read and Fisher.
5. *Secret Service*, Christopher Andrew, Chapter 4.
6. Dansey's early biographical details are well covered in *Colonel Z*, Read and Fisher.
7. *Colonel Z*, Read and Fisher.
8. ibid.

9. *MI6*, Nigel West, p. 69.

10. ibid.

11. The best account of the Venlo Incident is contained in the Payne Best papers held at the Imperial War Museum (IWM) under MSS 79/57/1.

12. *The Order of the Death's Head*, Heinze Hohne, pp. 214ff.

13. Record of International Military Tribunal, Nuremberg, Vol. XX, p. 194.

14. Shlomo Aronson, Heydrich's biographer, quoted in *The Order of the Death's Head*, Heinze Hohne.

15. *Colonel Z*, Read and Fisher.

16. André Dewarvrin (Colonel Passy), 4 January 1986.

17. Letter from Dansey to Payne Best, December 1945. IWM MSS 79/57/1.

18. Robin Cecil, personal assistant to Stewart Menzies, September 1943 to 1945. Interviewed 5 February 1986.

Chapter III

1. *The French and the Phoney War*, Fonvieille-Alquier, p. 78.

2. Bodington dispatches for Reuters.

3. Foreign Office, 28 November 1985.

4. Rolfe Boemelburg and the Boemelburg papers, Berlin Document Centre.

5. *État des Services* (essentially a military record), the Déricourt papers.

6. *Horoscope for a Double Agent*, Jean Overton Fuller.

7. Rémy Clément, 8 May 1982.

8. Déricourt's log, confirmed by SNCASE.

9. ibid.

10. ibid.

11. Mme Déricourt, 20 November 1982.

12. Rémy Clément, 8 January 1986.

13. Déricourt's log, authorized by SNCASE.

14. Mme Déricourt, 20 November 1982.

15. Déricourt's log, confirmed by SNCASE.

16. C. Besnard, December 1982.

17. ibid.

18. ibid.

19. Boemelburg papers, Berlin Document Centre.

20. *Codeword: Direktor*, Heinze Höhne, p. 85.

21. Carl Braun was Boemelburg's driver throughout the war. He disappeared in 1947 but was reached through a third party and eventually provided this account of Boemelburg's and Déricourt's reunion. The date is uncertain, but it was before the end of 1940.

22. Rolfe Boemelburg and *Codeword: Direktor*, Heinze Höhne.

23. Déricourt's log, authorized by SCLAM.

Chapter IV

1. Foreign Office, 28 November 1985.

2. *The Second World War*, Vol. 2, W. S. Churchill.

3. CAB 66/7, WP (40) 168 Meeting of the Chiefs of Staff, 25 May 1940, in the Public Records Office, Kew.

4. ibid.

5. Sir William Stephenson, telephone conversation with author, 10 January 1986.

6. *The SOE 1940-46*, M. R. D. Foot, p. 21.

7. ibid.

8. *Colonel Z*, Read and Fisher, p. 270.
9. J. G. Beevor, letter to the author, 3 September 1986.
10. Robin Cedi, 5 February 1986.
11. *Colonel Z*, Read and Fisher, p. 271.
12. ibid. Corroborated by Sir William Stephenson and General Sir James Marshall-Cornwall.
13. M/9, *Escape and Evasion*, Foot and Langley.
14. M. R. D. Foot, November 1985.
15. Foreign Office, 28 November 1985.
16. ibid.

Chapter V

1. Mme Déricourt, 9 May 1982.
2. Léon Doulet, 5 January 1986.
3. Arthur, Lord Granar, 6 January 1986; Sir Robert Maxwell, 11 February 1986.
4. Léon Doulet, 5 January 1986.
5. ibid.
6. Letter from H. M. Donaldson to unnamed officer in the Division of Foreign Activity Correlation of the US Department of State, 11 November 1942. 851.20241/2, in National Archive, Washington D.C.
7. ibid.
8. *I Was There*, Fleet Admiral William D. Leahy, p. 89.
9. Léon Doulet, 5 January 1986.
10. Two contemporaries at Marignon claim Déricourt boasted the Americans called him Henry.
11. Déricourt log, authorized by SCLAM.
12. Déricourt trial papers, Interrogation I, 1946.
13. Donaldson, see note 6 above.
14. Foreign Office, April 1986.
15. Donaldson, see note 6 above.

16. Dr Albert Guerisse (Pat O'Leary), March 1986.
17. Donaldson, see note 6 above.
18. Déricourt log, confirmed by SCLAM.
19. Mme Déricourt, 9 May 1982.
20. Léon Doulet, 5 January 1986.
21. Every detail of their journey to Britain comes from an interview with Doulet on 5 January 1986, and confirmed in innumerable letters and telephone conversations since.
22. The details of these messages from Dansey to his men in Gibraltar were relayed to me by a Foreign Office official, in April 1986. It was a rare insight into MI6 archives. I subsequently asked if I could have the text of Arthur (Lord Granar) Forbes' reply and, more importantly, Dansey's response to it. (In fact I already knew what Forbes' reply had been.) I was told that before any further information could be released from MI6 files, the matter would have to be referred to a higher authority. 'If you hear nothing further, that will be your answer.' I'm still waiting.
23. Arthur, Lord Granar, 6 January 1986.
24. Léon Doulet, 5 January 1986.
25. The fact that Déricourt declared his contacts with German intelligence from the very outset was confirmed in 1958 by Lord Lansdowne, a junior Minister from the Foreign Office. Since then, the Foreign Office have changed their position and now declare that Lansdowne was 'incorrectly briefed'. However, independent sources confirm that Déricourt did in fact make this declaration on a number of occasions to different people. A series of files concerned with his arrival in Great Britain

are listed at the Public Records Office. They are: Z 7300, Z 9571 and Z 9958. Unfortunately, the files themselves are not there. According to the Foreign Office (Foreign Office, 6 August 1986), they were destroyed some time ago.

26. Donaldson, see note 6 above.
27. Léon Doulet, 5 January 1986.

Chapter VI

1. Gubbins memo to Sir Charles Hambro, 8 August 1942.
2. M. R. D. Foot, November 1985.
3. *The SOE in France*, M. R. D. Foot, Chapter VII.
4. The growth of PROSPER is well chronicled in Foot's history *The SOE in France*, Cookridge's *Inside SOE* and Nogueres' *Histoire de la Resistance en France*.
5. Jacques Bureau, 24 February 1986.
6. For a more detailed account of French involvement in the Final Solution see Robert Paxton's *Vichy France*, and of course there is the French documentary *Le Chagrin et La Pitié*.
7. Jacques Bureau, 24 February 1986.
8. Dr Josef Götz, 28 February 1986.
9. Rolfe Boemelburg, 23 January 1986.

Chapter VII

1. Léon Doulet, 5 January 1986.
2. ibid.
3. I asked the Foreign Office in June 1986 for details of Déricourt's whereabouts during the period between his separation from Doulet and his arrival at SOE. No reply was received.

4. Foreign Office, 28 November 1985.

5. There is no reference to BOE/48 (Déricourt's German identification) before 1943 in any of Boemelburg's papers or any German papers now in the hands of the French authorities.

6. From an interview with Léon Doulet, 5th January 1986, and a subsequent letter to the author, 21 September 1986.

7. Dencourt's first statement to DST (Int.I). Undated, but 1946, in the Déricourt trial papers, Dépot Central d'Archives de la Justice Militaire.

8. Group Captain Frederick Winterbottom, Head of Section IV, Air Intelligence. Interviewed by the author July 1985.

9. Nigel West, 23 January 1986.

10. Marie-Madelaine Foucarde, 9 January 1986.

11. Winterbottom, July 1985.

12. See Read and Fisher's account of the Z Organization in *Colonel Z*.

13. Dansey lectured to American intelligence officers in May and June 1917: 'In any really delicate matter we always keep our fingers on every move in the game, and see the police do not spoil a good thing. If you catch one of their best men and can lead them to believe that he is still loose and operating, and they continue to rely on him for their information, and use his reports, it is of infinitely greater value than having a dead man.' See p. 111, *Colonel Z*, Read and Fisher.

14. British Intelligence in the Second World War, Vol. 2, Appendix 4, Prof. Hinsley *et al*.

15. ibid.

16. Memo from Group Captain Grierson to Air Ministry, 29 October 1942, AIR 40/2352/8B – in the PRO.

17. Foreign Office, 28 November 1985.

18. Letter from Jepson to author, November 1986.

19. Foreign Office, 17 December 1985. *SOE in France*, M. R. D. Foot, p. 291.

20. Interview with Buckmaster, October 1985.

21. Interview with Vera Atkins, February 1986.

22. Foreign Office, 28 November 1985.

23. Déricourt's log book was not authorized by any organization, French or British, from 6 August 1942 to 28 September 1945. According to Group Captain Hugh Verity (11 February 1986), 'If he had been a 161 Squadron pilot his log book entries would have been checked and countersigned each month by his Flight and Squadron Commanders.' Not until Déricourt joined Air France in October 1945 is there any kind of regular confirmation of his flights. The Air France authorities seem to have accepted his fictitious 'hours' concocted during the unauthorized period.

24. Air Historical Branch records. One curious thing about the RAF records is a strange number attached to Déricourt's name. According to Personal Records at RAF Barnswood, he had the number S 92908. It is not an RAF number; SOE did not use numbers at all; it is not his RPS file number; it is not his French pilot's licence number. Is it an MI6 number?

25. Harry Sporborg, 18 April 1983.

26. ibid.

27. Private information.

28. Déricourt correspondence with Jean Overton Fuller, undated.
29. Harry Sporborg, 18 April 1983.
30. 'There was no record at this (nor indeed at any later) stage of any pre-war contacts with German intelligence.' Foreign Office, 17 December 1985.
31. Vera Atkins, letter to the author, 11 January 1987.
32. Group Captain Hugh Verity, 31 October 1985.

Chapter VIII

1. C. Besnard, December 1982.
2. Déricourt family friend, Coulognes-en-Tardenois. Also Henri told JuJu he had given some of his cash to his mother and JuJu passed this on to Charles, her future husband, when finally she explained to him her involvement with SOE.
3. C. Besnard, December 1982.
4. Clément, 8 January 1986.
5. C. Besnard, December 1982.
6. Déricourt's second statement to DST (Int.II). Undated but 1946 in the Déricourt trial papers, Dépôt Central d'Archives de la Justice Militaire. *Int. II.* 1946.
7. Kopkow hinted at this story on 30 June 1983, but Dr Götz had the most complete version (3 December 1982):

   I remember being told then [1943] that Déricourt went to Boemelburg – that it was he who had sought contact with us. Which explains why Boemelburg had complete confidence in him, which he did. Boemelburg never wanted to believe he'd been tricked. Don't forget, at the beginning of '43, the German position was not totally lost. It was perfectly possible for Boemelburg to believe in a German victory at that time, to believe someone who said the same thing. To think – here's another one who wants to escape, who wants to choose the right side. Déricourt said to a devoted Nazi like Boemelburg, 'I believe absolutely that we must defeat the Russians, the real threat against Europe is Bolshevism.

I went to London and there were Communists everywhere, their terrible influence etc.' You must realize something, Boemelburg was no great thinker.

8. Mme Déricourt, 9 May 1982.
9. ibid.
10. This and subsequent accounts of Déricourt's operations have been compiled from the 161 Squadron and 138 Squadron Operations Record Books (PRO AIR 27/1068 and AIR 28/820 in the PRO), the memoirs of those who were carried by or worked with Déricourt, and, of course, *SOE in France*, by M. R. D. Foot.
11. A. Brooks, P. Culioli, A. Borrel, J. Barrett. These are some of the people on record about Déricourt's insatiable curiosity.
12. Unfortunately, unknown to Déricourt, the RAF had given the operation a black mark. Vaughan-Fowler claimed in his report that Déricourt's strip had been too bumpy, possibly because he had laid it across some cart tracks, and the violent buffeting had caused his engine to catch fire.
13. Horst Kopkow, 30 June 1983. According to Götz, Knochen and Kopkow, Boemelburg's first priority

was PROSPER and the invasion. Information about flights was secondary.

14. 'Boemelburg was a crack criminal investigator. He knew recruiting agents came down to two things: money and ideology. He always preferred the ideological to the scoundrel who was out for money. Someone else would come along and pay him more than you were offering. Some people like to think you can find recruits in jails. This is garbage, human garbage and they'll never produce anything for you.' Horst Kopkow, 30 June 1983.

15. A great many eminent people are on record about the playing of 'double agents'. Roger Hesketh describes in his unpublished book *Fortitude*, the process of playing the 'double', as does J. C. Masterman in *The Double Cross System*. Interviews with T. A. R. Robertson, Roman Czerniawski (BRUTUS), Ewen Montague and Roger Fleetwood-Hesketh have all contributed to this account of the role of the 'double'.

16. Private information.

17. Sporborg, 21 March 1983.

Chapter IX

1. *Winston Churchill and the Second Front 1940-1943*, Trumbell Higgins.

2. CAB 80/65 COS (42)399(0), Minute from Churchill dated 18 November 1942. (CAB – Cabinet papers, COS – COSSAC, in the PRO).

3. Press reports of Casablanca Conference, quoted in *The Pin-stripe Saboteur*, Charles Weighton.

4. A paper by the Joint Planners at Casablanca, CCS/167, 22 January 1943 – in the PRO.

5. *SOE in France*, M. R. D. Foot, pp. 233–4.
6. Ewen Montague, 26 May 1982.
7. *Fortitude*, Roger Hesketh, p. 20. This is an unpublished book which describes in some detail 'The History of Strategic Deception in North Western Europe April, 1943 to May, 1944'. Hesketh, who was posted to Section Ops (B) COSSAC, concerned with deception plans, and where he was eventually given charge of the 'Special Means' subsection, wrote this history at the request of the Ministry of Defence. A few copies were printed for official use and in 1976, Hesketh finally received official permission to publish. Curiously, in 1986, the MOD withdrew this permission and Hesketh has been 'debarred from even showing the book to anyone' or discussing its contents. This is a most extraordinary set of circumstances as Hesketh had already given hours of interview material on precisely this subject for Roy Davies' BBC documentary, 'Destination D-Day', transmitted in June 1984.

Chapter X

1. Joint memo from the Naval Staff and Chief of Combined Operations, 1 April 1943, COS (43)170(0) Ref CAB 80/68 (Cabinet papers) in the PRO.
2. Minute by Churchill, 10 April 1943, COS (43)194(0) Ref. CAB 80/68 (Cabinet papers) in the PRO.
3. Interview with Prof. Michael Howard, Oriel College, Oxford, 22 January 1986. 'COCKADE

had originally been devised to shroud a real invasion of France. Once the decision not to invade had been taken, the LCS had to throw COCKADE together at very short notice, but now not based on any real event, just a few spoof advances.' Prof. Howard has recently completed a history of Second World War strategic deception.

4. COS (43)219(0) (Final), Ref. CAB 80/69 (Cabinet papers) report to War Cabinet, 30 April 1943 – at the PRO.

5. This catalogue of *materiel* dropped by SOE's French Section to *all* the French networks was compiled from the archives of the Ministère de la Guerre at the Château de Vincennes in Paris (Ref. 13P68. *Materiel sur parachute et deportation*). The slight dip in the figures for July, before they resume their exponential rise, is explained by the events that occurred on the ground during that month.

1943	JAN	FEB	MAR	APR	MAY	JUN	JUL	AUG	SEP	OCT
Stens	87	64	32	644	1006	2353	2216	7378	2071	1915
Incendiaries	35	74	–	1044	1877	10,790	6533	13,288	2645	2785
Pistols	24	63	34	421	716	877	445	1740	480	481
Grenades	36	98	163	2508	4489	5537	2780	9527	2900	3270
High Exp. (kg)	88	253	162	1806	3872	10,252	6016	13,583	3380	3380

6. *Double Webbs*, Jean Overton Fuller, p. 196.

7. Clément, 24 February 1986.

8. Kopkow's post-war interrogation (27 January 1947) makes it quite clear Hitler had taken a deep interest in PROSPER from the very earliest reports. (Copy of this interrogation in SOE's archives at FO still restricted, and in Berlin Document

Centre.) Kopkow confirmed Hitler's obsession with PROSPER in another interview, 30 June 1983.

9. Kieffer papers, Berlin Document Centre.

10. 'Kieffer was an average police official. He had a very strong sense of duty which probably led him to the Nazi Party – more than any personal conviction. He was an indefatigable man, without any great skills. A bit simple in his intellectual process.' Interview with Dr Götz, 26 November 1982.

11. Dr Götz, 3 December 1982.

12. The precise details of Déricourt's arrangement with Boemelburg are described in the interrogations of Placke, Götz, Vogt *et al* in the Déricourt trial papers.

13. Taken from Kopkow's description of Boemelburg as a 'master controller' of double agents. These offers of help were standard. Kopkow expanded, 'If they were committed to us and Germany lost the war, we'd take care of them. Believe me, we did this in many cases.' Kopkow, 30 June 1983.

14. Rémy Clément, 8 May 1982.

15. *SOE in France*, M. R. D. Foot, p. 291. He refers to Frager's interrogation 22–26 October 1943.

16. There is evidence from Josef Placke's testimony to the DST in 1947 that the SD had known of this operation and followed 'a party of agents to a schoolhouse'.

17. Kopkow, 30 June 1983.

18. Dr Götz, 26 November 1982. He claims that the first clue they had that the Abwehr might have been making any inroads into PROSPER was by picking up someone else's *funkspiel* at the Boulevard Suchet.

19. *Colonel Henri's Story*, Hugo Bleicher, Chapter 6.
20. Hugh Verity, 31 October 1985.
21. Foot speculates in *SOE in France* that Bleicher used the CARTE list to get to them.
22. Carl Braun recalls a hasty meeting between Boemelburg and Déricourt during Easter.

Chapter XI

1. A remark often attributed to Boemelburg.
2. I have reconstructed these events from details contained in Charles Weighton's imperfect biography of Weil, *The Pin-stripe Saboteur*, pp. 129-50; a report by Cohen, the ROBIN radio operator, 11 October 1943; an interview with Mme Balachowsky by a French journalist in 1969 (not published); and some correspondence from Weil to Déricourt amongst the Déricourt papers.
3. Dr Götz, 26 November 1982.
4. Interviews with Atkins (January 1986) and Buckmaster (October 1985).
5. *Double Webbs*, Jean Overton Fuller, pp. 184–223.
6. Interview with Harry Sporborg, March 1982.
7. The Foreign Office, 17 December 1985.
8. ibid., 28 November 1985.
9. As Mme Déricourt described it, 9 May 1982.
10. Dr Götz, though rarely present at these meetings, knew the routine well enough.
11. Suttill spoke to Mme Balachowsky and others about his reservations concerning Déricourt.
12. Clément, 8 May 1982.
13. *Double Webbs*, Jean Overton Fuller, p. 192.
14. Besnard, December 1982.

15. *Most Secret*, COSSAC/18DX/INT. Titled: 'An examination of the effects of Operation STARKEY on Germany and the occupied countries.' Signed by Lieutenant Colonel J. E. Fass.

16. *Most Secret*, COSSAC (43) 15 FINAL.

17. Memo from Major General R. B. Woodruff, US Army, to the Commanding General, War Department, Washington DC, dated 23 September 1943, in which he describes British insistence on the classification, COCKADED or NOT COCKADED. The Americans found it very amusing.

18. Interview with Harry Sporborg, 21 March 1983. 'Of course it's wrong to say, as Foot did, that we weren't involved in deception. We dropped some people as a result of that, indeed. Clearly, however, if deception is involved, Buckmaster is the last person you want to know about it.' Sporborg was referring to the official history, *SOE in France*, by M. R. D. Foot.

19. Buckmaster, 31 October 1985.

Chapter XII

1. Colonel Reile, Head of the Abwehr's Ast III France, interviewed August 1982.

2. ibid.

3. Kopkow papers, Berlin Document Centre.

4. *Codeword: Direktor*, Heinz Höhne, pp. 171–2.

5. Kopkow, 30 June 1983.

6. 'Our relations with the SD were not close. We went our separate paths. Yes, we tried to burn GILBERT.' Interview with Reile, August 1982. On discussing the subject with a number of SD

veterans and with an ADC to Reile, they all conclude that such a move must have had backing from Berlin, if not an actual order.

7. Josef Placke was the SD man with the best links with the black market.

8. Christmann's own description of himself.

9. Christmann's testimony amongst the Déricourt trial papers, June 1948.

10. Richard Christmann was (and is) an unreliable witness. His explanation of what might have occurred had he caught up with Déricourt only leads to aimless speculation. He has claimed he was really interested in doing a genuine gem deal; he also claimed he 'made a report to London about the various traffickings' of Agazarian and Déricourt – in other words, alerting London to Déricourt's arrangements with the SD. An ADC to Reile, familiar with Christmann and his serpentine explanations, is in no doubt Déricourt would eventually have been shot. Interview with ADC (anon.), 2 March 1987.

11. Reile's ADC recalls hearing that Christmann was driven to 84 Avenue Foch, in the back of a BMW, escorted by two SD men.

12. 'Reile despised Boemelburg and the others from the SD – like amateurs who should have had nothing to do with all that.' Interview with Dr Götz, 26 November 1982.

13. *La Sologne*, Paul Guillaume, pp. 56-65.

14. Interview with Culioli, August 1986.

15. *SOE in France*, M. R. D. Foot, p. 309.

16. Mme Déricourt, 9 May 1982.

17. Bureau continues… 'All this was suddenly settled. He had received his orders. So it was normal that this man should appear a little troubled, a little worried, a little firmer. He deceived me then, he really made me believe in a September landing.' Jacques Bureau, 24 February 1986.

18. Mme Guepin's deposition to DST, 4 July 1947.

19. *La Sologne*, Paul Guillaume, p. 75.

20. *The Pin-stripe Saboteur*, Charles Weighton, p. 183.

21. *La Sologne*, Paul Guillaume, pp. 67–8.

22. *German Penetration of the SOE*, Jean Overton Fuller, p. 71.

23. *La Sologne*, Paul Guillaume, pp. 65-74.

24. Mme Balachowsky, quoted on p. 65 of *German Penetration of the SOE*, Jean Overton Fuller.

25. *La Sologne*, Paul Guillaume, p. 63.

26. ibid., p. 73.

27. Mme Guepin's statement to DST, 4 July 1947, in Déricourt trial papers.

28. Mme Fevre's statement to DST, April 1947, in Déricourt trial papers. A similar description is also on p. 76 of *La Sologne*, Paul Guillaume.

Chapter XIII

1. PROSPER's instructions to Bureau on what was expected of him, in the event of being arrested. Bureau, 24 February 1986.

2. PROSPER papers, 'Buckmaster Reseaux', Ministère de la Guerre Service Historique. 13P 18–64.

3. Kopkow was also the head of the department responsible for creating forged documents.

4. Culioli, August 1986.

5. The best account of the arrests is in the excellent *La Sologne*, Paul Guillaume.

6. Bureau, 24 February 1986.

7. ibid., and a letter from Bureau, December 1985.

8. 'I had a very comfortable war. I had my hotel, my food, a movie now and then. Sometimes I would go to Saint-Sulpice to listen to Marcel Dupré, the great organist. Compared with those who were at the Russian Front, I had an easy life.' Dr Götz, 26 November 1982.

9. Götz papers, Berlin Document Centre.

10. Götz, 26 November 1986; also well covered on p. 331 of *SOE in France*, M. R. D. Foot, based on Götz's post-war interrogation by the British, 3 September 1946.

11. PROSPER papers, 'Buckmaster Reseaux', Ministère de la Guerre. See note reference 2 above.

12. Letter from Sir Patrick Reilly, 15 September 1986.

13. *Colonel Z*, Read and Fisher, pp. 271-2; also conversation with Marshall-Cornwall on 7 July 1985.

14. According to Kieffer's post-war interrogation, Borrel was the best they ever saw.

15. Letter from Jean Savy, 17 August 1986.

16. According to Hugh Verity, SOE's returning agents were driven from the aircraft to Tangmere Cottage for a 'night-flying breakfast', then driven away by FANY girls. MI6 were free to drive their people away to their own safe-house at the base.

17. *SOE in France*, M. R. D. Foot, p. 293. Foot says his source was André Simon.

18. *Double Webbs*, Jean Overton Fuller, p. 210.

19. ibid., p. 189.

20. Foreign Office, 17 December 1985.
21. ibid.
22. Foreign Office, 16 January 1986.
23. *SOE in France*, M. R. D. Foot, pp. 329–30.
24. The Foreign Office claim that MI6 records identify only two agents outgoing that night. However, the 161 Squadron Records Book at the PRO clearly shows 'three' agents flown out to France on FLORIDE. MI6 veterans have also confirmed that it would have been absolutely impossible for anyone to get on an MI6 flight unless they were brought by an 'MI6 escorting officer'. There were no other flights that night.
25. Mme Déricourt, 9 May 1982.
26. Reile, August 1982.
27. *SOE in France*, M. R. D. Foot, p. 323; based on an interview Bodington gave to SOE's security section in April 1945.
28. Interview with Besnard, December 1982.
29. Foreign Office, 17 December 1985.
30. Foreign Office confirmed that Bodington warned Déricourt of Frager's accusations. The conversation, as I present it, comes from Roger Bardet, whose papers became available in 1986.
31. There is another canard that Bleicher placed a personal announcement in *Le Figaro*, welcoming Bodington to Paris and saying how much he (Bleicher) looked forward to meeting him. Then, so the story goes, just before he left for London, Bodington placed a reply in the same paper saying how much he regretted having to miss Bleicher this time round. A long search through newspaper archives failed to turn up these messages.

32. Reile, August 1982.
33. I quote from *SOE in France*, M. R. D. Foot, p. 278 (written ten years before any papers on COCKADE were released):

Only nine arms drops had been made by May, but by the end of August SCIENTIST and its sub-circuits had received as many as 121 aircraft loads of arms and stores, in nearly two thousand containers and packages. De Baissac could thus dispose of almost nine tons of explosive, and could provide about half his force with a personal firearm. 'Evidently something was building up', as Bourne-Patterson put it in retrospect. [Bourne-Patterson had written SOE's internal history.]

SCIENTIST in fact was snowballing, too soon for safety. Had the Allied invasion of France come in the early autumn of 1943, as many millions of people had hoped it would, SCIENTIST might have played an important role on the Biscay coast, distracting enemy attention from the main landing for a short but perhaps vital period of time. Twice that autumn the BBC broadcast warning messages to every active SOE circuit in France, indicating that the invasion would come within a fortnight; but the action messages that should have followed, on the night of the landing, were not sent.

With no other explanation to hand, Foot speculated that all this was designed to distract German attention from the landings at Salerno and the Italian surrender. No criticism intended – in 1964, very few people had ever heard of COCKADE.

34. Quoted in a letter from the Foreign Office, 16 January 1986.

35. Foreign Office, 28 November 1985.
36. Ref. CAB 79/63 (Cabinet papers). COS (43) 173rd Meeting (o). Minutes of Meeting of the War Cabinet, Chiefs of Staff Committee, 27 July 1943, in the PRO.
37. Quoted in CAB 79/63 (Cabinet papers). JIC (43) 325 (o). Report by the Joint Intelligence Sub-Committee on SOE activities in France, in the PRO.
38. ibid.

Chapter XIV

1. CAB 80/71 (Cabinet papers). COS (43) 302 (o) – in the PRO.
2. CAB 80/71 5360 (Cabinet papers). COS (43) 386 (o) – in the PRO.
3. ibid.
4. Memo from Lieut-Gen. Morgan to Chiefs of Staff, COSSAC/3122/Sec. Now in Modern Military Records – US National Archives (MMR US-NA).
5. Minutes of Meeting of Chiefs of Staff Committee, 22 July 1943. WO 106/4241 76289, COS (43) 386 (o) –23c in A6/2.
6. Director of Press and Publicity, War Office Report, 19-25 August 1943, in Intelligence Branch COSSAC/182X (now in SHAEF SGS 381, Pre-invasion File MMR – US NA).
7. *The New York Times*, 19 August 1943.
8. See note 6 above.
9. *The New York Times*, 19 August 1943.
10. See note 5, CHAPTER X. Note how all the figures peak during August, just prior to the COCKADE–STARKEY 'D-Day', then decline dramatically.

The dip in the July figures is accounted for by the PROSPER collapse. According to the Foreign Office (5 February 1986): 'by the first of June the organization… had received 254 containers and that during June it was to receive 190 more between the 12th and 21st'. By July, drops to PROSPER circuits had virtually ceased.

11. The 59th (Staffordshire) Infantry Division, p. 35 of its 'War Story', produced by Peter Knight. IWM Library.

12. Colonel Reile, August 1982.

13. Memo with report from Lieut-Colonel G.S., Army Intelligence Section. COSSAC/IX DX/1N (US-NA).

14. Enemy reactions to Starkey, COSSAC/41DX/Int. (MMR US-NA).

15. Records of the US JCS, CCS 385, MMR US-NA.

16. Von Runstedt's daily situation report, *Lagebeurteilungen OB West*, AL 1704 at Imperial War Museum.

17. Operation 'STARKEY' – Appreciation of Prospects. COSSAC (43) 44 in MMR US-NA.

18. Handwritten note from 'AB' to 'G1' (Intelligence Branch COSSAC HQ). Given seq number 60 1406 in MMR US-NA.

19. MOST SECRET CYPHER TELEGRAM, Concrete 736, WO 106/4241 – in the PRO.

20. Dr Götz, 26 November 1982 – and *Lagebeurteilungen OB West*, for September 1943. AL 1704 at the IWM.

21. Army Film Unit, Secret Dope Sheet, 9 September 1943, in the IWM Film Library.

22. The 59th Staffordshire Infantry Division's 'War Story', p. 35.

23. *SOE in France*, M. R. D. Foot, p. 308; 'D-Day 1943' by Campbell, p. 219, published in *The Canadian Journal of History*, 12: 207–37, December 1977.

Chapter XV

1. Amongst the Déricourt papers is a manuscript entitled, *De l'espionage, considere comme l'un des beaux arts*. It purports to be an account of one 'Gilbert' and his reflections on the work he does. It is a rough and aimless ramble, wherein Gilbert is clearly meant to be one of the greatest spies of all time. Not a source of factual material, but there is some insight into an attitude of mind. The MS is dedicated to: Colonel Boddington (sic). 'Sans lui, l'invraisemblable eut été moins vrai.' Loosely translated as: Without whom the improbable would have been less true.

2. 'I remember well when Boemelburg was telling me about GILBERT, I thought, Why me now?' Dr Götz, 26 November 1982.

3. ibid.

4. 'I was used for, say, routine contacts, Lysander dates etc. Boemelburg had contacts with Déricourt for much more important things: large war strategy etc.' Dr Götz, 26 November 1982.

5. Dr Götz, 3 December 1982.

6. Tony Brooks, December 1985. Brooks has always assumed that he was singled out for protection because he handled a lot of material for MI6.

7. ibid.

8. According to Clément, imprisonment by the SD was his most frightening experience of the war. He

still trembles when he describes it. Interview with Clément, 24 February 1986.

9. Interview with André Watt, January 1986.
10. This account was constructed from an interview with Clément in January 1986 and from *SOE in France*, M. R. D. Foot, pp. 295, 300-1, based on Frager's interrogation 22 October 1943.
11. Final report from Sentor on Frager's interrogation, 30 October 1943, from Foreign Office 28 November 1985.
12. ibid.
13. *SOE in France*, M. R. D. Foot, p. 299.
14. ibid., p. 311.
15. Foreign Office, 28 November and 17 December 1985.
16. Interview with Rolfe Boemelburg, December 1986.
17. *SOE in France*, M. R. D. Foot, p. 295 and Bony-LaFont interrogation, October 1945, in Déricourt trial papers.
18. Mme Déricourt, 9 May 1982.

Chapter XVI

1. The full text is published in *A Cross-Channel Attack*, Gordon Harrison, Appendix D. The shift in German priorities is discussed in *British Intelligence during the Second World War*, Hinsley *et al*, p. 23.
2. An informal committee meeting on 27 January 1944, chaired by Winston Churchill, at which representatives from the FO, MEW and de Gaulle were present. Bourne-Patterson and Sporborg were there to put the SOE case. Playing upon Churchill's

enthusiasm for unorthodox warfare the case was easily won. Churchill commented, 'Brave and desperate men could cause the most acute embarrassment to the enemy and it was right that we should do all in our power to foster and stimulate so valuable an aid to Allied strategy.'

3. Stephenson telexed me on 27 March 1986: 'It was common knowledge in the intelligence community that Dansey was intent on destroying the SOE. Gubbins discussed with me his concern about Dansey and I warned Menzies that I was going to have to report it to WSC [Churchill] unless he ordered Dansey to behave.

    'Gubbins came to me with his problems on my many visits to London because he knew of my close association with Winston.'

    Stephenson expanded in a separate telex, 'I came to the conclusion that a warning from Menzies to Dansey in May 1943, as a result of a threat from me at that time, resulted in Dansey intensifying his attacks on the SOE.' Stephenson then goes on to describe the subsequent SOS from Gubbins, which he received around September 1943, the text of which he sent to me on 18 March 1986.

4. Telex from Stephenson, 14 February 1986: 'I believe this final threat by me resulted in Menzies ceasing to be a puppet of Dansey, who, in my view and that of many others, was an evil man.'

5. Foreign Office, 28 November 1985.

6. ibid.

7. Foreign Office, 17 December 1985.

8. See note 5 above. The Foreign Office revealed, for the first time, that Déricourt was not recalled, as the

official history states, because of Frager's report, or Yeo-Thomas', or because of anyone from the SOE – but on the basis of reports from MI6.

9. Verity, 31 October 1985.

10. This account was compiled from an interview with Clément, 13 April 1982 and from *SOE in France*, M. R. D. Foot, p. 297, based on the Knacker report, 4 February 1944.

11. Dr Götz, 3 December 1982.

12. ibid.

13. Rolfe Boemelburg, who recalled Braun telling him: 'We were parked in a quiet spot. He handed over a huge sum of money. Imagine I could have killed Gilbert and taken all that money for myself.'

14. Mme Déricourt, 9 May 1982.

15. Clément, 24 February 1986.

16. Verity, 31 October 1985.

17. ibid.

18. Foreign Office, 17 December 1985.

19. *SOE in France*, M. R. D. Foot, p. 301.

20. Interview with Mr and Mrs Verity, September 1985.

21. Vogt's statement to the DST, undated but pre-21 January 1947.

22. Foreign Office, 17 December 1985.

23. Sporborg, 21 March 1982.

24. ibid.

25. ibid.

26. *Colonel Z*, Read and Fisher, p. 12.

27. Foreign Office, 28 November 1985.

28. Private information.

29. *SOE in France*, M. R. D. Foot, p. 301.

30. Vogt's statement to DST.

31. *Most Secret* – Security Clearance, SHAEF/17508/Ops(C) GCT 322-1 (SAS), issued from SHAEF HQ G-3 Division, 28 August 1944, in the Déricourt papers.
32. Déricourt's *État Des Services*, in the Déricourt papers.
33. Dr Götz, 26 February 1986.
34. Confirmed by Foreign Office, March 1986.
35. Sporborg, 21 March 1983.

Chapter XVII

1. An account of SOE personnel lost in German concentration camps is in *SOE in France*, M. R. D. Foot, Chapter XIII, 'Aftermath'.
2. There is some dispute over the date of this interview. According to Foot in *SOE in France*, it is 19 January 1947. However Atkins' own recollection, corroborated in no uncertain terms by the SAS man who arranged the interview with Kieffer, Freddy (Dusty) Rhodes, places it no later than Spring 1946. I am inclined to believe the latter.
3. Confirmed by UN Reference and Archives Unit.
4. Letter from Peter Belgeonne, 13 January 1986.
5. This account is compiled from the police report and the newspaper accounts of his hearing and trial – *Croydon Times*, 20 and 27 April 1946; *Croydon Advertiser*, 26 April 1946.
6. ibid.
7. Awarded 27 July 1946 and recorded in Déricourt's *État Des Services*, in the Déricourt papers.
8. DST report of their investigation, 23 September 1947, in the Déricourt trial papers.

9. Déricourt's first statement to the DST, undated 1946.

10. See note 8 above.

11. Knochen's DST interrogation, undated but pre-21 September 1947, DST investigation papers.

12. Placke's DST interrogation, 10 April 1946, DST investigation papers.

13. Dr Götz's deposition to the DST, 11 January 1946 plus additional questions, 24 July 1947.

14. Vogt's DST interrogation, undated 1946, DST investigation papers.

15. Letter from Henri to Jeannot, 29 January 1948.

16. Mme Déricourt, 20 November 1982.

17. Dr Götz, 26 November 1982.

18. Censored letter from Henri to Jeannot, 29 December 1947.

19. All the plans and specifications for 'Project Vega 439' have survived and are among the Déricourt papers.

20. Rolfe Boemelburg, January 1987.

21. *Double Webbs*, Jean Overton Fuller, pp. 47–9.

22. Copies of memos about British intransigence on this matter are among the DST investigation papers.

23. Mme Déricourt, 20 November 1982.

24. Vera Atkins, January 1986.

25. Transcript of Dr Götz's testimony in Déricourt trial papers.

26. Transcript of Bodington's testimony in Déricourt trial papers.

27. Mme Ddicourt, 20 November 1982.

28. Vera Atkins, January 1986.

Chapter XVIII

1. *SOE in France*, M. R. D. Foot, p. 302; from memo 5 December 1945.
2. Kopkow, 27 February 1986.
3. Déricourt compiled a large selection of newspaper reports of the accident.
4. Amongst the Déricourt papers is a false pilot's licence issued by Air Laos and a Lebanese passport.
5. *The Politics of Heroin in Southeast Asia*, Alfred McCoy *et al* pp. 254–5.
6. Clément described in great detail, during an interview on 24 February 1986, Déricourt's involvement in the heroin trade. Amongst the Déricourt papers are a dozen 'flight requisition forms', which state that the Beechcraft was owned by Francisci and flown by Déricourt.
7. Account statements and records of monies telegraphed to Jeannot amongst the Déricourt papers.
8. Clément was told all about the London account.
9. Translation of Reuters report to their Paris office. The Agence France version claimed he'd starred in the feature film about RAF pilots.
10. There has been a great deal of speculation about whether or not Déricourt was actually on the Beechcraft as it ploughed into the tree stumps at Sayaboury. There is a lot of circumstantial evidence to support the theory that he was not. Apart from the London bank account there is also the strange disappearance of his Vietnamese wife and child soon after the crash. However, Clément is certain Déricourt is dead. For those who are not,

an unreliable rumour has it that you should look for him in Barcelona.

11. Harry Sporborg, 21 March 1983.